Anxious Politics

Democratic Citizenship in a Threatening World

BETHANY ALBERTSON
University of Texas–Austin

SHANA KUSHNER GADARIAN
Syracuse University

CAMBRIDGE
UNIVERSITY PRESS

CAMBRIDGE
UNIVERSITY PRESS

32 Avenue of the Americas, New York, NY 10013–2473, USA

Cambridge University Press is part of the University of Cambridge.

It furthers the University's mission by disseminating knowledge in the pursuit of education, learning, and research at the highest international levels of excellence.

www.cambridge.org
Information on this title: www.cambridge.org/9781107441484

© Bethany Albertson and Shana Kushner Gadarian 2015

First published 2015
Reprinted 2015

Printed in the United States of America by Sheridan Books, Inc.

A catalog record for this publication is available from the British Library.

Library of Congress Cataloging in Publication Data
Albertson, Bethany.
Anxious politics : democratic citizenship in a threatening world / Bethany Albertson, University of Texas-Austin, Shana Kushner Gadarian, Syracuse University.
   pages   cm
Includes bibliographical references and index.
ISBN 978-1-107-08148-2 (Hardback) – ISBN 978-1-107-44148-4 (Paperback)
1. Political culture – United States.   2. Political psychology – United States.
3. United States – Politics and government – Psychological aspects.
4. United States – Politics and government – Public opinion.
5. Fear – Political aspects – United States.   6. Medical policy – United States.
7. United States – Emigration and Immigration – Government policy.
8. Terrorism – Government policy – United States.   9. Climatic
changes – Government policy – United States.   I. Gadarian, Shana Kushner, 1979–
II. Title.
JK1726.A426   2015
306.20973–dc23
2015012310

ISBN 978-1-107-08148-2 Hardback
ISBN 978-1-107-44148-4 Paperback

Anxious Politics

Democratic Citizenship in a Threatening World

Emotions matter in politics – enthusiastic supporters return politicians to office, angry citizens march in the streets, a fearful public demands protection from the government. *Anxious Politics* explores the emotional life of politics, with particular emphasis on how political anxieties affect public life. When the world is scary, when politics is passionate, when the citizenry is anxious, does this politics resemble politics under more serene conditions? If politicians use threatening appeals to persuade citizens, how does the public respond?

Anxious Politics argues that political anxiety triggers engagement in politics in ways that are potentially both promising and damaging for democracy. Using four substantive policy areas (public health, immigration, terrorism, and climate change), the book seeks to demonstrate that anxiety affects how we consume political news, who we trust, and what policies we support. Anxiety about politics triggers coping strategies in the political world, where these strategies are often shaped by partisan agendas.

Bethany Albertson is an assistant professor of government at the University of Texas, Austin. She received a PhD in political science from the University of Chicago. Previously, she was a visiting scholar at the Center for the Study of Democratic Politics at Princeton and on faculty at the University of Washington, Seattle. Her research has been funded by the National Science Foundation and the Harrington Foundation. Her work has been published in the *American Journal of Political Science, Political Behavior, Political Psychology,* and *American Politics Research.*

Shana Kushner Gadarian is an assistant professor of political science at the Maxwell School of Citizenship and Public Affairs, Syracuse University. She received a PhD in politics from Princeton University. Previously, she was a Robert Wood Johnson Scholar in Health Policy Research at the University of California–Berkeley. Her research has been funded by the National Science Foundation, Robert Wood Johnson Foundation, Campbell Public Affairs Institute, and the

Bobst Center for Peace and Justice. Her work has been published in the *American Journal of Political Science, Journal of Politics, Political Psychology, Political Communication, Perspectives on Politics*, and volumes on experimental methods and political psychology.

To Mike, Jonah, Ethan, Josh, and Will – five charming men who elicit positively valenced emotions

Contents

Contents

Tables

Figures

Acknowledgments

As many projects do, this book started as a series of conversations, and now – after seven years, four cross-country moves, four jobs, fourteen experiments, countless phone calls and presentations, two book conferences, one wedding, and three babies later – these conversations are in print. The path to this point was not always linear, but working together has made the process much less lonely and much more fun, and made for a much better book overall. Along the way, we have been incredibly fortunate that many people generously provided feedback, funding, and support, and we have accumulated many intellectual and personal debts that we will attempt to acknowledge here.

During academic year 2005–2006, Bethany was a fellow at the Center for the Study of Democratic Politics (CSDP) at Princeton University and Shana was in graduate school at Princeton. Our first and most profound debt of gratitude is to Larry Bartels for introducing us, providing us an intellectual home at CSDP, and supporting our endeavors even these many years later. We were both working on dissertations focused on the political psychology of the American public and, over the course of the year, had many fruitful conversations about research design and how voters think. When Bethany accepted a job across the country at the University of Washington, we decided that we should work on a project together so that we would stay in touch. After several years, several rounds of pretesting, experiments, and many, many rewrites, our initial idea to test how immigration anxiety affected news seeking turned into an article published in *Political Psychology* in 2014 and Chapter 3 in this book. Our initial findings that immigration anxiety prompted people to seek out threatening immigration news raised a series of questions that clearly needed more studies and more articles: was this the case only for certain people? How did this work in other policy areas? What were the consequences for public opinion?

When Shana accepted a Robert Wood Johnson Fellowship in Health Policy Research at the University of California–Berkeley, we added public health issues to the growing list of policies in our project. Many thanks to John Ellwood, Alan Cohen, and the Robert Wood Johnson Foundation for providing two years to study public health. Time is an invaluable resource, and the years in Berkeley allowed us time to think broadly about anxiety and provided the opportunity to meet and work with amazing scholars across disciplines. Plus, a view of the Bay Bridge is always good for productivity. Thank you to Rene Almeling, Jack Citrin, Sean Gailmard, Jack Glaser, Ben Handel, Vince Hutchings, Jonah Levy, Eric McDaniel, Helen Marrow, Ted Miguel, Colin Moore, Ryan Moore, Marco Gonzalez Navarro, Brendan Nyhan, Rashawn Ray, Maria Rendon, and Neil Smelser for providing comments and ideas during that time. After Shana arrived at Syracuse University and Bethany accepted a Harrington Faculty Fellowship and then a faculty position at University of Texas–Austin, we decided that these many articles and conference presentations were a book and went through the process of connecting the chapters through a more general theory about protection.

Over the course of the project, we had a great number of people who read, commented, and provided excellent feedback. We were privileged to present various pieces of this project at the American Political Science Association Annual Meeting, Harvard Political Psychology Workshop, International Society of Political Psychology Annual Meeting, NYU-CESS Experiments Conference, Robert Wood Johnson Foundation Health Policy Scholars Annual Meeting, Midwest Political Science Association Annual Meeting, the Political Psychology Workshop at the University of Chicago, Research Workshop in American Politics at the University of California–Berkeley, the Social Psychology Brown Bag at Syracuse University, West Coast Experiments Meeting, and the Western Political Science Association Annual Meeting. Thank you to the attendees of those meetings for their thoughts. Thanks especially to Emily Baceltis, Antoine Banks, Matt Barreto, Matthew Baum, Adam Berinsky, John Brehm, Tereza Capelos, Ryan Enos, Cengiz Erisen, Martin Gilens, Howard Lavine, Michael MacKuen, George Marcus, Jennifer Merolla, Tali Mendelberg, W. Russell Neuman, Laura Stoker, Dustin Tingley, Josh Tucker, Penny Visser, and Elizabeth Zechmeister. Thank you to the Department of Government at the University of Texas–Austin and the

Department of Political Science at Syracuse University for hosting two book manuscript conferences that helped to make a series of connected papers into a compelling narrative. Many thanks to Josh Blank, Terry Chapman, Stephen Jessee, David Leal, Tasha Philpot, Daron Shaw, Brian Roberts, and Matt Vandenbrock at UT and to Kristi Anderson, Kris Byron, Matt Cleary, Jon Hanson, John Hanley, Seth Jolly, Tom Keck, Quinn Mulroy, Tom Orgazalek, Leonard Newman, Grant Reeher, Breagin Riley, Brian Taylor, and Stu Thorson at Syracuse. For serving as discussants at the manuscript conference at Syracuse and prompting us to weave partisanship more clearly into the theory, thank you to Rose McDermott and David Redlawsk. Special thanks to Ted Brader and Nick Valentino for constructive criticism and wholehearted support over many phases of this project.

For funding the fourteen experiments and pretests that we ran over the course of this project, we thank the National Science Foundation's Time Sharing Experiments in the Social Sciences for grants in 2007 and 2011, along with Principal Investigators Skip Lupia, Diana Mutz, James Druckman, and Jeremy Freese, the Institute for Ethnic Studies at the University of Washington, and the Princeton Policy Research Institute for the Region at Princeton, the Harrington Foundation at the University of Texas, and the Robert Wood Johnson Foundation. For assisting us in navigating the workings of five different universities, thank you to Candy Brooks, Kelley Coleman, Michele Epstein, Sally Greenwald, Jacqueline Meyers, Tess Slater, Seana Van Buren, Ann Buscherfeld, Ling Fu, Nancy Moses, Annette Carlile, Katie Beth Willis, Carolina Villanueva, Bethany Walawender, and Brianna Weishuhn. For excellent research assistance, thank you to Ruth Chan, Ben Gonzalez, and Logan Strother. Thank you to our editor Robert Dreesen and Cambridge University Press for excellent guidance along the way.

We also want to thank our larger community who make it possible to be working parents and scholars. Without the help of Micaela Cooper, Amanda Eckrich, Deanna Payson, Kalsang Sangmo, and the Early Childhood Development Program at the Jewish Community Center of Syracuse, none of this would be possible. Many thanks to the Child Development Center at UT Austin, Nasreen Bhatti, Christine Martinez Serra, Yesenia Prieto, Julian Villagomez, Sandra Hammer, Tori Baker, and Bianca Bidiuc. Thank you to all of these hardworking and compassionate caregivers who care for our children so that we can research, write, and attend conferences.

Shana wishes to thank Barbara and Steve Gadarian for visiting, supporting us, and helping with the boys. Thank you also to my parents Robin and Gary Kushner for your continual love and support for our whole family, for reminding me to do my homework that one time in second grade, and for being wonderful examples of the rewards of hard work. My deepest debt and most profound thanks go to the Gadarian men, Jonah, Ethan, and Mike. To Jonah and Ethan for allowing me to experiment as a parent and providing me welcome distractions from the study of politics. To Mike, for your willingness to support my career by moving across the country (twice!), being an amazing father to our boys, and reminding me that if it were easy, everyone would write a book, there are no adequate words so I will simply say, thank you.

Bethany wishes to thank family near and far who provided such strong support throughout this long road – Linda Albertson, Lenore McHenry, Brian Albertson, Linda Busby, and Mark Busby. I'm also forever indebted to Melissa Harris Perry for getting me started and for sticking by me every step of the way. To Will Busby, thank you for being a goofball, and thanks to Josh Busby for being the crazy man I married.

Of course, we're anxious that we forgot names, but perhaps with a project this big in terms of studies, institutions, authors, and years, that's just inevitable. We are deeply thankful to the political psychology community that helped us along, even those not singled out here.

Prologue

The only thing we have to fear is fear itself – nameless, unreasoning, unjustified terror which paralyzes needed efforts to convert retreat into advance.

Franklin D. Roosevelt (1933)

"THE MOST FEARED DISEASE"

In summer 1916, the United States experienced its first major outbreak of polio, a viral disease that mainly affected children, leaving survivors with paralysis and wasted limbs. Concentrated around New York City, the outbreak would claim 27,000 lives before running its course. As historian David Oshinsky noted, polio was

the most feared disease of the middle part of the 20th century. It was a children's disease; there was no prevention; there was no cure; every child everywhere was at risk. And what this really meant was that parents were absolutely frantic. And what they tried to do was to protect their children the best way they could. (Dentzer 2005)

Anxiety surrounding the disease led to demand for public policies to combat the outbreak along with private behaviors to avoid contraction. With the cause of the disease shrouded in mystery, the public initially blamed Italian immigrants for the 1916 outbreak, focusing on their hygiene. Anxious parents cautioned their children not go swimming in pools or lakes (Youngdahl 2012). Armed police patrolled roads and rails around New York to ensure that travelers could prove their children were polio-free (Oshinsky 2006, 20–22).

In the wake of these disease outbreaks, politicians advocated public health policies to protect the public from polio. President Franklin D. Roosevelt, who himself was afflicted with the disease, launched a campaign against polio through the National Foundation for Infantile Paralysis. The campaign, more commonly known as the March of Dimes, called for citizens to send their dimes directly to the president. In 1938, that effort would yield more than two and half million dimes in addition to bills and checks. Such was the popular nature of the fight against polio that politicians of both parties sought to be associated with it. For example, in 1954, Republican vice-presidential candidate Richard Nixon was famously photographed pumping gas in a fundraising effort for the fight, "Fill 'Er Up for Polio" (Oshinsky 2006). In 1955, those efforts bore fruit, and a vaccine was created that was rolled out nationwide by the Eisenhower administration to rid the United States of this deadly disease.

AN IMMIGRANT THREAT?

Some threats like polio imminently endanger the lives of citizens, triggering visceral reactions on the part of the public and generating bipartisan support for action. Other threats emerge in a more politically charged environment in which partisans of different political parties may see an issue like immigration differently. They may even differ on whether immigration is a threat. In the mid-2000s, immigration was a contentious political issue in the United States, particularly in Western states like Arizona and California where demographic change and cross-border migration began to stoke fears among some. One response to this potential threat came from groups such as the Minuteman Project, who led vigilante border enforcement efforts. Others, like Ray Ybarra of the ACLU, were more afraid of overzealous efforts. Describing the Minuteman, Ybarra said: "I don't think these guys are all evil racists or anything. I just think the fact they see every migrant coming across as an object and as something to fear that is going to ruin our society is scary" (Wood 2005).

Although immigration reform failed at the federal level in 2007, at the state level, restrictive immigration policies gained traction. Advocates of these policies argued that they were necessary to protect both public safety and the economic structure of the United States. In 2009, Republican Secretary of State Jan Brewer succeeded Democrat Janet Napolitano as governor of Arizona. Virtually unknown outside of Arizona, Brewer shored up her support in the party by promoting highly restrictive immigration policies. In April 2010, those efforts culminated in SB 1070, a bill that would require police officers to request the immigration papers of anyone they thought might be in the country illegally (Allan 2010). Using threatening language, Brewer justified support for that bill by tying immigrants to drug trafficking: "They're coming here, and they're bringing drugs. And they're doing drophouses, and they're extorting people, and they're terrorizing families" (Rough 2010). Other politicians cautioned that the law itself was a threat. President Obama decried the Arizona law for potentially undermining "basic notions of fairness that we cherish as Americans, as well as the trust between police and our communities that is so crucial to keeping us safe" (Archibold 2010).

Immigration dominated the headlines again in the summer of 2014, as tens of thousands of children, many of them unaccompanied, crossed from Mexico into the United States illegally, most of them originating from El Salvador, Honduras, and Guatemala (Kuhnhenn 2014). The influx of immigrants was widely covered in the news, with the surge driven in part by drug violence in Central America alongside a misinformation campaign from human traffickers that the Obama administration was accepting Central American minors. Many Americans took to the streets in rallies and protests, with some advocating stronger borders and others hoping for a humanitarian response and a resolution to the wider immigration problem. President Obama asked for $3.7 billion to deal with the problem, while other politicians tried to position themselves as "tough" on immigration. In July 2014, Texas governor Rick Perry ordered 1,000 National Guard troops to defend the border, arguing, "Drug cartels, human traffickers, and individuals are exploiting this tragedy for their own criminal opportunities. ... I will not stand idly by while our citizens are under assault, and little children from Central America are detained in squalor"[1] (Fernandez and Shear 2014). The American public remains decidedly anxious about immigration.

* * * * *

As these vignettes illustrate, whether the issue is an infectious disease like polio or new immigrants, American life is often threatening. Crisis, threat, and worry are relatively common phenomena in the American landscape.

---

[1] Prior to this event, Governor Perry was perhaps best known nationally for his failed 2012 presidential run. He was widely criticized for his support of in-state tuition for undocumented immigrants and his comments regarding those who didn't agree with him on the issue: "I don't think you have a heart."

In the past century alone, the country experienced numerous occasions of peril – the Great Depression, Pearl Harbor, World War II, the Cold War, the Cuban Missile Crisis, gas shortages, the Iran hostage crisis, the Oklahoma City bombing, September 11, and the 2008 economic collapse. On these occasions, the public turned to the government for guidance about how best to protect and preserve the United States and its people. Contemporary American life is no exception to this pattern. Immigrants stealing American jobs, swine flu sickening thousands, floods and storms brought on by global warming, and terrorists plotting to kill innocents are just some of the many purported dangers of modern American existence. Politicians and the news media regularly sound warnings about threats to the nation and citizens' lives and safety. Candidates running for office and elected leaders warn the public of risks to health, safety, and security. It is difficult to turn on a news channel without hearing about the latest virus, food, political regime, or ideology that is an imminent threat to one's life and the security of the nation. The mass media disproportionately cover threatening issues such as crime and terrorism (Iyengar 1991), and, even within newscasts, the media focus prominently on the most threatening aspects of stories and spend far less time providing reassuring information to the public (Nacos, Bloch-Elkon, and Shapiro 2011).

What are the consequences for an American public besieged with emotional appeals, evocative imagery, and threatening news? In this book, we explore how political anxiety shapes how the American public engages with politics. Political thinkers and democratic theorists express concern that the anxiety created by contemporary politics may undercut citizens' abilities to make rational political choices (Edelman 1985; Hamilton, Jay, and Madison 1961). Yet recent research from political science and psychology paints a more hopeful picture of anxiety, suggesting that political fears may lead to more knowledgeable and trusting citizens (Brader 2006; Garsten 2006; Marcus 2002; Marcus, Neuman, and MacKuen 2000; McDermott 2004; Neuman et al. 2007).

Anxiety signals to individuals that a threat is present in the environment that is personally relevant to them and motivates a desire and need for protection. Our fundamental argument is that political anxiety shapes how individual citizens interact with politics by affecting how they search for information, who they trust in times of crises, and their political attitudes. By political anxiety, we mean simply anxiety felt on the individual level about political issues. People vary in what makes them anxious – one person's threat can be another person's hope. The problems causing anxiety might exceed individual or community coping capacity, and anxious people often want government intervention to protect them from harm. The uncertainty and negative feelings that accompany anxiety are unpleasant, and individuals are motivated to regulate this emotion through strategies that restore a sense of security and affective balance. Citizens cope with this anxiety in a number of ways that we trace through the book. Coping mechanisms can take on a variety of forms, including bolstering self-esteem or putting more trust in neighbors and friends. We expect, though, that when anxiety comes from the world of politics, ultimately, the resolution of anxiety comes from political rather than private behaviors and attitudes.

Our focus in this book is on a variety of anxieties that motivate citizens to engage with the political world. Throughout this book, we explore how the public's anxieties about immigration, public health, terrorism, and climate change shape our current politics. Some political anxieties, like the fear of infectious disease, originate from the fear of illness and physical violence and need no framing from elites to frighten the public. Other anxieties, like fears about immigration and climate change, are what we called *framed threats*, those related to uncertainty over one's place in society, the quality of that society, or the economic health of the country, and require more explanation from elites about why the public should be worried. Americans made anxious by elites, events, and issues seek protection from threats to their lives, livelihoods, planet, and culture by seeking information, putting their trust in select political institutions and leaders, and supporting policies framed as protective.

Anxiety might cause us to engage in politics, but it can also alter the shape of that engagement. Our research reconciles the generally normatively positive portrayal of anxiety in political psychology with the strategic uses of threatening appeals by political elites. Anxious citizens learn, trust, and hold political attitudes. Campaigns can take advantage of an anxious politics, and even help to create it because there are systematic ways in which these processes occur. In an anxious politics, we learn threatening information, we trust certain expert or relevant figures at the expense of others, and we hold political attitudes that are framed as protective.

Political anxiety occurs in a partisan world. Politicians compete over the emotional agenda, telling the public what to be anxious about, as well as what policies will ultimately alleviate their anxiety. Politicians have an incentive to both make the public anxious and to tap into their anxiety on policies where their party is perceived as having expertise and the most effective solutions. Republicans generally benefit when the public worries about the ill effects of immigration, future terrorism, or crime, whereas Democrats are more trusted when the public is concerned about the environment or education. Partisanship and other political identities can act as a bulwark against anxiety's persuasive power, though. Elites are not equally successful at making all citizens anxious, particularly about framed threats. Scaring the public may help a politician persuade partisans across the political spectrum to elect him or support her favored policy when threats are new, uncertain, and not yet associated with only one political party. Yet repeated use of threatening appeals may lessen the effectiveness, both because the public begins to tune out warnings for threats that may not occur (i.e., the Chicken Little phenomenon) and because the anxious appeal becomes associated with one political party. When the sky does not fall or when anxiety seems overtly partisan, sections of the public may refuse to become anxious. During times of crisis, though, anxiety can lead citizens to set aside partisanship and their own policy predispositions and follow political leaders who they normally would not, thus making an anxious politics very appealing to political elites.

Partisan politics shape not only who becomes anxious but also what types of solutions anxious citizens support. When an issue is closely associated with a political party (e.g., immigration for Republicans and climate change for Democrats), partisanship can shape the ways that anxious people engage in politics. Anxious people seek out threatening news, but partisanship affects who remembers that news. Anxious people put their trust in relevant, expert figures, but on partisan issues, anxious people trust the political party seen as more effective on that issue. Finally, anxious people are drawn to policies that protect them from threat, and parties compete to offer protection.

Anxiety in Democratic Life

Passion is a sort of fever of the mind, which ever leaves us weaker than it found us.

William Penn (1909), *Fruits of Solitude*

Anxiety is the hand maiden of creativity.

T. S. Elliot

Emotions matter in politics – enthusiastic supporters return politicians to office, angry citizens march in the streets, a fearful public demands protection from the government. Yet, in much of Western political thought, emotions are either ignored or derided as destructive to democracy. Until recently, scholarship in political science paid little sustained attention to how emotions such as anxiety affect political life, focusing instead on the cognitive and rational aspects of politics. We explore the emotional life of politics in this book, with particular emphasis on how political anxieties affect public life. When the world is scary, when politics is passionate, when the citizenry is anxious, does this politics resemble politics under more serene conditions? If politicians use threatening appeals to motivate and persuade citizens, how does the public respond?

Throughout this book, we show that political anxiety triggers engagement in politics and that it does so in ways that are potentially both promising and damaging for democracy. Using four substantive policy areas (public health, immigration, terrorism, and climate change), we demonstrate that anxiety triggers learning, but it also prioritizes attention to threatening information. Anxiety can push citizens toward trusting the government in times of crisis, but this can leave people open to manipulation. We also find that political anxiety increases support for protective and potentially anti-democratic policies. Anxiety about politics triggers coping strategies in the political world, where these strategies are often shaped by partisan agendas.

This book provides a fuller picture of anxiety in politics and gets us closer to reconciling the current normative appreciation of anxiety with the political uses of anxiety. Emotions like anxiety may benefit citizens by increasing attention and making political choices easier, but we doubt that political elites and the news media evoke fear in order to create better citizens. Democratic citizenship in an anxious world can be a deeper, more informed citizenship. Without a full spectrum of voices from partisan political elites, though, anxious citizens in search of protection from threats to their health and way of life may support charlatans or madmen who offer bodily protection while destroying the body politic.

In much of foundational Western thought, emotion plays a role in conceptions of citizenship and the correct form of government, and it rarely is viewed in a positive light. In Plato's parable of the cave, human beings are trapped by desire and prevented from moving up into reason, thus underscoring the idea that emotion undermines rational thought. In Plato's conception of democracy, the rulers are defined by emotional disorder, an unstable system that would eventually lead to tyranny or rule by fear (Neblo 2007). For Thomas Hobbes, emotion is a universal experience and fundamental to the formation of governance. For Hobbes, the fear of death is a motivating force in political life, encouraging and indeed compelling individuals to form a government to protect themselves from anarchy and its dangers. Hobbes argues that fear of physical violence made the state of nature intolerable, leading citizens toward endowing a government with authority to rule and keep citizens safe. In order to escape this fear, those in the state of nature were motivated "to seek and accept a sovereign who will ensure public peace and mutual compliance with freely made arrangements and their resulting obligations" (Hobbes 2008). Anxiety thus leads to support for a sovereign who can ensure public safety; yet, this is not always a democratically elected or accountable leader.

American political philosophy perpetuated the notion of emotion as destructive and destabilizing of governance. Much of the focus in the *Federalist Papers* is on how to build institutions that can limit the force of passion in the newly formed American government. In *Federalist 71*, Alexander Hamilton argues that government should only respond to the true opinions of the community, not to "every sudden breeze of passion or to every transient impulse which the public may receive from the arts of men who flatter their prejudices to betray their interests" (Hamilton, Jay, and Madison 1961, 432). Twentieth-century scholars concerned about the rise of totalitarianism, fascism, and the atrocities of two world wars also suggested that emotions, cued by political propaganda, affected mass behavior in damaging ways (Lasswell 1927; Lippmann 1943) and that the public can be convinced to act, often violently and against their interests, through the manipulation of affect (Edelman 1985). Contemporary deliberative theories (Ackerman and Fishkin 2004; Fishkin 1995; Habermas 1989) generally consider emotion as an impediment to reasoned discussion, the recognition of one's true interests, and deliberation as a democratic practice.

Whereas political philosophers focused on emotion's role in society, for many decades, empirical social science ignored emotion, instead focusing on a colder, calculating politics. Much of the political science literature on mass political behavior emphasizes cognition – what citizens know or do not (Berelson, Lazarsfeld, and McPhee 1954; Converse 1964; Delli Carpini and Keeter 1996), how citizens learn about politics (Gilens and Murakawa 2002; Iyengar and Kinder 1987; Prior 2007), and how they utilize information in making political decisions (Campbell et al. 1960; Lau and Redlawsk 2006; Lupia 1994; Zaller 1992). The rational choice perspective, in particular, underscores how individuals weigh cost-benefit information in making political decisions (Downs 1957; Fiorina 1981; Lupia, McCubbins, and Popkin 2000) and rarely considers how emotions may inhibit or enhance decision making (but see Lupia and Menning 2009). For decades, psychology's cognitive revolution similarly undervalued emotions, placing the focus instead on processes like perception and memory, which were conceived of as separate from emotion (LeDoux 2000). If emotions are epiphenomenal, this underemphasis on emotional processes may be sensible, but recent work shows the systematic effects of emotion on political life.

This is not to say that emotion was wholly ignored in psychology or political behavior research. In cognitive psychology, Abelson's concept of "hot cognition" (1963) called for closer attention to affective processes. Taking up Abelson's call, Zajonc (1980) argued that affect is primary, basic, and inescapable in how individuals judge the world around them. Emotion also appears in earlier work on political behavior. Research on the authoritarian personality (Adorno et al. 1950), Lane's investigations of the common man (1962), and Sears's theory of symbolic politics (1986, 1993; Sears et al. 1980) all consider emotion's place in political life, although emotion rarely plays a constructive role in these works.

In recent decades, though, social scientists have turned their attention back to emotion's role in a wide variety of phenomena such as voting (Abelson et al. 1982; Marcus and MacKuen 1993), candidate and presidential evaluations (Conover and Feldman 1986; Steenbergen and Ellis 2006), information processing (Redlawsk, Civinetti, and Lau 2007), framing effects (Dillard et al. 1996; Druckman and McDermott 2008; Huddy and Gunnthorsdottir 2000), and public opinion (Brader 2002, 2006; Huddy, Feldman, and Cassese 2007; Huddy et al. 2003; Kinder 1994). In addressing the serious concern of political observers about emotion's destructive capacity, research in the past two decades reveals that emotion may be a useful and constructive part of political life. As Kinder (1994, 310) put it, "Emotion is, in some respects, an inevitable natural force. And nothing that is so essential to the human experience is likely to be all bad." Recent psychology, neuroscience, and political science work finds that emotion may be integral to learning (Marcus, Neuman, and MacKuen 2000; Redlawsk et al. 2007; Valentino et al. 2008), attitude formation (Brader, Valentino, and Suhay 2008; Zajonc 1980), and even reasoning (Damasio 1994; Lodge and Taber 2005; McDermott 2004). Even political theorists are touting the potential benefits of anxiety to the American public. Bryan Garsten (2006) argues in *Saving Persuasion* that anxiety might actually be a key to deeper reflection:

Deliberation and judgment therefore seem to emerge not in sedate citizens who reason, as Rousseau once proposed in the "silence of the passions" but instead in citizens who have been disturbed out of their calm and made attentive by sharp feelings of anxiety. Partiality and passion together, in the form of anxiety, can prod reflection. (Garsten 2006, 196)

We also see emotion as inextricable to political life. Furthermore, we believe that a focus either on how emotions can undercut rationality or on how emotions can cure democratic malaise can only tell half the story.

We argue that citizens think and act differently when they are emotionally involved in politics – particularly when they are anxious – than when emotion is less intense or absent. Fear does not paralyze the need for action, for turning passivity into activity, for advancing against an unseen enemy on foreign shores, as suggested by Franklin Roosevelt's famous quote. Anxiety prompts a need and desire for protection, and this motivates citizens to seek out this protection by utilizing coping mechanisms. Threats and the anxieties that accompany those threats lead to a public more engaged with politics, more trusting of expert political actors, and more supportive of public policies they believe will return security. Anxiety also leads to a bias toward threatening news, less trust in a range of political actors perceived as less expert, and increased support for denying rights in the name of safety.

UNDERSTANDING EMOTION AND ANXIETY

We are concerned with how anxiety affects a set of political outcomes – information processing, trust, and attitudes. Because our focus is on the substantive effects of one emotion, we do not offer a general theory of emotion in political life. Rather, we rely on previous scholarship in psychology and political science to illuminate the broad role of emotions in conditioning citizens' opinions and behavior and instead concentrate on how anxiety influences citizen motivations and conduct. As Kinder (1994) mentions, theories of emotions abound, and we heed his call for more empirical investigations of the consequences of emotion. In this section, we define emotion, differentiate emotion from other phenomena like moods, and describe differences across emotions.

Emotions are "multi-faceted, whole-body phenomena" (Gross and Thompson 2009, 5) that occur when individuals evaluate a situation as relevant to their goals and involve changes in perceptions, behavior, and physiology (Clore and Isbell 2001; Gross and Thompson 2009). Emotions are internal states that represent an "evaluative, valenced reaction to events, agents, or objects" (Nabi 1999, 295) and may vary in intensity. Emotions are made up of five separate components: (1) an appraisal or evaluation of the situation, (2) a physiological reaction, (3) a change in cognitive activity, (4) an action tendency, and (5) a subjective feeling state. Whether cognition precedes emotion or the converse, emotions are a central feature not only of social experience (Damasio 1994; James 1884), but, as we show, also of political experience because they influence political thoughts and motivate behavior. Not only do emotions make us feel something, they also encourage us to *do something*.

Emotions are related to but distinct from mood and affect. Mood represents diffuse states that are not attached to any particular objects and are longer lasting than emotions (see Gray and Watson 2007, for a review). Because moods are not tied to a specific provoking stimulus, they involve less thinking than emotions (Cassino and Lodge 2007; Forgas 1995) but can bias cognition (Clore, Schwarz, and Conway 1994). Emotions are generally more intense than moods, are shorter lasting, and have a more definite cause. *Affect* is often used as a broader term that encompasses emotions and mood, as well as other phenomenon such as liking and disliking, pain, arousal, stress, and the like (Gross and Thompson 2009; Petty, Baker, and Gleicher 1991). Affect is a "physiological state that is experienced as either pleasant (positive affect) or unpleasant (negative affect)" (Ottati and Wyer 1993).

Drawing on functionalist approaches to emotion (Frijda 1988) and appraisal theory (Arnold 1960; Lerner and Keltner 2000; Roseman and Evdokas 2004; Smith and Ellsworth 1985), we use the idea that emotions serve to coordinate responses to circumstances that individuals confront and that their effects often persist past the original emotion-evoking event. Rather than being a mysterious process unrelated to reason or cognition, we agree with previous scholars that emotions evolved to assist humans in negotiating a complicated and sometimes dangerous environment. Simon (1967) claims that emotions act as an alarm system and direct people to redirect plans and efforts to goals they prioritize. Similarly, Dillard and colleagues tout the importance of emotion in evolutionary terms:

> Emotions function to enhance the likelihood of survival of individual organisms and, by extension, the species. The advantage of emotions over careful cognitive analysis is the rapidity and globality of response. In fact, one function of emotion is to alert the system to the state of the organism-environment relationship. (Dillard et al. 1996, 46)

Tooby and Cosmides (2008) also argue that emotions are fundamentally important to the human experience because they have evolved to solve adaptive problems and guide a host of other systems. Emotions, in this framework, are superordinate programs designed to direct the activities over other bodily processes including attention, perception, learning, physiology, reflexes, behavioral decision rules, communication processes, energy allocation, probability estimates, values, and regulatory variables such as self-esteem.

Emotional reactions provide individuals feedback about the nature and potential urgency of the contexts that they are in (Damasio 1994; Schwarz and Clore 1983a; Zajonc 1980). Positive affect and emotions signal that a situation is safe and heuristic thinking is adequate. Negative affect signals a problem in the environment that should be attended to more systematically (Clore and Isbell 2001). Feelings of risk are experienced rapidly and include often unconscious responses to perceived danger or threat (Slovic 1993; Slovic et al. 2005). The information provided by emotions is not duplicative of consciously acquired information, but instead these two systems are reinforcing. This is not to say that experienced emotions are always appropriate for a given situation or that emotions are always attributed to the correct cause. Emotional misattribution or the inability to regulate emotions can be the cause of psychopathology (Gross and Thompson 2009), social struggles, and changes in memory and perception (Schwarz and Clore 1983b; Tversky and Kahneman 1973).

Early studies of emotion by both political scientists and psychologists focused broadly on two qualities of emotions: *valence* (ranging from pleasant to unpleasant) and *arousal* (ranging from calm to excited) (Abelson et al. 1982; Bradley and Lang 2000; Osgood, Suci, and Tannenbaum 1957). Valence models allow researchers to show how positive or negative evaluations of candidates or issues affect attitudes in a relatively low-effort way (Bargh et al. 1996; Sniderman, Brody, and Tetlock 1993). In the "affect as information" model (Forgas 1995), individuals are able to use mood or general affective states as substitutes for detailed information in making judgments. Rather than relying on memories or conscious thoughts about a policy, individuals base their evaluations on their positive or negative feelings about groups affected by the policy. Affectively charged information can be embedded in the judgment process and influence the encoding and use of information (Bargh et al. 1996; Forgas 1995). These valence models are useful in tracing out how sets of emotions shape evaluations and attitudes, but they are unable to differentiate how specific emotions may influence behaviors in different ways. Our focus on the discrete emotion of anxiety draws most heavily from the cognitive appraisal approach but recognizes the importance of valence and arousal.

Theories in the cognitive appraisal family emphasize how perception of the environment affects the formation and application of emotion (Frijda 1988; Lazarus 1991; Nabi 1999; Ortony, Clore, and Collins 1990; Roseman, Spindel, and Jose 1990; Smith and Ellsworth 1985). Frijda, Kuipers, and ter Schure (1989) contend that "events are appraised as emotionally relevant when they appear to favor or harm the individual's concerns: his or her major goals, motives, or sensitivities" (1989, 213). These goals may include meeting societal and personal ideals, and appraisal is a key step between a situation and emotion (Scherer 2003). Similarly, Clore and Isbell (2001) state that appraisals "reflect one's goals and concerns, and are therefore as important in guiding human behavior as is a rudder in guiding the ship" (Clore and Isbell 2001, 106).

Once an appraisal of relevance and either benefit or harm is made, emotions can be signaled that then determine other responses. Note that this appraisal process does not need to occur consciously and that attributions are not always accurate. Misattribution of emotional states from one situation to another may result because it is often difficult to separate how one feels about a candidate, policy, or piece of information from how one feels more generally. Although individuals may misattribute their anxiety about their job to anxiety about national economic conditions, we are interested in how expressed anxiety matters for politics, even if the emotional accounting is off.

Anxiety occurs when individuals appraise a situation as being unpleasant, highly threatening and uncertain (Lerner and Keltner 2000, 2001; Roseman and Evdokas 2004), and when the situation seems out of control (Smith and Ellsworth 1985). Anxiety is not merely a threat to a disliked consequence but also is a reaction to a perception that a situation, person, or object poses a threat to one's own well-being. We rely on Eysenck's definition of anxiety as an "unpleasant and aversive state" with the purpose of detecting threat and danger in the environment (Eysenck 1992). Anxiety is a negatively valenced emotion but differs from other negative emotions such as anger, sadness, and disgust, which involve different cognitive appraisals (Lerner and Keltner 2001). Anxiety involves uncertainty (Steenbergen and Ellis 2006), whereas anger involves certainty over obstacles blocking progress toward a desired goal and blame on harm inflicted by others (Brader 2011). Sadness comes from an inability to achieve goals and the loss of valued objects and people. Like anxiety, sadness often causes attention to information, but this attention is often backward looking and reflective rather than directed at ameliorating future threats. Disgust is a reaction to "the presence of noxious conditions (e.g., rotting food, bodily excretions)" (Brader 2011, 195) and comes from an evolutionary urge to remain clean and safe (Smith et al. 2012). Shame comes from the recognition of one's inability or unwillingness to meet standards and motivates individuals to hide, but it also enforce these standards on others. We focus on anxiety because it is a common phenomenon in politics, and it has important political effects.

Political scientists are increasingly interested in how anxiety affects political life. One of the most influential theories of emotion within political science is Marcus, MacKuen, and Neuman's theory of *Affective Intelligence* (AI), a theory that focuses on three major emotions: anxiety, enthusiasm, and anger/aversion. AI posits that two emotional systems, the dispositional and the surveillance systems, help citizens to organize the political environment (Marcus and MacKuen 1993; Marcus et al. 2000; Neuman et al. 2007). The dispositional system regulates the execution of previously learned behavior and receives feedback from the environment about the success of those behaviors that make up habits. The surveillance system provides citizens with warnings about novel situations and potential threats, signaling that an innovative response is necessary. When the surveillance system senses a threat in the environment, it signals that citizens should pay closer attention and gather more information in order to counter the threat. Citizens mainly rely on their political habits to guide new decisions unless they are made anxious about candidates or issues. A major implication of the AI theory is that, once anxious, citizens are motivated to learn, pay attention to news coverage, and base political decisions more heavily on contemporary information rather than partisanship. Brader's (2006) experimental study of how emotive campaign ads influence learning, participation, and voting also emphasizes how anxiety can increase learning and the potential for persuasion. Scholarship on Americans' reactions to the 9/11 terrorist attacks highlights the important role of anxiety (Huddy et al. 2005a, 2005b, 2007; Schlenger et al. 2002; Schuster et al. 2001; Skitka et al. 2006) as does recent work on topics as varied as immigration attitudes (Brader et al. 2008), health behaviors (Gravatt and Brown 2011; Green and Witte 2003; Groenendyk, Brader, and Valentino 2011; Witte 1992), and environmental risks (Meijnders, Midden, and Wilke 2001).

ANXIETY AND POLITICS

Because typically anxiety is unpleasant for those people experiencing it, we expect that citizens will try to cope with this emotion in a variety of ways. Individuals do not merely passively experience emotions; they also try to regulate those emotions by increasing pleasant emotions and decreasing unpleasant ones like anxiety (Gross 2009; Gross and Thompson 2009). Emotions are motivating, meaning that they cause us to want to act. In particular, anxiety motivates individuals to avoid danger, seek protection, and create a safer environment (Jarymowicz and Bar-Tal 2006; Nabi 1999; Roseman and Evdokas 2004). When the emotion that we feel is negative, misplaced, or destructive to the situation, we often do something to reduce the intensity or the valence of the emotion that we feel. Emotional regulation can range from unconscious, automatic techniques developed in childhood (i.e., avoiding upsetting information or steering attention to pleasant faces) to more effortful, conscious processes such as hiding one's anger at immigrants in particular company. When anxiety originates from political life, we expect that individuals will employ more conscious processes connected to politics (i.e., calling a Member of Congress) more often than interpersonal methods (i.e., calling a friend).

We focus on three ways that citizens may cope with political anxiety: (1) seek information, (2) endow trust in government, and (3) support protective public policies. These behaviors need not all occur for an anxious citizen to feel better about politics. Nor do we assume that some methods are better than others. Here, we describe each coping process in turn and further lay out our expectations of how anxiety shapes these processes in specific cases in Chapters 3–5.

Information Seeking

As one way of regulating emotion, individuals may seek information, which we explore in Chapter 3. Both seeking information and avoiding information may serve to lessen anxiety either by resolving uncertainty or ignoring the cause of anxiety (Gross and Thompson 2009). As Maslow (1963) stated, "we can seek knowledge in order to reduce anxiety and we can also avoid knowing in order to reduce anxiety" (1963, 122). When individuals feel they are ill-equipped to deal with harms or the information environment, they may simply avoid information as a coping mechanism (Green and Witte 2003). However, based on previous scholarship that shows increased attentiveness under conditions of political anxiety (Brader 2006; Huddy et al. 2007; Marcus et al. 2000; Valentino et al. 2008), we expect that anxiety will tend to increase attention, particularly when information provides solutions. Political anxiety caused by a variety of sources such as ads (Brader 2006), candidates (Kinder, Abelson, and Fiske 1979; Valentino et al. 2009), policy changes (MacKuen et al. 2010), and threatening events (Boyle et al. 2004) increases both the desire for information and the active search for information.

Although individuals seek information in the pursuit of lowering anxiety, the information that they are attracted to may not help them accomplish this goal. As individuals pursue information, we expect that their search will concentrate on threatening information because this information may seem more relevant to avoiding future harms and thus potentially reducing anxiety than positive information (Cacioppo and Berntson 1994; Lau 1982). From an evolutionary standpoint, anxiety motivates shifting perception and attention toward the source of a threat, reweighting safety as the highest goal, directing memory toward useful retrieval tasks, and activating specialized learning systems (Tooby and

Cosmides 2008). In the throes of political anxiety, citizens seek information that is relevant to the source of their anxiety (Brader 2006) and use information more efficiently (Valentino et al. 2009). When losses loom larger than gains in judgments (Kahneman and Tversky 1979), avoiding future harm and reducing uncomfortable feelings make useful information imperative. Negative, threatening pieces of news provide an efficient way to evaluate whether anxiety is warranted and what the potential remedies are for it.

Political Trust

For representative government to function properly, citizens must put at least minimal trust in the actors who govern on their behalf. We argue that another method by which people cope with the uncertainty and negative affect that underlie political anxiety is to trust expert political actors to protect them from threats. We investigate trust in Chapter 4. Trust acts as an emotional regulation technique, a palliative for citizens made anxious by events and elites. As Levi and Stoker (2000) so aptly put, "If trusting, an individual is freed from worry and from the need to monitor the other's behavior or to extricate herself from the relationship" (495).

Trust helps individuals to manage and mitigate risks. In a society with complex and potentially perilous threats, citizens must put their trust in institutions to handle these risks. Complex policy problems such as environmental disasters, disease outbreaks, or confronting terrorism demand collective rather than personal solutions. As Merolla and Zechmeister (2009) write:

Collective crises tend to have solutions that lie beyond the control of any given individual or household. Individuals might take certain measures to in order to mitigate the personal damage that occurs in the face of a collective crisis (e.g., stocking the house with gas masks in the face of a terrorist threat) but these individual measures are unlikely to forestall or resolve the crisis condition entirely. (27)

As such, we concentrate on how anxiety influences trust in political actors rather than interpersonal trust (Putnam 1994). Hand-washing is a potentially effective behavior that can lessen the threat of any individual getting sick from the flu or other infectious diseases, but without organized vaccine programs or quarantine plans, quelling disease outbreaks is unlikely. Similarly, some individuals might take action against illegal immigration (i.e., participating in Minutemen militias), but only coordinated governmental policy can resolve immigration problems. This means that citizens must turn toward government actors to help lower anxiety.

Trusting involves believing that others will act "as they should" (Barber 1983) and that a person or institution will "observe the rules of the game" (Citrin and Muste 1999). Hetherington defines political trust as the "degree to which people perceive the government is producing outcomes consistent with their expectations" (2005, 9). Cleary and Stokes see trust as relational, "trust involves a relationship between actors regarding an action. ... Trust is a belief (that is, A's beliefs that B will do X)" (2006, 12). As Levi and Stoker (2000) note, political trust judgments reflect citizens' evaluations of the current political context rather than their social characteristics or political identities.

We argue that judgments of government trust depend on individuals' emotional state as well. General trust judgments are more than ideological or partisan reactions to specific political figures or incumbent administrations (Levi and Stoker 2000). This suggests that a political environment of crisis, threat, and anxiety should influence trust in government broadly among the populace. When governments appear unable or unwilling to handle societal problems such as the economy and crime, trust in government wanes (Chanley, Rudolph, and Rahn 2000; Hetherington and Rudolph 2008; Mansbridge 1997). Whereas inefficient government tends to decrease trust, perceptions of procedural fairness in distributing benefits (Tyler, Rasinski, and McGraw 1985) and competence augment trust (Barber 1983; Levi 1988).

Political trust is a crucial component of governance (Citrin 1974; Hetherington 1998). As Hetherington (1998) argues, political trust is both a cause and by-product of how citizens evaluate the government and incumbent elites, and political distrust creates an environment where it is difficult for political leaders to successfully implement policy. Trust increases compliance with a wide range of government policies that call for sacrifice, including taxation (Scholz and Lubell 1998), cooperation in collective action problems (Tyler and Degoey 1995), public health mandates (Leavitt 2003), and support for economic redistribution (Chanley, Rudolph, and Rahn 2000; Hetherington 2005; Rudolph and Evans 2005). Trust is useful for both constituents and legislators because it fosters political accountability by providing citizens a low-effort heuristic for sanctioning or rewarding elected officials (Bianco 1994).

More trusted politicians are endowed with more leeway to exercise power and judgment even when their actions may be at odds with or more extreme than what the constituency wants (Bianco 1994; Egan 2012; Ferejohn 1999) because officials can be discovered and punished. We expect that anxious citizens put their trust in experts who can handle the threats that create anxiety.

Political Attitudes

Just as anxiety drives people to pay attention to threatening information and trust relevant figures, we also expect that it leads them to support policies that they think of as protective. Anxiety motivates individuals to seek safety, and this can take the form of either flight or fight mechanisms (Halperin, Sharvit, and Gross 2011; Jarymowicz and Bar-Tal 2006; Nabi 1999; Roseman and Evdokas 2004). Anxiety also increases the potency of frames (Druckman and McDermott 2008) as well as increases the potential for persuasion by elites (Brader 2006; Marcus et al. 2000). Together, this suggests that the motivation to seek protection may lead citizens to follow the policy prescriptions of the most prominent elite voices, particularly if those policies seem effective at lessening threat (Rogers 1975). Policy solutions may appear to be particularly effective because of the character of the policy itself, because the elite offering it has an advantage in that policy domain, or because few other solutions are offered by other elites.

Previous research suggests that threat and anxiety increase support for protective policies across a variety of policy areas. Citizens who feel threatened by crime and terrorism are more supportive of civil liberties restrictions on fellow citizens than are those who are less threatened (Berinsky 2009; Davis 2007; Marcus et al. 1996; Mondak and Hurwitz 2012). Worry about violence tends to increase support for more punitive crime policy (Page and Shapiro 1992) as well as lower support for the consolidation of democracy in the developing world (Merolla, Montalvo, and Zechmeister 2012). Anxiety over immigration from Mexico increases support for restrictive immigration policies (Brader et al. 2008).

Although these examples all suggest that anxiety increases support for policies on the right, not all anxiety leads to support for more conservative policies. The political environment shapes whether anxiety may increase support for protective policies offered from the right or the left. Days after the 2004 Madrid bombings, Spanish citizens voted in a socialist government that promised to pull Spanish troops from Iraq (Rose, Murphy, and Abrahms 2007). The Great Depression ushered in an era of liberal government in the United States and Sweden, but led to conservative governments in Australia and Britain (Achen and Bartels 2005). Natural disasters like droughts and floods tend to decrease the vote share of sitting incumbents of both parties (Achen and Bartels 2002), suggesting that anxiety may not consistently favor one side of the ideological spectrum but rather depend on political context.

What sorts of policies are best suited to offer protection? Answers to this question vary in the population, and they also vary by policy area. Political elites play a significant role in drawing the link between public anxiety and proposed solutions, especially in portraying their recommended policy action as effective and protective. Edelman's theory of symbolic politics (1985) also suggests that, in a political world where crisis is ubiquitous, public anxiety produces a desire for reassurance and placation to quiet doubts. Political leaders offer this reassurance through attaching emotion to abstract symbols such as groups, leaders, and political enemies. For Edelman, the myth and ritual surrounding symbols provide meaning to the anxious person's life, creating reassurance and contentment:

Politics is for most of us a passing parade of abstract symbols, yet a parade which our experience teaches us to be a benevolent or malevolent force that can be close to omnipotent. Because politics does visibly confer wealth, take life, imprison, and free people, and represent a history with strong emotional and ideological associations, its processes became easy objects upon which to displace private emotions, especially strong anxieties and hopes. (1985, 5)

For Edelman, anxious citizens are ripe for manipulation by elites who use symbols to divert the public's attention from self-interest into actions that facilitate the interests of elites. Our view is more optimistic about how elites help the public to regulate and resolve their anxiety. In our model, political figures offer to a worried citizenry not only symbols but also tangible policy framed as protective. Worried citizens will support these protective policies when they believe the policies are effective and that the government is capable of implementing them.

This is not to say that policies framed as protective are necessarily the best possible policy options, that public anxiety cannot be channeled into democratically questionable behavior such as racial prejudice or violence, or that the public cannot be manipulated. Using a game theory model, Lupia and Menning (2009) predict that politicians can send unwarranted fear signals (i.e., claim that there is a threat when none exists) when citizens cannot receive feedback about the true threat and thus manipulate the public into supporting bad policies. This is most likely to occur for distant, abstract, or ambiguous threats because these issues are less likely to provide the type of feedback for citizens to "realize, rethink, and change previous behaviors" (2009, 101). In addition, convincing an anxious public to support a particular set of protective policies should prove easier when one policy option dominates elite discussion and has few dissenting voices (Zaller 1992). However, for some policy areas with more elite divergence, persuasion should be more difficult even when anxiety is high.

COPING IN A PARTISAN WORLD

Some threats are not heavily debated. In some situations, everyone experiences anxiety, and political elites agree on a solution. For example, a tornado warning will cause people to worry and government officials to urge people to take cover. However, many threats in politics are more nuanced. An economic crisis will generate anxiety, but not everyone will worry about her own job or wealth, and political elites might fight over whether increased spending or austerity will bring the economy back. In a political context where political elites disagree over which actors are responsible for the source of threat and solutions to the anxiety-causing threats, we expect partisanship to shape which actors citizens turn toward to alleviate anxiety.

Generally, when citizens see similarity between their own policy preferences and government outputs, they are more satisfied with policies and are more trusting of government (Citrin 1974; Miller 1974); they become less satisfied as policies appear further from their ideals (Hetherington 1998). As the parties vocally disagree about the resolutions to threats and policy issues become politicized, we expect that individuals will turn toward expert elites for guidance about what policies to support that they perceive will keep the public safe and improve their emotional state. For example, in Israel, after rocket attacks, support for right-wing parties increases because these parties are seen as more capable of handling security (Getmansky and Zeitzoff 2014). In more politicized policy areas, those actors who come from the party that "owns" the policy area may be deemed more expert and therefore more trustworthy in times of threat (Egan 2013, Petrocik 1996).

Partisanship and Information Seeking

Anxiety may free individuals from partisan biases in how they search for information, or it may serve to reinforce their predispositions. Partisans exhibit resistance to information inconsistent with beliefs, as well as factual information that would necessitate updating evaluations, and this bias is not mitigated by political knowledge (Bartels 2002; Shani 2006; Zaller 1992). Bartels argues that partisanship "is ... a pervasive dynamic force shaping citizens' perceptions of, and reactions to, the political world" (138). Partisanship not only shapes attitudes but also how partisans search for and retain political information. Partisans are motivated to seek out and evaluate information in ways consistent with their partisan identities, which may include ignoring or discounting information that would challenge their previous views (Klapper 1960; Lord, Ross, and Lepper 1979; Vallone, Ross, and Lepper 1985). Together, these biases suggest that partisans may be immune to the effects of anxiety on information seeking if the threatening news that they encounter disagrees with their political predispositions. Yet, anxiety may also break through the partisan wall to free individuals to more broadly seek information to balance their anxiety, even if that information leads to updating beliefs. Marcus et al. (2000) state the proposition this way: "when anxious, people would no longer rely on their political habits (thus mindless partisanship would no longer figure in the vote equation)" (61). They argue that, in a threatening political environment, political identities such as partisanship and group membership are set aside and that these identities do not affect information processing. In Chapter 3, we test how partisanship shapes the type and valence of information that partisans seek.

Partisanship and Trust

Anxiety may either increase or decrease trust in a variety of political actors, conditional on whether the government is the source of the anxiety, whether the actor has expertise in the area of concern, and whether one party is advantaged on the policy. Political elites help citizens to link their own anxiety into trust in the various elements that make up the American government. When the government is not blamed as the cause of anxiety and can offer solutions to threats and, citizens may increasingly trust government actors. When political anxiety stems from government policy failure, though, this anxiety may lead citizens to decrease trust in the political actors responsible for the anxiety, not necessarily the whole political system.

Actors who come from the party who "owns" that issue should be advantaged on expertise grounds. Political parties maintain "issue owning" advantages on select policy areas (Petrocik 1996; Petrocik, Benoit, and Hansen 2003; Simon 2002), areas where the party is seen as more competent, consistent, and more active based on the party's priorities and constituency (Egan 2013). On owned issues, parties appear more sincere and committed to delivering policy (Egan 2013; Rabinowitz and Macdonald 1989) and generally focus rhetoric on owned issues (Petrocik 1996). If anxious respondents consider the owning party to be the most knowledgeable about the policy and have the most capacity to give useful information, then trust should be higher in the owning party than in the less expert/non-owning party.

Partisanship and Political Attitudes

There is widespread consensus about what will keep us safe in some policy domains. For example, in the realm of public health threats, there are generally agreed upon "best practices" designed to keep the public safe. Although even best practices can be debated in the public, such as whether to immunize girls against human papilloma virus (HPV) (Haber, Malow, and Zimet 2007), there is likely to be more of a consensus at the professional/elite level. In other policy areas, protective measures are more contested. People argue over whether undocumented immigrants pose a threat in the United States, and some Americans think that access to government services (education, welfare) creates a "magnet" that attracts more immigrants (Frey et al. 1996). Along this line of reasoning, denial of government services may help protect Americans from undocumented immigrants. When it comes to climate change, is it individuals, the U.S. government, or the international community that has to act? Activists would argue that all three are needed to combat global warming, but even they face disagreement over the best policies (nuclear power vs. renewable energy sources, cap-and-trade measures vs. carbon taxes). Finally, most Americans have experienced some level of anxiety over terrorism since 9/11 and wondered what sorts of policies will keep us safe. In the simplest comparison, we can think of hawkish foreign policy response versus a more dovish policy. Although certain elites advocated liberal internationalism after 9/11, we contend that the dominant framing was of a global "War on Terror", and that this hawkish policy was successfully framed as protective (Entman 2004).

Protective policies may originate from both parties, but we expect that policies that originate from an "owning" party may be deemed more attractive and effective at regulating anxiety. Over the past several decades, the Republican Party has "owned" the issues of taxation, terrorism, national security, and crime, whereas Democrats have been advantaged on the environment, education, and healthcare (Egan 2013). J. M. Miller (2007) notes that negative emotions mediate agenda setting, meaning that when anxiety is high, individuals are more likely to prioritize that issue as nationally important. If anxiety leads citizens to prioritize particular policies in judgments of leaders, and the parties themselves prioritize different issue areas, then anxious citizens may end up trusting an elite and supporting his or her policies even if they do not normally agree with that party. Given that anxiety stems from uncertainty and that owning parties seem able to deliver policies that can fix anxiety-producing problems, supporting the policies offered by the owning party may be an appealing way to lower anxiety (Egan 2013). Overall, we note that what counts as "protective" is malleable and subject to framing, but, with particular policies in particular contexts, we use our theory to construct workable hypotheses. Taken together, we expect that evoking anxiety should increase support for more protective public policies.

CONCLUSION

Anxieties about contemporary political issues such as immigration and climate change shape how Americans think and act in political life. Because anxiety is uncomfortable, we expect that individuals utilize a variety of mechanisms to regulate anxiety – seeking additional information, putting trust in government, and supporting protective policies. We explore each of these coping mechanisms in turn in the remainder of the book. Chapter 2 describes the four policy areas that we use and explains the basic contours of our experimental studies. Chapter 3 explores how anxiety influences the content of information seeking using immigration as a case study. In Chapter 4, we explore anxiety's effect on trust in both the areas of immigration and a public health outbreak. Chapter 5 utilizes all four policy areas (immigration, public health, terrorism, and climate change) to trace out anxiety's effects on attitudes. Last, Chapter 6 concludes with a discussion of the implications of anxiety for democratic theory.

2

What's Your Worry?

Finding and Creating Anxiety in the American Public

> *It did what all ads are supposed to do: create an anxiety relievable by purchase.*
>
> David Foster Wallace, *Infinite Jest* (1996)

A survey of American politics offers an embarrassment of riches when looking for anxiety. Anxiety appears to be everywhere, especially during campaign seasons. Terrorist attacks, crime waves, not to mention economic downturns, are just a few of the many areas of politics that are infused with anxiety. We chose four areas to focus on in our research: immigration, public health, terrorism, and climate change. Our case selection was driven first by a very practical concern: the policy areas had to trigger anxiety at least among a subset of the population. Then, we sought variation on two important dimensions for our theory: (1) whether the issue is inherently threatening or threatening dependent on framing and (2) the partisan dimensions of the issue (e.g., whether anxiety is concentrated on the left, the right, or spread among the population evenly, and whether a party is more closely associated with the issue). Public health crises and terrorist threats trigger widespread anxiety (although as these issues move further away from the crisis moment, they often become politicized). On the other hand, climate change tends to trigger more anxiety on the left, and immigration worries are more prevalent on the right. This variation is used to demonstrate the potential for and limits on anxiety as a persuasive tool. In subsequent chapters, we use experiments to study the relationship between anxiety and three coping mechanisms (learning, trust, and attitudes) across these different issue areas.

Our goal in this chapter is to offer an overview of our substantive cases. We begin by explaining our choice of policy areas and the important dimensions on which they differ. We also establish that each case has been the subject of considerable anxiety for the mass public through survey data. Finally, we describe our approach to studying the effects of anxiety on the mass public. We use three different experimental techniques to generate anxiety: (1) thought listings, (2) news stories, and (3) campaign ads. Together, these offer a full picture of how anxiety can affect the ways that citizens engage with politics.

ANXIETY-INDUCING THREATS

Societal upheavals, epidemics, wars, and campaigns possess the ability to force the public to stop, pay attention, and react emotionally. Some events are obvious and widely recognized as threats. Events that evoke dread and fear of death, that seem uncontrollable, that have catastrophic consequences for individuals and society (Lichtenstein et al. 1978) can create anxious feelings for everyone. Floods, the bubonic plague, terrorist bombings, or even shark attacks are threatening because they can cause imminent bodily harm and possibly death. These threats do not need to be framed, or, in other words, they do not have to rely on elite messaging to rattle our nerves. Other possible threats have a more subjective quality. Do immigrants make the United States economically strong and culturally enriched, or do they take American jobs and commit heinous crimes? Are gun control laws a common-sense public safety measure, or are they chipping away at our basic freedoms? Whether these topics trigger anxiety, apathy, or even enthusiasm depends on the way they have been framed by news media and political parties and what people care about. In Table 2.1, we outline our conceptualization of different types of threat.

Our two main cases occupy different cells, with disease outbreaks (threats to public health) as our unframed threat and immigration as our framed threat. Public health crises can evoke citizens' existential fear of death, a powerful force in shaping perceptions and behaviors (Cohen et al. 2005; Greenberg et al. 1990; Landau et al. 2004). Immigration, on the other hand, is a mixed case. Whether Americans feel anxious about immigrants depends on how immigrants are portrayed, as well as on contextual factors such as economic conditions and security issues. The separation between unframed and framed threats is not perfect. After all, some Americans will downplay the risk of a widely accepted health threat like the flu that actually causes sickness or may worry more about

TABLE 2.1: *Types of threats*

	Unframed Threats	Framed Threats
Definitions	Widely agreed upon cause of harm. Harms may include imminent bodily harm and/or death	Debated cause of harms (not necessarily physical), where harms can be delayed.
Examples	Disease Outbreaks Terrorist Attack Flood Attacks on border guards	Obesity Epidemic War on Terror Climate Change Immigration

* Underlined topics are our issues.

the harms of childhood immunization rather than the illnesses that vaccines are given against. Still, these debates tend to occur on the fringe, and the vast majority of the public is alarmed in the face of illness and death, at least when the illness is visible and imminent. It is also worth noting that the vast majority of threats that trigger anxiety in American politics depend upon framing. Events that trigger imminent death and destruction are (thankfully) exceptional.

An Unframed Threat: Public Health

For our public health studies, we use a real public health threat (H1N1) and a fictionalized account of a smallpox outbreak. In the late twentieth and early twenty-first centuries, a host of new flu outbreaks emerged and spread rapidly across an increasingly globalized world. These influenzas were known popularly by their animal carriers (such as birds and pigs), although scientists gave them scientific names like H1N1 to specify the specific strain and subtype. In the early days of these emergent public health risks, conflicting reports about the number of people affected and the relative lethality of the illnesses evoked fears of a novel and deadly illness that could spread to many people quickly. Each new strain brought with it the risk of a pandemic flu potentially killing millions, as the Spanish flu epidemic did in the wake of World War I; that epidemic killed on the order of 20 million people.

The U.S. Centers for Disease Control and Prevention (CDC) declared a U.S. Public Health Emergency for H1N1 influenza in 2009, as the so-called swine flu emerged from Mexico and then spread around the world. By 2010,

the outbreak was under control but not before there were 18,500 confirmed
deaths as a result worldwide (Dawood et al. [2012] argue that real number is
fifteen times higher). This unusual respiratory flu, which could lead to
seizures and changes in mental status, prompted school closures in the
United States. Although H1N1 was actually a mix of human, avian, and
pig flus, such was the fear that the Egyptian government took the unusual
step of having 300,000 pigs killed (Garrett 2009).

Anxiety over the disease was widely felt in the United States. In May
2009, the Harvard School of Public Health reported that 48 percent
of parents of school-aged children were worried that they or a family
member would contract H1N1. Thirty-nine percent of people were worried that they or someone in their immediate family would get H1N1 in
September 2009, and, in October 2009, 76 percent of Americans thought
there would be widespread cases of H1N1 over the fall and winter, with
people getting very sick (Blendon et al. 2009). There was also anxiety over
the vaccine. Some Americans worried about sufficient supply – 82 percent
of Americans said the United States had shortages of the vaccine in
November 2009 (Steinhauser 2009). One-third of Americans worried
that the vaccine itself was dangerous (Langer 2009). Late 2009 and
early 2010 was a time of great anxiety over H1N1.

Our other public health issue is smallpox, a highly infectious viral
disease that dates back to early human civilizations. In the twentieth
century alone, smallpox claimed the lives of hundreds of millions. It was
a scourge that left its survivors blind or disfigured from scars. Although a
vaccine for smallpox dates back to the late 1700s, it was not until the
twentieth century that a push to eradicate the disease worldwide took on
new urgency.

Although the World Health Organization declared that smallpox was
eradicated globally in 1980, the public may not widely appreciate this
fact. Blendon et. al (2003) found that 30 percent of Americans thought
there had been a case in the United States in the past five years. What's
more, in the wake of 9/11, officials in the U.S. government were sufficiently concerned about the threat of lab samples of smallpox being
disseminated as a bioterror threat that they spent billions of dollars to
vaccinate health workers and stockpile the vaccine (Broad 2002). In
2003, 64 percent of Americans thought that an attack by terrorists
using smallpox would be likely if the United States took military action
against Iraq (Blendon et al. 2003). These types of fears prompted
major responses from governments. In 2011, the Obama administration
advocated for a $433 million dollar plan to purchase an experimental

smallpox drug (Willman 2011). In addition, more than 500 medical personnel were vaccinated against smallpox in advance of the 2012 London Olympics to prepare for a potential biological terror attack (Malnick 2012). By international agreement, the last samples of smallpox are housed in secure repositories in the United States and Russia, but, in 2014, vials of smallpox were discovered in unsecured storage rooms at the National Institutes of Health, prompting renewed concern about the security of this disease (Centers for Disease Control and Prevention 2014).

Like H1N1, a lack of trust in vaccinations and government more generally could hinder any government response to disease. In the past, government action has made the isolation and treatment of smallpox more difficult. During a smallpox outbreak in Milwaukee in 1894, public health officials isolated poor immigrants in low-quality hospitals while allowing wealthy families to stay in their homes, thus creating a sense of inequity and distrust that led to riots and only exacerbated the outbreak (Leavitt 2003). In a 2002 survey of support for possible quarantine and mandatory vaccination policies in the event of a smallpox attack, the perception that the government would abuse its authority significantly increased opposition to both quarantines and vaccinations (Taylor-Clark et al. 2005). In the 2014 Ebola epidemic in West Africa, distrust of health workers and government facilitated the spread of the deadly disease because citizens refused to be tested or treated. Religious leaders as well as public figures urged the public to trust the government in the face of the threat of Ebola (Fessy 2014).

Framed Threats

Public health scares often trigger widespread anxiety, whereas framed threats involve more subjective or temporally removed harms that generate anxiety for some. By calling them "framed threats," we do not mean to say that these threats are fake and not worth worrying about. Rather, once we are out of the realm of imminent death and destruction, we have more complex phenomena, where some see risks and costs and others see gains and benefits. With framed threats, we differ in terms of the things that make us anxious. We argue that, in American politics, partisanship is a key variable that shapes whether a framed threat elicits anxiety. Both Rush Limbaugh and Rachel Maddow would experience heart palpitations and sweaty palms in the event of a tornado or bubonic plague, but they would have very different reactions to a new law that offered undocumented immigrants a path to citizenship.

No issue area is fixed as either an unframed or a framed threat. When harms become unclear or remote, politicians and media elites can play a crucial role in creating anxiety. Political elites evoke threat in rhetoric and campaign ads to inform the public of danger, to explain the need for policy change, and to persuade. Arousing anxiety is a common campaign strategy (Brader 2006; Kern 1989), but politicians may use anxiety-inducing language and images outside campaign times as well to attract attention and garner influence. Urging the public to pay attention to looming risks and enhancing those messages with powerful language and visuals is generally a smart strategic choice so long as anxiety appeals enhance citizens feelings of efficacy (Witte 1992; Witte and Allen 2000) and do not appear manipulative (Dillard and Shen 2005). In addition, if the policy area is one where the public believes one's party can best handle the issue, making the public anxious can increase the party's legislative flexibility in pursuing its favored policies, even when those solutions are not the public's ideal policies (Egan 2012).

Political elites, particularly election-seeking elites, have an incentive to warn the public of risks. The consequences for downplaying the risk of future terrorism, viral pandemics, hurricanes, or economic crises may be more serious than the political consequences for hyping threats, an asymmetry that elites realize. As Jessica Stern notes, "those who publicly underestimate threats are far more vulnerable than those who exaggerate them" (2006). No elected official wants to seem indifferent to or flatly wrong about the probability of a risk. Appearing to be or being unprepared for crises affects approval ratings and votes for individual politicians (Berrebi and Klor 2007; Malhotra and Kuo 2008) and may damage party reputations (Goble and Holm 2009) as well as lower trust in government (Hetherington and Rudolph 2008). For example, in 1995, Conservative prime minister John Major told the House of Commons that there "is no scientific evidence that B.S.E (bovine spongiform encephalopathy, also known as 'mad cow disease') can be transmitted to humans or that eating beef causes it in humans" (*New York Times* 2000). A year later, an outbreak of BSE resulted in the deaths of ten young people and a three-year ban on beef sales to the European Union (Green 1999). The Conservatives would lose a series of local elections due in part to their handling of mad cow disease (Lyall 1996) in a prelude to losing their majority in Parliament to the Labour Party in 1997, thus ceding control of government for the first time since 1979.

Political leaders who make threatening appeals are not always in the wrong, and they are not always able to use anxiety to get what they want. Their appeals might be strategic, but they can also be sincere. Some threats are real, and politicians need to warn citizens to take precautions. Second, political leaders using threatening appeals may be met with a disbelieving or skeptical audience. Finally, emotion does not simply convince citizens to support any candidate or adopt any policy sold as a solution. Anxiety does increase the potential for persuasion by making contemporary information more appealing and by increasing the desire for protection. Under some circumstances, anxiety decreases the weight of standing political predispositions like partisanship in opinion formation (Brader 2006; Marcus, Neuman, and MacKuen 2000). However, the potential for persuasion is not the same thing as persuasion itself.

The mass media are also a source of the public's anxieties. The news tends to favor negativity and conflict in coverage (Baum and Groeling 2010). Focusing on new, unique events is a journalistic norm (Bennett 2012) that may lead to a focus on unusual and unlikely events like hurricanes, school shootings, bombings, and clashes between immigrants and law enforcement (Stern and Fineberg 1996). In a media environment where newspaper readership and television audiences are down and many citizens choose to opt out of news altogether (Arceneaux and Johnson 2013; Prior 2007), journalists and editors have incentives to use emotionally powerful visuals and storylines to maintain ever-shrinking news audiences. As market pressures increase and competition over views increases, so do the incentives for journalists to produce sensationalistic coverage of policy (Zaller 1999).

In an industry where "news dramas emphasize crisis over continuity, the present over the past or future, conflicts" and "downplay complex policy information, the workings of government institutions, and the bases of power behind the central characters" (Bennett 2012: 46), stories that focus the public's attention on problems like immigration and climate change tend to focus on the most vivid and striking frames, thus increasing public anxiety. As Nelson and Kinder point out, "Graphic and arresting pictures of menacing criminals, butchered seals, or presidents in heroic pose are standard features of political communication" (1996, 1061). Coverage of our substantive cases tends toward sensationalism in both the amount of coverage as well as the tone. Hayes (2011) finds that the most prominent frames in television news coverage of immigration reform efforts in 2005–2007 focus on threats that illegal immigration posed to law enforcement and national security. Even before the recent focus on terrorism, news coverage of terrorism predominated on the airwaves even over other types of potentially threatening news. In the early part of the 1980s, Iyengar found that ABC, NBC, and CBS broadcast more stories on hijackings and hostage situations than on poverty, unemployment, racial inequality, and crime combined (Iyengar 1991). Whereas media coverage of climate change often features skeptics due to the journalistic norm of balance (Feldman et al. 2012), coverage of extreme weather events like floods and droughts that show evidence of climate change are regular news features, giving these stories the potential to influence public fears (Hendrickx, Vlek, and Oppewal 1989).

Immigration

Immigration is our major case of a framed threat. The United States, it is often said, is a nation of immigrants. Indeed, the Statue of Liberty and Ellis Island are paradigmatic examples of the United States' history of welcoming immigrants. However, immigration has periodically been a politically salient issue throughout U.S. history (Tichenor 2002), and public support for immigration ebbs as new immigrant groups enter the country in large numbers. In the early 1900s, the country of origin of immigrants began to change from traditional sources such as Britain, Ireland, and Germany to southern and eastern Europe; this new group of immigrants was poorer, less educated, and more Jewish than previous immigrant waves, provoking concern and increased nativism among the public. Indeed, previous waves of largely Catholic migrants in the 1850s triggered a similar reaction. In the wake of the Russian Revolution, the threat of communism and potential communist infiltration became a more salient concern, triggering a number of congressional actions like a literacy test and quotas to make it more difficult for successive waves of migrants to the make it to the United States. In the wake of the Second World War, the United States took in hundreds of thousands of refugees. By the 1950s, the tide had turned against immigration, with some of the first measures to return immigrants of Mexican origin back to their home country (the name applied to this effort to send hundreds of thousands of Mexican immigrants home was the racist moniker Operation Wetback). In the 1980s, the partisan politics of immigration were still sufficiently consensual that President Reagan, a Republican, would push through an amnesty law that ultimately legalized the status of about 3,000,000 immigrants, many of them of Mexican origin (NPR 2010).

In discussing immigration, political elites often evoke the language of risk and peril. Anxiety-inspiring language and foreboding imagery are also used to great effect in ads and political rhetoric about immigration, focusing particularly on illegal immigration. By the 1990s, as the demography of California had changed with waves of migration, politicians, particularly Republicans, began to highlight immigration as a threat to the country. As Governor, Pete Wilson claimed that California had an "immigration emergency" and backed Proposition 187 in 1994, designed to deny social services to illegal immigrants. Commercials supporting the proposition featured the voice over "They just keep coming" coupled with images of people running across the freeway, dodging cars. The *Los Angeles Times* describes a similar ad run by the 1996 Dole presidential campaign as follows:

[T]he viewer sees a sea of menacing Latino faces – only Latino faces – invading the state, filling its schools and prisons and victimizing a non-Latino "we." "We pay the taxes. We are the victims. Our children get shortchanged," the ad says as the camera zooms in on a classroom full of white teenagers. (*Los Angeles Times* 1996)

By the 2000s, fears of immigration, particularly from Mexico and Latin America, had taken on increasingly apocalyptic tones. Indeed, even the prominent scholar Samuel Huntington warned that the "Hispanic challenge" threatened to divide the country in two based on culture and language and imperiled the American dream (Huntington 2004).

Even Senator John McCain of Arizona, a supporter of more progressive immigration reform efforts and a member of the bipartisan Gang of Eight Senate group that sought to craft a legislative compromise, has used threatening language about immigration. When facing a challenger in the Republican primary going into the 2010 election, McCain blamed illegal immigrants for "drugs and human smuggling, home invasion [and] murder" before calling for Arizona to "complete the danged fence." As we noted in our vignette on immigration in the prologue, Arizona's governor Jan Brewer also drew international attention for her anti-immigrant positions. In response to the general tone of political rhetoric about immigration, Representative Chris Cannon (R-Utah) criticized politicians for "playing to primal fear" (Kiely 2006). In particular, many of the fears evoked by immigration ads and rhetoric implicitly or explicitly reference Latinos as the source of the anxiety. Although Republicans have run notable campaigns invoking anti-illegal immigration rhetoric, the issue sometimes cuts across partisan lines. For example, President Bill Clinton portrayed threatening scenarios involving illegal immigrants in his 1995 State of the Union address:

All Americans are rightly disturbed by the large numbers of illegal aliens entering our country. The jobs they hold might otherwise be held by citizens or legal immigrants; the public services they use impose burdens on our tax payers. That's why our administration has moved aggressively to secure our borders more by hiring a record number of new border guards, by deporting twice as many criminal aliens as ever before, by cracking down on illegal hiring, by barring welfare benefits to illegal aliens. (Clinton 1995)

Clinton offers as a given that "all Americans" share these concerns, referencing job competition, abuse of public services, criminality, and "alien" status. In addressing the surge of unaccompanied minors apprehended at the U.S. border in 2014, Barack Obama noted that his administration increased the number of Border Patrol agents to historically high levels and deported 400,000 migrants before discussing the humanitarian situation, framing the enforcement actions as protection from an immigration crisis.

There is evidence that this type of rhetoric connects with the public. Between 2001 and 2012 Gallup has asked about immigration worries almost every year.[1] Their polling shows an extremely worried citizenry. Every time Americans are asked whether they are worried about illegal immigration, more than half of the public responds that they worry either a great deal or a fair amount (in contrast to only a little or not at all).

When people are made anxious by framed threats, partisanship can play a significant role. There can be partisan differences over what generates anxiety and even whether we ought to worry. For example, although Americans across the political spectrum express worry over immigration, these worries are both more extreme and more clearly tied to elite politics in the Republican Party. In March 2012, 50 percent of Republicans worried "a great deal" about illegal immigration compared to 24 percent of Democrats, reflecting a 26 percentage point difference (Saad 2012). With an unframed threat such as a disease outbreak, we do not expect partisan differences in who experiences anxiety. After all, a smallpox outbreak does not distinguish based on political attachments.

SUPPLEMENTARY CASES

Although public health threats and immigration are our two main case areas, we bring two other cases into our chapter on political attitudes:

---

[1] Question text: "how much do you personally worry about ... illegal immigration? A great deal, a fair amount, only a little, or not at all?"

climate change and terrorism. Both climate change and terrorism have elements of unframed threats because both the extreme weather caused by climate change and violence perpetrated by terrorists can inflict bodily harm, and neither distinguish victims based on political affiliation. However, because the risks associated with climate change are temporally remote and a sizable minority of Americans express doubt that climate change is occurring, we place climate change in our framed threats category. Similarly, although terrorist attacks themselves evoke dread and fear of death, terrorism became a framed threat as time since 9/11 passed. During the Bush presidency, the solutions offered to counter terrorism were closely associated with the Republican Party, although that, too, has changed.

Climate Change

We use climate change because it offers a look at anxiety that is concentrated on the left of the political spectrum. The Democratic Party has positioned itself as the party that both recognizes the threat and has the appropriate solutions. Climate change has much in common with unframed threats because the scientific consensus is that climate change is occurring and will bring with it significant destruction without intervention. However, climate change is experienced as a framed threat. Democrats are more anxious about climate change, and the parties differ both on the nature of the problem and on policy solutions.

In June 1988, in the midst of a cripplingly hot summer, climate change burst on to the political scene in the United States. NASA scientist James Hansen was asked to testify to a Congressional hearing. He warned:

Number one, the earth is warmer in 1988 than at any time in the history of instrumental measurements. Number two, the global warming is now large enough that we can ascribe with a high degree of confidence a cause and effect relationship to the greenhouse effect. And number three, our computer climate simulations indicate that the greenhouse effect is already large enough to begin to effect the probability of extreme events such as summer heat waves. (Hansen 1988)

In the wake of Hansen's testimony, environmentalists in the United States and beyond unsuccessfully sought to push the George H. W. Bush administration to accept a binding international treaty with targets and timetables for rapid emissions reductions of greenhouse gases. Attention to global warming would wax and wane over the course of the next decade, with a sympathetic Democratic administration under President Bill Clinton unable to generate sufficient support for either domestic legislation or ratification of the Kyoto Protocol. The partisan divide on this issue would reach its high water mark in the 2000s, when climate change was elevated to an important partisan marker, distinguishing the two parties in terms of the appropriate policies and, at a more fundamental level, the causes of climate change. Still, extreme weather events occasionally had the power to cut through the partisan rift on climate change, first in 2005, in the wake of Hurricane Katrina that buffeted New Orleans. Former vice president Al Gore created a groundswell of public support through his documentary and slide show tour in which he described climate change as a "planetary emergency" demanding action:

The climate crisis is, indeed, extremely dangerous. . . . The voluminous evidence now strongly suggests that unless we act boldly and quickly to deal with the underlying causes of global warming, our world will undergo a strong of terrible catastrophes, including more and stronger storms like Hurricane Katrina, in both the Atlantic and the Pacific. (Gore 2006, 10)

That movement would fall short of achieving legislative change, and, by the late 2000s, public attention and anxiety about the threat of climate change would pale in comparison to worries generated by the housing bust and global economic crisis of 2008. The steep divide between the two parties would widen further. Not until Hurricane Sandy bore down on the East Coast in 2012 would public concern about climate change recover in any significant way. Still, preoccupation with the problem primarily resides on the left.

One of the major challenges that advocacy groups face is that the effects of climate change are both physically and temporally remote, and although the long-term consequences of climate change are terrifying, the threat appears removed from the daily life of many Americans.[2] Gallup has asked respondents how much they worry about global warming since 1989, and the percent who worry either a fair amount or a great deal never dips below 50 percent, indicating that climate change anxiety is fairly widespread. Gallup's data also show a rising percentage of Americans who are not at all worried about climate change – only 12 percent of respondents fall into this category in 1989, as compared to

---

[2] Of course, there are numerous impacts that are not remote. Americans have experienced more record high temperatures in recent years, and rains have been heavier and more frequent throughout much of the United States. These extremes have been coupled with drought conditions in the southwest (Karl et al. 2009).

29 percent in 2010 (J. Jones and Saad 2013). This shift coincides with the growing partisan divide in climate change attitudes. In a 2012 survey, 40 percent of Republicans reported that they were "not at all" concerned about climate change, as compared to 10 percent of unworried Democrats. In contrast, 34 percent of Republicans worry a great deal or fair amount, whereas 74 percent of Democrats report this level of anxiety (Newport 2012).

Terrorism

In addition to climate change, we selected a second issue, terrorism, which is also increasingly refracted through a partisan lens. The events of September 11, 2001, initially were sufficiently shocking and immediate to constitute an inherent threat and generate cross-party support for measures to address the problem. Over time, as no new attacks occurred on U.S. soil and the "War on Terror" was used to justify an intervention in Iraq, terrorism increasingly took on the attributes of a framed threat, seen increasingly through a partisan filter. Like the other issues in our book, it is useful to step back and understand a bit about the history of the phenomenon and how the issue came to generate an incredible outpouring of national anxiety in the wake of the 2001 attacks.

In 1972, Palestinian terrorists captured global attention by abducting and murdering eleven Israeli athletes at the Munich Olympic Games. Although terrorist events preceded this event (indeed, the word itself dates back to the French Revolution), global awareness of politically motivated attacks on civilian targets with the intent to coerce and scare the populace seized the popular imagination. A series of evocative events brought the issue to greater public consciousness, such as the 1976 hijacking of an Air France plane that was taken to Entebbe, Uganda, and stormed successfully by Israeli commandos, and the 1985 hijacking of the *Achille Lauro* cruise ship that saw one elderly man killed by the terrorists and thrown overboard. Still, most of these events, for Americans, were "over there," rather than at home. Although homegrown terrorist events like the 1995 Oklahoma City bombing would bring the issue more to the fore among Americans, the international implications of terrorism for the American people remained a low priority, even after the first attack on the World Trade Center in 1993. It was not until the events of September 11, 2001, that the specific risks for American citizens at home were brought into sharp relief with the attacks on the World Trade Center and Pentagon.

As a case, terrorism bolsters our research because of its prominence in the literature on anxiety (Feldman and Huddy 2005; Huddy et al. 2005a, 2005b; Landau et al. 2004; Mueller 2006; Nacos, Bloch-Elkon, and Shapiro 2011; Rubin et al. 2003; Skitka et al. 2006). Terrorism is also a useful case from a partisan perspective: although 9/11 initially triggered widespread anxiety, over time, the threat of terror took on partisan dimensions, where anxiety became more concentrated on the right (Gadarian 2014). In addition, the solutions to terrorism proffered by the parties differed at the time of the study, although they are more similar now.

On September 11, 2001, after the terrorist attacks on the United States, 87 percent of Americans expressed worry about another terrorist attack on the United States in a *Washington Post* poll (Cohen 2013). Fifty-eight percent of Americans were worried that they or a member of their family would be a victim of a terrorist attack (Jones 2001). On the day of the attacks, there was widespread anxiety, reflecting the inherent nature of the terrorist threat that had, in a single day, claimed the lives of 3,000 people.

President George W. Bush and members of his administration took to the air often to warn the public about the threat of terrorism and to offer policies to lessen the threat. From 9/11 onward, George W. Bush and members of his administration gave more than 700 speeches and addresses on national security ranging from briefings on the Patriot Act to broader discussions on the War on Terror (Gadarian 2008). These speeches often invoked the 9/11 attacks and the potential for future attacks as a rationale for the president's proposed policies. For example, in a February 2008 speech arguing that the federal government should be allowed to continue wiretapping suspected terrorists, the president began with these words,

At this moment, somewhere in the world, terrorists are planning new attacks on our country. Their goal is to bring destruction to our shores that will make September the 11th pale by comparison. To carry out their plans, they must communicate with each other, they must recruit operatives, and they must share information. The lives of countless Americans depend on our ability to monitor these communications. (White House 2008)

The president's speech did not simply explain that wiretapping is an essential counterterrorism tactic, but rather it also reminded the public of the continuing and ever present threat to their safety. The speech used language and imagery to induce memories and emotions linked to September 11 to not only inform citizens about wiretapping, but to also surround the issue with anxiety-inducing uncertainty.

Almost half of the American public named terrorism as the country's most important problem in the days immediately following 9/11, but just 3 percent held that view in 2008 and 2009 (Bloch-Elkon 2011). Americans' anxiety over terrorism also declined, although to a lesser degree. In the immediate aftermath of the attacks, 53 percent of Americans reported being very or somewhat worried that they themselves or a member of their family would be a victim of terrorism. Eight years later, this figure ranged from 30 to 40 percent of the American public (Bloch-Elkon 2011). As worry over terrorism dropped, the War on Terror divided the public, and feelings about terrorism took on partisan dimensions. In July 2007, 63 percent of Republicans thought that the United States was winning the War on Terror, whereas only 27 percent of Democrats shared that belief (although, in 2010, under a Democratic administration, there was no partisan difference) (Pew Research Center for the People and the Press 2010c). While partisans converged on the beliefs about the War on Terror, anxiety over terrorism has become more common on the right. In 2012, 48 percent of Republicans and 27 percent of Democrats worried "a great deal" over the possibility of future terrorism in the United States (Saad 2012).

These four issue areas offer interesting variation on anxiety-inducing threats in American politics. We have taken care to include issues from across the ideological spectrum and with varying degrees of threat. Of course, there are many other topics that make Americans uneasy – the economy, the national deficit, the rise of China, the changing job market, genetically modified foods, the decline of the nuclear family, and the death of bees are just a few of the many threats that grace our headlines. We contend that our argument that anxious citizens seek protection is generalizable beyond our four policy areas. American politics can be a threatening environment, and anxious citizens need to cope.

OUR APPROACH

Survey data are useful in many ways for studying anxiety. Surveys can tell us about the distribution of anxiety in the mass public, and we can use surveys to track shifts in anxiety over time. Although we use existing surveys to establish that our four case areas generate anxiety, surveys are not well suited to understanding the causal relationships between anxiety and other attitudes and behaviors. Take, for instance, economic anxiety. People who are more aware of a struggling economy might also be more anxious about the economy. If both measures are taken in a single survey, then it is impossible to know whether knowledge of the economy is causing anxiety, anxiety is causing learning about the economy, or both are caused by a third factor, such as personal economic loss. Even if we were to take advantage of a two-wave survey, where emotion is measured in time 1 and the relevant attitude or behavior is measured in time 2, we still could not be certain that emotion played a causal role. A panel survey design addresses the temporal issue (surely the attitude or behavior at time 2 could not cause the emotion at time 1), but it does not allow us to isolate emotion as the causal mechanism. For example, a third factor such as a personal economic loss could cause economic anxiety at time 1 and learning about the economy at time 2. This would be particularly problematic if the third factor is not measured or even considered. We can control for many possible correlates with a survey design, but we cannot control for the correlates we have not considered.

We therefore adopt an experimental approach in which we randomly assign anxiety-inducing stimuli to a subset of our respondents. We use three methods of inducing anxiety in experimental subjects: (1) A bottom-up, subject-directed emotional listing task; (2) news stories (newspaper and television); and (3) campaign ads. There are strengths and weakness in each approach, and they complement each other. Table 2.2 outlines the major studies that make up our original research. We also conducted six pretests with convenience samples (see Table A2.1 in the Appendix).

Method 1: Thought Listings

We used a bottom-up manipulation in Immigration KN Study 2007 and in Public Health – H1N1 Study 2010. In these studies, respondents in the treatment condition are asked to focus on an object, person, or policy area that causes them to feel a distinct emotion – in this case, anxiety. In the immigration study, we asked respondents to focus on what made them worried about immigration.[3] We modeled this manipulation on those used by social psychologists as well as political scientists (Valentino et al. 2008, 2009) who found that, by asking respondents to go through an exercise of listing their worries, individuals experienced increased

---

[3] Prompt Wording, Control Group: "First, we'd like you to take a moment to think about the debate over immigration in the United States. When you think about immigration, what do you think of? Please list everything that comes to mind." Treatment Group: "First, we'd like you to take a moment to think about the debate over immigration in the United States. When you think about immigration, what makes you worried? Please list everything that comes to mind."

TABLE 2.2: *Seven main studies*

Name of study	Immigration KN Study 2007	Immigration MT Study 2011	Immigration KN Study 2011
Date	Spring 2007	Winter 2011	Summer 2011
Sample	384 Adults, representative. Knowledge Networks (KN)	174 Adults, online opt-in convenience. Mechanical Turk (MT)	1053 Adults, representative. KN
DVs	Info seeking, Attitudes	Trust, Attitudes	Trust, Attitudes
Anxiety manipulation	Thought listing	Campaign ad (video)	Campaign ad (video)

Name of study	Public Health – H1N1 Study 2010	Public Health – Smallpox Study 2011	Terrorism YG/P Study 2006	Climate Change PMR Study 2012
Date	Spring 2010	Spring 2011	Fall 2006	Summer 2012
Sample	156 Students, convenience. University of Texas lab	600 Adults, representative. YouGov/Politmetrix (YG/P)	809 Adults, representative. YG/P	250 Adults, online panel. Pacific Market Research (PMR)
DVs	Trust	Trust, Attitudes	Attitudes	Attitudes
Anxiety manipulation	Thought listing	Newspaper story	TV News	Cross sectional

Note: Immigration MT Study 2011 and Immigration KN Study 2011 rely on the same stimulus materials.

anxiety. One advantage of this method is that emotion generation using language increases self-reported negative affect as well as amygdala activation more consistently than do methods that include visual stimulation (McRae et al. 2011). An additional advantage of this manipulation is that we do not need to assume what dimension of the policy issue makes people anxious, which is particularly important with multidimensional issues such as immigration because there are individual differences in what evokes emotion (Kahan et al. 2010). We share the concern with Ottati (1997) that there are individual differences in what aspects of political issues and candidates are emotionally relevant. The ability of an ad or news story to generate anxiety would depend on the particular issues related to immigration that we chose (economic competition or language) and may not resonate with all respondents. We also use a bottom-up manipulation in our H1N1 study, which relied on a student population. This health scare was particularly prevalent among young people, and we were interested in how their anxieties over their own health affected their levels of trust in others.

We use Immigration KN Study 2007 to demonstrate that a bottom-up manipulation can effectively raise anxiety. We had two separate research assistants unaware of our hypotheses code the degree of anxiety and anger in each respondent's thought listing. We include anger in our testing because it often occurs with anxiety in response to immigration. We measure anger in addition to anxiety for two reasons: (1) to show that the manipulations heighten anxiety more than anger and (2) for mediation models that demonstrate that anxiety and not anger mediates the relationship between the manipulation and the dependent variables. These mediation models are presented in subsequent chapters.

Responses were coded as 0 (none), 1 (some), or 2 (extreme) for each emotion.[4] Coders showed a great deal of agreement for both anxiety (70 percent agreement, Cohen's kappa = .53, z = 15.01, p<.01) and anger (78 percent agreement, kappa = .52, z = 13.05, p<.01), so we averaged across the codes to create one anger score and one anxiety score for each respondent. On average, respondents in the control condition had an anger score of .29 (standard deviation [sd] = .49) and an anxiety score of .48 (sd = .58). Consistent with other work on immigration

---

[4] To differentiate between anxiety and anger, the coders were told to code responses in which the respondent appears to directly blame immigrants for negative consequences for America as anger. Responses that showed concern about negative consequences without blame attribution were coded as anxiety.

(Groenendyk, Brader, and Valentino 2011), the treatment condition increased both anxiety and anger. The average level of anger in the treatment condition was .42 (t = 2.42, p<.02), whereas the average level of anxiety in the treatment condition increased by more than twofold to 1.02 (t = 8.57, p<.01). Although the treatment condition did raise some anger in addition to the targeted emotion of anxiety, average levels of anxiety are more than twice those of anger, and the treatment condition increased anxiety significantly more than it did anger (χ^2 = 21.24, p<.01).

Bottom-up manipulations are especially useful when the sources of anxiety on a particular topic are varied, and the anxiety-arousing events are highly personal. They are also ideal for establishing a causal link between anxiety and the relevant attitudes and behaviors because of their ability to trigger emotion in diverse populations. Although we think the bottom-up manipulations are ideal for demonstrating internal validity, these studies might be criticized for lacking relevance to the political world. Individuals might experience anxiety when you ask them to reflect on what makes them worried but not under more ordinary circumstances. Our other two types of manipulations are designed to address this concern.

Method 2: News Stories

We rely on news to generate anxiety in Public Health – Smallpox YG/P Study 2011 and in Terrorism YG/P Study 2006. We relied on newspaper stories to trigger anxiety in the smallpox study and a television news program in the terrorism study. These manipulations establish that real-world stimuli can generate both anxiety and our hypothesized effects. Newspapers and television news are two of the dominant ways that citizens can stay informed about politics, and both are facing increased competition from other media. These media have incentives to attract audiences with threatening headlines and emotionally powerful visuals. Beyond market incentives, the media has a responsibility to cover the news, which can be terrifying. Public health threats and terrorist attacks arguably need no embellishment in order to scare the mass public.

Another strength of our news manipulations is that they provide a tough test for our hypotheses involving partisan effects. One component of our argument is that partisanship conditions the coping strategies that anxious citizens pursue. For example, in an immigration crisis, we hypothesize that partisanship affects whether a person trusts a partisan leader. An emotional prime coming from a political actor like the president might trigger partisan effects, whereas a less overtly political messenger would not. News manipulations offer a less political or partisan trigger of anxiety.

We rely on a pretest that uses the same stories as Public Health – Smallpox YG/P Study 2011 to demonstrate one of our news story manipulations. In this study, participants in the treatment condition read about a smallpox outbreak that was the first in thirty years, whereas subjects in the control condition read about the twenty-fifth anniversary of a smallpox outbreak. The articles were roughly the same length (435 words vs. 455 words) and had largely the same content except for verb tense (see Appendix for full transcript of stories). Our goal was to hold the salience of smallpox constant across the two conditions while increasing anxiety in the treatment condition. After participants read their story, we asked a subset of the sample (n = 51) whether they felt a variety of emotions on 9-point scales, ranging from not at all to felt very strongly. We used three variables to tap anxiety (worried, anxious, and fearful; Cronbach's alpha = .92), and we combine these in an additive scale. Participants in the treatment condition were significantly more anxious than participants in the control condition ($M_{control}$ = 10.64 vs. $M_{treatment}$ = 15.88, p<.01). We also tested whether the treatment raised levels of two other negative emotions: anger (angry, mad, furious; Cronbach's alpha = .97) and sadness (sad, depressed, grief stricken; Cronbach's alpha = .82). The treatment condition did not affect anger ($M_{control}$ = 4.88 vs. $M_{treatment}$ = 5.62, p = .68), but it did increase sadness ($M_{control}$ = 6.80 vs. $M_{treatment}$ = 11.27, p<.01).

Method 3: Campaign Advertisements

Our final type of manipulation relies on campaign advertisements. Political actors (both candidates and interest groups) use emotional messages in constructing campaign ads. Ads evoke emotions ranging from hope and enthusiasm for recent accomplishments to anger over injustices to fear of a bleak future. From the classic "Daisy Girl" ad run by Lyndon Johnson's 1964 campaign featuring a nuclear countdown and mushroom cloud to George W. Bush's 2004 terrorism ad including a pack of menacing wolves, fear ads are an increasingly common feature of modern campaigns (Brader 2006). Ridout and Searles (2011) estimate that 23 percent of ads for Senate races in 2004 used fear appeals, with the majority of those appeals being strong emotional appeals, and more than 60 percent of ads in the 2008 presidential campaign took a negative tone (Geer 2012). Whether through ominous sounding music, grainy photographs, or menacing voice-overs, across a wide range of policy areas and candidates, fear ads highlight current bad conditions and/or warn of rough sailing ahead for the country if X policy is not enacted or X candidate is not (re)elected. The effects of anxiety in a political context depend in part on the political resonance of the message. For example, a political appeal about the dangers of immigration or climate change will spark anxiety for some audience members and fall flat with others. This work establishes some of the boundaries around the effects of anxiety-inducing appeals in politics, and, in doing so, provides an important element to the normative debates over emotion in politics: individuals' characteristics moderate whether they experience anxiety in the face of a threatening campaign appeal.

We use Immigration KN Study 2011 to illustrate our approach to using campaign ads to raise anxiety. In order to evoke anxiety about the detrimental effects of illegal immigration on the United States, we created a thirty-second ad that detailed arguments against illegal immigration. We chose to create an ad that outlined the costs of illegal immigration because this is a prominent part of political rhetoric about immigration (Simon and Alexander 1993), and immigration attitudes are significantly shaped by concerns over the costs of immigration (Alvarez and Butterfield 2000). The ad highlighted the public's main areas of concern about illegal immigration (Pew Research Center for the People and the Press 2006a): (1) illegal immigrants take American jobs, (2) open borders bring crime and a national security threat, and (3) illegal immigrants take healthcare, education, and welfare funding from Americans. Across the control and treatment conditions, the verbal script remained the same while the images and presence of threatening music varied.[5] In the control condition, the ad featured neutral imagery of children in school or hospital waiting rooms and no music. In the treatment condition, the ad featured evocative images of border crossings and arrests and included a musical track composed for negative ads by a political media firm. To the extent that there are differences in trust or attitudes across the conditions, they are due solely to the evocative images and music.

To ensure that the music and evocative imagery primarily evoked anxiety, we asked respondents how strongly they felt anxiety, anger, and enthusiasm on a 9-point scale from "did not feel this emotion at

---

[5] See the Appendix for the full script of the ad, which is based on one of the commercials run by California Governor Pete Wilson in his 1994 campaign.

all" to "felt this emotion very strongly" after viewing the videos. To capture anxiety, we asked how afraid, worried, and anxious respondents felt (Cronbach's alpha = .81); to capture anger, we asked how irritated, angry, and upset they felt (Cronbach's alpha = .86). To capture enthusiasm, we asked respondents how excited, eager, hopeful, confident, enthusiastic, and reassured they felt (Cronbach's alpha = .93). Factor analysis revealed three separate emotions, so we created three indices (Fear, Anger, Enthusiasm) that varied from 0 to 8.[6] Like other work that uses media to elicit discrete emotions, we found that the negative emotions of anger and anxiety co-occurred among our respondents (Brader, Valentino, and Suhay 2008; Gross and Levenson 1995). The anger and anxiety indices were correlated at .52 (p<.01), so to calculate the effect of the treatment on each emotion, we controlled for the other two emotions in three separate ordinary least squares (OLS) models. On average, respondents felt more angry (M_{anger} = 4.26, sd = 2.24) than anxious ($M_{anxiety}$ = 2.66, sd = 1.94) or enthusiastic (M_{enthus} = 1.94, sd = 1.90), but the treatment condition did not significantly affect how angry respondents felt (b_{anger} = −.35, se = .28). In contrast, the treatment condition increased respondents' anxiety by .43 (p<.09) or 5 percent of the scale, and decreased enthusiasm by .56 (p<.04) on the 0 to 8 scale. Using a simultaneous equations model, we find that the treatment condition increased self-reported anxiety significantly more than anger (χ^2 = 2.87, pr = .09), indicating that our manipulation worked as intended by increasing anxiety about immigration without affecting anger. Please see the Table A2.2 in the Appendix for an OLS model that formally shows this manipulation check.

One of our main goals is to study the effects of anxiety in an explicitly political context. The political ad manipulations are important for this purpose. Although the bottom-up and news media manipulations demonstrate the causal relationships between anxiety and our dependent variables, the political ad manipulations speak to whether these relationships play out when politicians and interest groups incite anxiety.

MOVING AHEAD

The next three chapters draw on our seven studies, which rely on a variety of samples and experimental settings (see Table 2.2). Although this

---

[6] Using factor analysis with orthogonal varimax rotation, there were three factors with eigenvalues of more than 1 that explain 95 percent of the variance (eigenvalues = 4.41, 2.16, 1.46). These factors corresponded to anger, enthusiasm, and anxiety.

TABLE 2.3: *Sample characteristics for studies*

	Immigration KN Study 2007	Immigration KN Study 2011	Immigration MT Study 2011
Female	53	49	48
White	82	72	83
Black	5	12	6
Latino	7	10	4
Democrats	48	51	52
Independents	7	4	18
Republicans	44	47	30
College degree	41	32	51
Liberal	24	28	41
Moderate	39	33	35
Conservative	37	40	24
N	384	1,053	174
DVs	Info seeking, Attitudes	Trust, Attitudes	Trust, Attitudes
Manipulation	Thought Listing	Campaign ad	Campaign ad

	Public Health – H1N1 Study 2010	Public Health – Smallpox Study 2011	Terrorism YG/P Study 2006	Climate Change PMR Study 2012
Female	56	54	52	54
White	60	73	80	78
Black	10	10	6	10
Latino	18	10	6	6
Democrats	35	46	43	56
Independents	24	16	23	12
Republicans	42	39	34	27
College degree	N/A	29	23	55
Liberal	28	26	27	48
Moderate	46	34	42	25
Conservative	26	40	31	27
N	156	600	818	250
DVs	Trust	Trust, Attitudes	Attitudes	Attitudes
Manipulation	Thought Listing	Newspaper story	TV News	Cross-sectional

diversity has advantages in terms of external validity, it is particularly important given our hypotheses regarding partisanship. Of the seven studies, four were run with nationally representative online samples through either YouGov/Polimetrix or through Knowledge Networks with Time-sharing Experiments in the Social Sciences (TESS) grants. We ran two additional studies with online opt-in adult convenience samples, either through a marketing firm with an online panel or through Amazon's Mechanical Turk marketplace. Finally, one of our studies took place in a political science lab at the University of Texas, with students compensated through extra credit.

A final methodological note that is important for our approach is that anxiety does not occur in a vacuum. For example, anger often co-occurs with anxiety but has different origins and effects on attitudes. One of the advantages of focusing on a variety of policy areas is that although anger and anxiety are likely to be highly correlated in some policy areas like immigration and terrorism, we expect there to be less correlation in other policy areas, such as public health. In order to identify the discrete effects of anxiety, we also measure other emotions including anger, sadness, and enthusiasm. It is the case that anger and anxiety co-occur in some of our studies, as they do in the real world, but we believe that our manipulations were able to substantially increase anxiety with no or more muted effects on anger. Several of our pretests were designed to choose manipulations that meet this goal. In addition, we use mediation models to show the causal path between our manipulations, anxiety, and our outcomes of interest, while controlling for anger. We also, whenever we can, use mediation models to rule out anger as an alternative mediator.

We focus on a key consequence of anxiety in politics in each subsequent chapter: learning, trust, and political attitudes. The relevant pretests are referenced each time a study is first mentioned, and we offer mediation models when appropriate. This chapter demonstrated that each of our cases has incited anxiety in the American public. Whereas no book could cover an exhaustive list of all the things that make Americans anxious, our four issues offer variation across important dimensions that will allow us to generalize to many other policy areas. In our approach, emotions are induced through a variety of stimuli. This allows us to be very careful regarding the connection between anxiety and the relevant attitudes and behaviors, but also to be relevant to the way anxiety is incited by news media and political campaigns. Our next task is to see if anxiety changes the way that citizens engage in politics in systematic ways.

3

Anxiety, Immigration, and the Search for Information

The ability of the press to present us with bad news, with news meant to disquiet us, though unpleasant . . . serves us well.

George Marcus, *The Sentimental Citizen* (2002)

Fear is the most powerful enemy of reason.

Al Gore, *The Assault on Reason* (2007)

How does anxiety affect information processing? We argue that anxious citizens are motivated to seek political information but are attracted to threatening news. Anxiety serves to motivate learning by increasing interest, the desire for information, and information gathering itself (Brader 2005, 2006; Gross 2009; Marcus and MacKuen 1993; Marcus, Neuman, and MacKuen 2000). In a public where the average person has little factual knowledge about politics (Delli Carpini and Keeter 1996), political appeals that increase individuals' anxiety can increase political knowledge and help people come closer to the democratic ideal of engaged citizens. Previous research finds that anxiety motivates citizens to learn about politics, but the act of simply gathering more information may not necessarily create better democratic citizens. We know very little about the kind of information that anxious citizens pay attention to or how they engage with political information. If anxious citizens seek more information but demonstrate biases in information processing, then the consequences of anxiety for citizen learning are more complex than suggested by political commentators and previous work on emotion and politics.

In the realm of politics, some issues may be inherently threatening, whereas others are framed threats and may be made threatening by news media and strategic campaigns. The contemporary political debate over undocumented immigration in the United States is infused with these framed threats – the threat that "illegals" pose to Americans' economic well-being, their security, and their way of life are all evident in campaign advertisements and candidate speeches. Politicians, political pundits, and some political thinkers regularly sound alarm bells about the dire effects of immigration on the economic health and cultural fabric of the United States (Borjas 1999; Huntington 2004). To test the consequences of anxiety on political learning, we use Immigration KN Study 2007. The American public is torn on immigration policy, but a significant portion of the public believes that immigrants, particularly undocumented immigrants, burden the country's economy and social system (Pew Research Center for the People and the Press 2006c) and worry about the consequences of immigration. Our hypothesis testing in this chapter is confined to the immigration study, but we expect that same dynamics would play out across other issue areas.

ANXIETY AND INFORMATION PROCESSING

Anxious citizens are more likely to engage with and learn more about politics by seeking information (Brader, Valentino, and Suhay 2008; Kubey and Peluso 1990; Valentino et al. 2008). Crises like terrorist attacks and pandemics send people to their television and computer screens to find information (Althaus 2002; Bar-Ilan and Echerman 2005; Boyle et al. 2004; Ginsberg et al. 2008), as do potentially significant policy changes (Pantoja and Segura 2003). Concerns over anthrax in October 2001 increased visits to the Centers for Disease Control and Prevention (CDC) website by 115 percent over the previous week and made "anthrax" the top search term in Google (Bar-Ilan and Echerman 2005). Marcus, MacKuen, and Neuman's theory of *affective intelligence* (AI) offers an explanation for this increased engagement. AI theory posits that two emotional systems, the dispositional and the surveillance systems, help citizens to navigate the political environment (Marcus and MacKuen 1993; Marcus et al. 2000). When the surveillance system senses a threat in the environment, it signals that the citizen should pay closer attention and gather more information in order to counter the threat. A major implication of the AI theory is that citizens mainly rely on their political habits to guide new decisions unless they are made anxious about candidates or issues. Once anxious, citizens will be more motivated to learn, will pay attention to news coverage, and will base political decisions more heavily on contemporary information rather than partisanship.

Experimental work demonstrates that anxiety causes citizens to search for information relevant to the threat, and this information seeking is not simply opinion confirming. Brader's study of campaign advertising (2005, 2006) shows that anxiety appeals steer citizens' attention toward information relevant to the threat. Exposure to campaign fear appeals increased respondents' desire for information relevant to the issues covered in the advertisement. Redlawsk, Civettini, and Lau (2007) find that voters search for additional information about candidates who make them anxious, even if they are otherwise positively evaluated. MacKuen et al. (2010) examined how varying news presentations affected emotional reactions and learning. Anxious experimental subjects were more willing than subjects in the control condition to learn about policy changes and were more willing to learn from opponents of their policy preferences. Valentino et al. (2009) demonstrates that citizens made worried about the 2004 presidential campaign sought out useful information on the Internet. When anxious respondents knew they needed to defend their candidate choice, they sought balanced political information, but, absent that motivation, their information search was one-sided. We expect that anxiety causes people to focus their attention on threatening information because this information may prove more useful in avoiding future harm than positive information (Lau 1982). Attention to threatening information need not be a conscious choice.

We argue that even in a world with a poorly informed citizenry, more political information may not always lead to better democratic outcomes. A large body of literature on public opinion demonstrates that levels of political knowledge are quite low and that motivation and interest are key factors in explaining political knowledge (Delli Carpini and Keeter 1996). Marcus et al. (2000) and Marcus (2002) argue that anxious citizens are closer to the democratic ideal of motivated and interested citizens who gather new information in order to make political decisions. Although anxiety increases the desire to learn more, its effect on actual learning and information processing might not be necessarily positive. There are three circumstances under which information seeking may not be a normatively good end in and of itself. First, citizens may seek out information but not retain it or not be open to it. Feldman and Huddy (2005) found that, after 9/11, individuals most anxious about terrorism claimed to be most attentive to politics but actually retained less factual information than nonanxious individuals. Civettini and Redlawsk (2009) found that anxiety also increases voters' recall of campaign information, although it does not enhance correct recall, thus suggesting that information seeking does not necessarily lead to learning when anxiety is high. Anxiety may also reduce openness to new ideas through cognitive freezing and a resistance to change (Jost et al. 2003). Alternatively, if anxious people only expose themselves to views that conform to their previously held attitudes or if citizens pay the closest attention to threatening, anxiety-enforcing information, then anxiety-driven learning might not create better citizens. People do not have the luxury of infinite attention – we might direct our limited attention toward only one area of a policy debate, and that focus is politically consequential (Jones 1994). As Jones writes, "in mass politics, preferences change glacially but focus changes rapidly" (1994, 29). We argue that anxiety shifts focus toward threatening information, and whether or not this information will lead to good decision making is an open question.

Our research takes up the third possibility – that anxiety may lead citizens toward threatening news. We argue that the desire to regulate the unpleasant emotion of anxiety, coupled with the vigilance toward threat that accompanies anxiety, will increase citizens' motivation to seek information but will lead them toward news that is threatening. Anxiety increases individuals' sensitivity to risk (Fischhoff et al. 2003; Huddy, Feldman, and Cassese 2007; Lerner and Keltner 2000, 2001; Renshon and Lerner 2012; Skitka, Bauman, and Mullen 2004), and we suggest that this results in increased attention to threatening information. In societies with high threat, individuals may become oversensitive to danger signals and exist in a readiness state to defend themselves (Bar-Tal, Halperin, and De Rivera 2007; Halperin, Canetti-Nisim, and Hirsch-Hoefler 2009). We argue that this hypervigilance to risk may occur even when threats are less existential than in high-threat societies and when anxiety is induced situationally.

Literature in cognitive psychology demonstrates that high stress and anxiety are associated with biased information processing; that is, with a tendency to pay closer attention to threatening information (Eysenck 1992; Mathews 1990; Mogg et al. 1990; Pratto and John 1991; Yiend and Mathews 2001). Cognitive theories of anxiety emphasize the role of anxiety in the selective processing of information. Anxiety heightens attention to threat and prioritizes the processing of threat cues (Mathews 1990). The same vigilance to threatening information is found among both individuals who are naturally prone to anxiety (i.e., high in trait anxiety) and in individuals made anxious by extant circumstances (i.e., high state anxiety) (Spielberger, Gorsuch, and Lushene 1984). Clinically anxious individuals are slower than nonanxious individuals in performing a task when simultaneously listening to threatening words (Mathews and MacLeod 1986), even though none of the participants could identify the threatening words. Individuals high in trait anxiety are also more likely to perceive a threatening meaning in ambiguous stimuli (Wood, Mathews, and Dalgleish 2001). Using a nonclinical sample, Mogg et al. (1990) found that high stress was associated with the bias toward threat, regardless of whether subjects were prone to anxiety. In subsequent work, Mogg and Bradley (2002) showed that as the threatening value of stimuli increases, all individuals tend to pay closer attention to it, regardless of trait anxiety.

We expect that citizens not only seek and remember information, but that they also engage with the news that they gather. Little previous research considers what happens after anxious individuals find information: are they likely to agree with the information they find, or do they poke holes in it? Indirect evidence from the literature on threat and tolerance suggests that citizens made anxious about immigration will be more likely to agree with information that portrays immigration as a threat. Jost et al. (2003) argue that a motivation to manage uncertainty and anxiety underlies citizens' endorsement of conservative ideologies. They point out immigration as a policy area that is often portrayed as "frightening, confusing, and potentially threatening to the status quo" (Jost et al. 2003, 351). Kuklinski et al. (1991) found that when asked to focus on their feelings about a variety of social groups, individuals focused on the potential negative consequences of granting civil liberties and subsequently decreased their support for civil liberties like freedom of speech, particularly when the group they considered was disliked. Although these studies do not directly address the link between anxiety and engagement, we propose that agreement with threatening information is a plausible link between anxiety and anti-immigration attitudes. More directly related to our study, Brader et al. (2008) find that subjects made anxious about the costs of immigration are likely to request immigration information from anti-immigration groups. Although this research is highly suggestive, it's unclear if subjects would actually read the information they requested, and, if they did, what they would think about it. Our study allows us to trace each step in information processing.

HYPOTHESES

Based on the literature on emotions and information processing, we derive three main hypotheses about the effect of anxiety on information.

We predict that *manipulating anxiety about immigration will lead citizens to seek out information* and that anxious individuals will seek more information than will individuals in the control condition. We predict that *manipulating anxiety about immigration will lead to biased attention,* in which anxious individuals pay the closest attention to threatening information. Additionally, we predict that *anxious individuals will be more likely to agree with threatening immigration stories than will nonanxious individuals.*

Biased information processing may occur either because anxious citizens selectively expose themselves to more threatening information than those with less anxiety or through a process of selective attention, whereby anxious people pay closest attention to and recall a higher proportion of threatening information (Vallone, Ross, and Lepper 1985). In order to test these hypotheses, our experiment measures both information exposure and recall, which allows us to empirically demonstrate whether anxious citizens read more threatening news about immigration than do less anxious citizens and whether anxious citizens are more likely to remember threatening information. To test our last hypothesis, we examine the consequences of anxiety on how individuals evaluate information by asking if people agree or disagree with the stories they read.

In addition to these three main hypotheses, we also examine the role that partisanship plays in information processing. Because we separate out information seeking, attention, and agreement with information in our hypothesis testing, we are able to see if and when partisanship matters. It is possible that Democrats and Republicans have different reactions at every stage of information processing or that partisan predispositions only enter into information processing in later stages, such as memory and agreement with information.

METHODOLOGY: HOW TO MEASURE INFORMATION SEEKING

One of the innovations of Immigration KN Study 2007 is that we track not only if anxious individuals seek information, but also what they seek out and read. With the exception of Valentino et al. (2008, 2009), MacKuen et al. (2010), and Redlawsk et al. (2007), most previous studies of anxiety's effect on information seeking rely on self-reports of how interested respondents are in learning more about the issues presented in an experiment. Self-reports are not always reliable reflections of behavior and tend to overestimate media exposure by large magnitudes

(Prior 2009; Zaller 2002). Even if subjects reported an interest in learning in an experimental environment, it is unclear whether they would actually research these issues on their own. We also do not know anything about media content when we rely on self-reports of news exposure. For example, Marcus et al. (2000) measure the number of days a week respondents read a newspaper and magazine about the campaign and demonstrate that anxiety is associated with an increase in newspaper and magazine reading. However, this measure does not reveal *what* citizens were reading.

Rather than relying on self-reported intentions to gather information, our experiment simulates an information environment in order to monitor actual information consumption (Lau and Redlawsk 2001; Mintz 2004; Mintz et al. 1997). In this controlled political "world," subjects can choose what type of information they are interested in and spend as much or as little time with each piece of information as they choose, and behavioral measures can be collected unobtrusively. The main advantage of this design is that the researcher does not need to make assumptions about the type or content of information that subjects read. Mintz and colleagues (1997) used a similar dynamic information environment to explore how military leaders acquire information and make foreign policy decisions. Valentino and colleagues (2009, 2008) utilized this type of design to test the effects of anxiety, anger, and enthusiasm on information-seeking behavior in a campaign. Subjects were given an opportunity to visit a closed web domain modeled after the presidential candidates' websites. Yet, even with this design, the question still remains concerning what citizens are most attracted to when their choice includes more explicitly emotive information. Subjects in these studies could learn about the biographies and issue positions of the presidential candidates, but one could imagine that, in the political world, anxiety might push citizens to seek solace from more affectively charged sources such as interest group websites or sensationalistic news coverage, thus reinforcing anxiety. These dynamic environments are a significant methodological advance over self-reports, and our design pushes further by providing a more affective information environment that has both policy-relevant and less relevant stories.

RESEARCH DESIGN

In our study, respondents were randomly assigned to either a treatment condition that induced anxiety over immigration or to a control condition. Respondents came from Knowledge Networks' (KN) panel of respondents with web access. The 384 subjects in our sample are drawn from KN's panel members who access the Internet through a computer (see Chapter 2, Table 2.3, for sample characteristics). Because of the large amount of text used within the study and the limitations of screen size and legibility of text on WebTV, those KN participants whose only access to the Internet is through WebTV were excluded from the sample frame for this study.[1]

Immigration KN Study 2007 relied on a bottom-up manipulation of anxiety. In the control condition, participants were asked to list their thoughts about immigration; in the treatment condition, participants were asked to list their worries about immigration.[2] Responses in the control condition ranged from just simple phrases such as "illegal" and "social security" to paragraph-long explanations of the differences between illegal and legal immigration. Several respondents told their own immigration stories or those of family members. Although the control prompt did not mention worry, some respondents mentioned why they thought that immigration was problematic or spontaneously mentioned their concerns, such as illegal immigrants driving down wages or taking jobs from Americans. The amount of worry about immigration that occurred in the control group without prompting suggests that the baseline level of anxiety about immigration is relatively high in the American public. This makes our experimental design a hard test of the hypotheses and should make showing the expected effects in the treatment condition more difficult.

Within the treatment condition, worries about immigration focused almost exclusively on illegal immigration, although our prompt did not separate legal and illegal immigration. Worries fell into four major

---

[1] We excluded WebTV respondents from the sample frame because we believed that the experience of selecting and reading newspaper articles on a television screen was sufficiently different from reading newspaper articles on a computer screen, and we did not want the mode differences to affect the results. One of the advantages of an Internet-based platform for our study is that this is the way many people gather their news – the computer screen offered a realistic test of information seeking.

[2] A randomization check showed that the conditions were balanced on age, race, gender, region, education, partisanship, and ideology. Using a logit model to predict whether a respondent was assigned the treatment condition, we found no significant effects for partisanship ($p<.99$), ideology ($p<.32$), age ($p<.64$), whether a respondent was white ($p<.87$), female ($p<.88$), whether the respondent was the head of household ($p<.38$), region of residence ($p<.60$), or level of education ($p<.13$).

categories: (1) economic concerns; (2) concerns about exploitation of the social welfare system; (3) culture worries, such as the loss of English as a dominant language; and (4) security concerns that included both crime and terrorism. Respondents were also likely to mention particular immigrant groups (such as Mexican immigrants) in elaborating their worries. Several respondents also mentioned worries about immigrants themselves – worries about immigrant families or discrimination against immigrants. Worries over the costs of immigration, though, far outweighed worries over the treatment of immigrants.

We had three research assistants unaware of our hypotheses code how many unique worries about immigration each respondent listed in the open-ended prompt in the KN sample.[3] We expect that the act of listing worries will make respondents feel more anxious about immigration and cause them to list more immigration worries than will respondents in the control condition. The number of worries listed ranged from 0 to 8, with an average of 1.56 worries and a standard deviation (sd) of 1.49 worries. On average, respondents in the control condition mentioned 1.18 worries with an sd of 1.36 compared to 1.95 worries in the treatment condition with an sd of 1.52 ($t = 5.24$, $p<.01$). It is important to note that these worries do not simply reflect respondents' predispositions toward immigration policy. The only significant predictor of the number of worries mentioned is whether a respondent was assigned to the treatment condition. The demographic and political characteristics correlated with immigration attitudes (race, gender, education, region of the country, partisanship, and ideology) do not predict the number of worries that subjects mention.[4] Our mediation models in this chapter rely on both this number of worries manipulation check and on the coder rating manipulation check in which coders rated each response as expressing none (0), some (1), or extreme (2) levels of anxiety and anger, outlined more fully in Chapter 2.[5]

---

[3] Two research assistants coded all respondents, and the third coded a subset of respondents. Coders were in agreement 63 percent of the time on the number of worries in the treatment condition, compared to 17 percent expected by chance (Cohen's kappa for all respondents = .48 (se = .03)).

[4] We modeled the number of worries mentioned by respondents as a function of gender ($p<.45$), the highest level of schooling completed ($p<.15$), region of the country ($p<.19$), partisanship ($p<.25$), ideology ($p<.26$), and treatment condition using ordinary least squares (OLS). The only significant predictor of worries was whether a respondent was in the treatment condition ($b_{treatment} = .75$, $se_{treatment} = .15$, $p<.01$).

[5] We include other manipulations checks in the Appendix (Tables A3.1, A3.2, A3.3).

TABLE 3.1: *Information search stories*

Immigration Stories: Threatening	Gangs in the U.S.: How Illegal Immigrants Complicate Law Enforcement
	Why Unskilled Immigrants Hurt America
Immigration Stories: Nonthreatening	Immigrants to Be Proud Of
	A Story of Two Immigrants
Non-Immigration Stories	One in Five Children Will Become Obese
	Mysterious Stone Slab Bears Ancient Writing

INFORMATION PROCESSING

After the manipulation, the KN respondents were invited to read news stories and informed that they would answer questions about the stories later in the survey. Each respondent was presented with a story set consisting of six randomly ordered headlines linked to full articles – four of which were about immigration and two of which were on unrelated topics (Table 3.1). Of the immigration stories, two stories focused on the benefits of immigration and how immigrants enrich the United States. The other two immigration stories reflected the more typical threatening and negative framing of immigration that dominates news coverage (Simon and Alexander 1993) – immigrants take resources and jobs from Americans and contribute to crime in large cities.[6] The headlines make clear both the subject and the tone of the stories. Subjects also had the ability to opt out of reading anything about immigration – respondents could choose to ignore all the stories and proceed to the second part of the survey or to read one of the two unrelated stories on childhood obesity or an ancient language.[7] All the stories were uniform in length, and the story headlines appeared in random order on respondents' screens. This limited but

---

[6] One could imagine also including threatening stories that focused on threats to immigrants themselves (e.g., exploitation, the possibility of deportation) that would be more in line with less restrictive immigration policy. We chose to include these threatening stories that are more consistent with calls for more restrictive immigration policy because they are the most frequent types of frames utilized by political elites in the immigration debate and create an external validity to our information environment. Hayes (2011) finds that, in the 2007 immigration reform debate, frames that focused on immigration in terms of law enforcement (crime), national security, and the burden on taxpayers made up 46 percent of all frames used on television news, whereas frames focusing on humane treatment of workers and the disruption to families made up roughly 7 percent of frames and were more likely to be utilized by pro-immigrant interest groups rather than by political leaders.

[7] Before selecting the news stories, we had twenty-one outside raters rate a variety of story titles on how interesting and threatening they seemed. We chose these story titles because the raters rated them as equally interesting but with varying levels of threat.

competitive information environment allowed subjects to exercise a multitude of choices in seeking news. On average, respondents read 2.79 stories out of the 6 offered, and although 14 percent of respondents chose to read none of the stories, 23 percent read all 6 stories.

We examine biases in information processing in three ways. The first is information seeking: when subjects are made anxious about immigration, are they more likely to look at immigration stories that portray immigration as a threat? We test our information-seeking hypothesis through tracking information-seeking behavior – both by the number of stories read and the time spent on stories. The next opportunity for bias in information processing is attention. Perhaps threatened subjects are no more or less likely to look at threatening information, but, when they do, they are prompted to pay closer attention and store threatening information in their memories. We measure attention through recall: what information do subjects say that they remember?

We also examine how subjects evaluate immigration news. Respondents were asked to evaluate the stories that they chose to read in an open-ended way, and their answers were coded for whether respondents agreed or disagreed with the content of the stories they read. The effect of anxiety on information seeking has been well documented, but we do not know what anxious people think about the new information they read. The engagement measures allow us to examine differences in the way that subjects evaluated stories about immigration.

INFORMATION SEEKING

Participants were given the opportunity to read any or all of the six stories. Subjects in the control condition read an average of 2.89 stories whereas subjects in the treatment condition read an average of 2.67 stories (n.s.). At first glance, it does not appear that anxiety triggered information seeking. However, the experiment specifically triggered anxiety related to immigration, and a more appropriate test is whether anxiety about immigration caused subjects to seek out more information about immigration. To test this idea, we compared the proportion of the stories each subject read that were about immigration out of all stories (Figure 3.1). On average, respondents in the treatment condition read a greater proportion of immigration stories than did respondents in the control condition. Out of all stories read by control condition subjects, on average, 65 percent of those stories were about immigration, whereas treatment condition respondents averaged 72 percent of their searching on

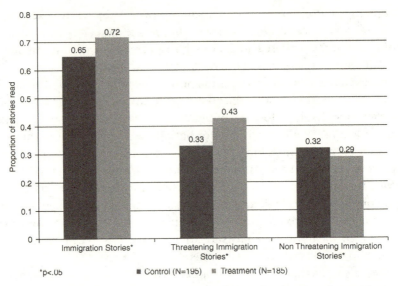

FIGURE 3.1: Anxiety increases exposure to threatening immigration stories

immigration stories (F(1, 327) = 4.58, p = .033[8]).[9] This finding is consistent with previous literature that anxiety increased the seeking of relevant information. Anxiety triggered exposure to information about immigration, but our study allows us to break immigration stories by whether they were threatening or nonthreatening.

So far, our findings are in line with previous work: people who are anxious seek out more information about the source of their anxiety. However, these subjects were presented with an emotionally charged information environment that allows us to see if anxious subjects were driven to seek out a particular kind of information about immigration. We find that the increase in information consumption about immigration was entirely driven by exposure to threatening stories (Table 3.2). For control condition subjects, threatening immigration stories represented just 33 percent of all the stories they looked at, whereas threatening immigration stories represent 42 percent of the stories that treatment condition subjects looked at (F(1, 327) = 7.77, p = .01). Treatment condition subjects are not significantly less likely to look at nonthreatening stories about

---

[8] Subjects choosing stories randomly would have chosen 67 percent immigration stories, so it appears that thinking about immigration did not, by itself, increase the probability of choosing an immigration story to read.

[9] Significance testing is based on ANOVAs, and full results are presented in the Appendix (Table A3.4).

TABLE 3.2: *Immigration anxiety increases exposure to threatening immigration news*
Proportion of stories read

	All Immigration Stories	Negative Immigration Stories	Positive Immigration Stories	All Immigration Stories	Negative Immigration Stories	Positive Immigration Stories
Basic Model:						
Treatment condition	0.09	0.10	-0.02			
	(0.05)	(0.05)	(0.04)			
Constant	0.51	0.28	0.23			
	(0.04)	(0.04)	(0.03)			
N	384	384	384			
R²	0.01	0.02	0.00			
Mediation Models:						
Treatment condition	-0.01	0.03	-0.04	-0.04	0.01	-0.04
	(0.04)	(0.04)	(0.04)	(0.05)	(0.03)	(0.04)
Number of worries	0.06	0.04	0.01			
	(0.01)	(0.01)	(0.06)			
Anxiety				0.11	0.09	0.02
				(0.03)	(0.03)	(0.02)
Anger				0.10	0.10	0.00
				(0.03)	(0.04)	(0.03)
Constant	0.63	0.31	0.32	0.61	0.28	0.32
	(0.10)	(0.09)	(0.10)	(0.10)	(0.09)	(0.10)
N	384	384	384	384	384	384
R²	0.08	0.09	0.02	0.07	0.08	0.01

Source: Immigration KN Study 2007.
Model specification: OLS with mediation effect calculated using algorithm in Imai, Keele, and Tingley (2010a). Coefficients in bold indicate p<.05, based on a two-tailed test. The dependent variables are the proportion of all stories read that were about immigration, the proportion of all stories read that were threatening about immigration, and the proportion of all stories read that were nonthreatening about immigration. If a respondent did not read any stories, they are set to 0. The mediating coefficients for anger and anxiety come from separate models. These are the second stage of the mediation models and also include controls for partisanship, ideology, race, gender, and education (coefficients not shown). For full models with controls, please see Table A3.7 in the Appendix.

immigration than are control condition subjects (32 percent [control] vs. 29 percent [treatment], F(1, 327) = 0.79, p = .38) though. We replicated this analysis with the amount of time spent on immigration stories measured in seconds and obtained largely similar results. Treatment condition respondents spend 28 percent of their total time on threatening immigration stories compared with control condition respondents who spent 23 percent of their time on threatening immigration stories (based on between subjects analysis of variance (F(1, 279) = 4.02, p = .05). The differences in time spent on nonthreatening information are again statistically insignificant (18 percent for the treatment condition vs. 21 percent for the control condition, F(1, 279) = 1.32, p = .25). Subjects in the treatment condition spent more of their time reading threatening stories about immigration in addition to simply clicking on a greater proportion of negative stories. Anxiety about immigration led people to read more about immigration, but we find that they focused on threatening stories.[10] We attribute the difference in exposure to threatening information between the treatment and control conditions to different levels of anxiety generated by the worries listing exercise. To test this causal mechanism directly, we use a mediation model that accounts for the level of anxiety each respondent expressed. As a robustness check, we use two different measures of immigration anxiety in these models – the number of worries listed by respondents and their level of anxiety. As a reminder, the number of worries range from 0 to 8, whereas the level of anxiety is coded as either 0 (none), 1 (some), or 2 (extreme). We also include respondents' level of anger in the mediation models and check that the treatment condition influences information seeking through anxiety rather than through anger. By using these measures, we can test whether anxiety is mediating the relationship between the experimental manipulation and the bias toward threatening information.

Table 3.2 demonstrates that the treatment condition led respondents toward threatening stories by increasing immigration anxiety. Using the causal mediation approach advocated by Imai et al. (2010a, 2011),

---

[10] We also conducted a 2 × 2 repeated measures ANOVA to test the proposition that respondents spent a larger proportion of their total reading on threatening immigration stories relative to the other stories (nonthreatening immigration stories and irrelevant stories) when anxiety was elicited but not in the control condition. The factors were condition (control, treatment) by valence (threatening stories, nonnegative stories [positive and irrelevant stories]), and the analysis revealed a significant interaction for condition × valence, F(1, 382) = 4.04, p = .05. The main effect for valence (F(1, 382) = 157.72, p<.00) was significant, and the main effect for condition was not (F(1, 382)= .38, p = .54).

Table 3.2 shows the effect of being in the treatment condition and immigration worries on three measures of information seeking: (1) the proportion of all stories read that focused on immigration, (2) the proportion of all stories that were threatening, and (3) the proportion of all stories that were nonthreatening.[11] To satisfy the statistical assumptions underlying this model,[12] we also include pretreatment variables (gender, education, ideology, and partisanship) that may be related to immigration information seeking, as well as anxiety in both the models predicting the mediator and the models predicting the outcomes of interest.[13] Using this causal mediation framework, we calculate three quantities of interest: (1) the direct effect of being in the treatment condition on information seeking, (2) the mediating (indirect) effect of anxiety on information seeking, and (3) the total effect, which is the sum of the direct and indirect effects.[14] The direct effect can be interpreted as the causal effect of the treatment (being asked to worry about immigration) on the proportion of stories read that is *not* due to anxiety. The mediating effect can be interpreted as the effect of the treatment on the proportion of stories read due to a change in the level of anxiety. These quantities can be found in the Appendix in Table A3.7.

The models in Table 3.2 show that immigration anxiety mediates the effect of the treatment condition on the proportion of immigration stories read and, specifically, on the proportion of threatening immigration stories read by respondents. In other words, the treatment condition increases exposure to news stories about the negative consequences of immigration through heightening anxiety. These findings are consistent

[11] Because we established in the manipulation check section that the treatment condition significantly increased both the number of worries listed by the respondents as well as the level of worry, we do not show the first-stage models here. Please see Table A3.3 in the Appendix for the manipulation checks. If respondents did not read any stories, they are set to 0.

[12] The mediation models rely on two ignorability assumptions made sequentially. The first assumption is that the treatment is exogenous to the outcomes of interest. In an experiment, this assumption is expected to hold because the treatment is randomly assigned. The second assumption is that the observed mediator is independent from the pretreatment and treatment confounders (Imai et al. 2010b). It is because of this second assumption that we include covariates that were measured prior to the treatment in the models predicting the mediator as well as information seeking and remembering.

[13] We include anger only in the second-stage model that predicts information seeking as a function of emotions and the treatment. Including anger as a predictor of anxiety would imply that anger was a cause of anxiety and would thus be a post-treatment confounder, which would violate the sequential ignorability assumption that underlies these mediation models.

[14] We calculate these effects using the "mediate" command in Stata (Hicks and Tingley 2011).

across both measures of anxiety.[15] On the other hand, anxiety does not mediate the relationship between the treatment condition and exposure to nonthreatening immigration stories. These models also show that anger over immigration does increase the proportion of threatening immigration stories that subjects read, but its effect is not due to the experimental treatment. Anger, in contrast to anxiety, is an emotion associated with certainty (Lerner and Keltner 2001), so the fact that our experimental treatment influenced information seeking through anxiety rather than anger gives credence to our claims that one of the motivations of information seeking is to resolve uncertainty.

We find no evidence for mediation for nonthreatening stories, thus confirming our claim that immigration anxiety increase biased attention, not just overall attention. When we include a measure of thinking about immigration (word counts) as a mediator, we find no mediation effect, suggesting that simply thinking more about immigration does not influence the proportion of threatening or nonthreatening stories read by respondents. As predicted, anxiety, rather than thoughts about immigration, carries the causal impact of the treatment condition on exposure to threatening information.

ATTENTION

We found that subjects in the treatment condition were more likely to look at threatening information about immigration than were subjects in the control condition, but did they pay attention to this information? Information seeking and attention are two ways in which bias may creep into anxiety-driven learning, and they do not necessarily go together. People might read plenty of information and remember little (Feldman and Huddy 2005), or they may read very little and remember all of it

---

[15] The magnitude of the causal mediation effect of anxiety on our outcomes is similar in size to those of Brader et al.'s (2008) as calculated in Imai et al. (2011) and anxiety's effect on trust in Myers and Tingley (2011). The sensitivity analysis also reveals that the alternative anxiety measures have sensitivity parameters of equal size. To conclude that the true causal mediation effect is not significantly different from zero, we must assume that an unobserved confounder that affects both anxiety and information seeking in the same direction makes the correlation between the two error terms greater than .19 for the number of worries and .18 for the level of anxiety. These results are more sensitive to potential confounders than those of Brader et al. (2008); however, using the product of coefficients method of mediation proposed by Baron and Kenny (1986), we find that both measures of anxiety mediate the effect of the treatment on the outcome, giving us more confidence that these results hold. Please see Table A3.5 in the Appendix for those results.

(Valentino et al. 2008). There are multiple ways that previous research has conceptualized attention, such as tracking subjects' eye movements toward or away from an anxiety-producing stimulus (Yiend and Mathews 2001) or measuring how anxiety interferes with processing (Pratto and John 1991). We rely on an open-ended question that asked subjects which stories they remembered best. We asked, "Of the stories you read, what stories do you remember best? (If you don't remember the names, just describe the stories.)" The simple self-report is an appropriate measure for our purposes because we are interested in what subjects took away from their reading.[16]

We compared the recall of immigration stories between the treatment and control conditions in multiple ways, first focusing on whether subjects recalled immigration stories, and then whether they recalled threatening or nonthreatening stories about immigration. The dependent variables are the proportion of all stories recalled that are about immigration, the proportion of all stories that are threatening, and the proportion of all stories that are nonthreatening. We use proportions for hypothesis testing because we expect that anxiety shifts attention. Subjects in the treatment condition remembered a larger proportion of immigration stories ($M_{control}$.51 vs. M_{treat} = .60, $F(1, 384)$ = 5.38, p = .02). When we break apart the immigration stories by tone, we find that subjects in the treatment group remembered a higher proportion of threatening stories ($M_{control}$ = .29 vs. M_{treat} = .39, $F(1, 382)$ = 6.36, p = .01), but that the groups did not differ in their tendency to recall nonthreatening immigration stories (.23 vs. .21, $F(1, 382)$ = .13, p = .71).[17]

Next, we examine the effect of the treatment condition on recall, using a mediation model with ordinary least squares (OLS) that controls for the number of immigration stories read in order to further disentangle attention from exposure (Table 3.3). As in the previous mediation models,

---

[16] Additionally, because the measure followed closely after subjects selected and read the experimental stories and because we can verify which stories respondents chose, we are less concerned about projection or subjects forgetting what they read.

[17] If we restrict the analysis to those 266 respondents who read an immigration story, the findings are substantively identical. In the threatening bias analysis, we include only those subjects who read a threatening story (N = 232), and our nonthreatening bias analysis includes only those subjects who read a nonthreatening story (N = 200). We first compare the treatment and control groups using ANOVAs, and we find that subjects in the treatment condition remembered a larger proportion of immigration stories (.74 vs. .85, $F(1, 266)$ = 5.90, p = .02). When we break apart the immigration stories by tone, we find that subjects in the treatment group remembered a higher proportion of threatening stories (.60 vs. .47, $F(1, 232)$ = 5.78, p = .02), but that the groups did not differ in their tendency to recall nonthreatening immigration stories (.44 vs. .40, $F(1, 200)$= .43, p = .51).

TABLE 3.3: *Immigration anxiety increases memory for threatening immigration stories*

	All Immigration Stories	Threatening Immigration Stories	Nonthreatening Immigration Stories	All Immigration Stories	Threatening Immigration Stories	Nonthreatening Immigration Stories
Basic Model:						
Treatment condition	0.09	**0.10**	-0.02			
	(0.05)	(0.05)	(0.04)			
Constant	0.51	0.29	0.23			
	(0.04)	(0.04)	(0.03)			
N	384	384	384			
R^2	0.01	0.02	0.01			
Mediation Models:						
Treatment condition	0.07	0.08	0.00	0.07	0.05	0.01
	(0.05)	(0.05)	(0.04)	(0.05)	(0.05)	(0.04)
Number of worries	**0.04**	**0.04**	0.00			
	(0.02)	(0.02)	(0.01)			
Anxiety				0.04	**0.08**	-0.03
				(0.04)	(0.04)	(0.03)
Anger				0.09	0.08	0.00
				(0.05)	(0.05)	(0.04)
Number of stories read	**0.13**	**0.05**	**0.07**	**0.13**	**0.05**	**0.07**
	(0.01)	(0.02)	(0.01)	(0.01)	(0.02)	(0.01)
Constant	0.09	0.03	0.06	0.08	0.14	0.06
	(0.10)	(0.09)	(0.09)	(0.11)	(0.05)	(0.08)
N	384	384	384	384	384	384
R^2	0.26	0.12	0.15	0.26	0.13	0.15

Source: Immigration KN Study 2007.

Model specification: OLS with mediation effect calculated using algorithm in Imai, Keele, and Tingley (2010a). Coefficients in bold indicate p<.05, based on a two-tailed test. The dependent variables are the proportion of all stories recalled that are about immigration, the proportion of all stories that are threatening, and the proportion of all stories that are nonthreatening. If a respondent did not read any stories or did not remember any stories, they are set to 0. The mediating coefficients for anger and anxiety come from separate models. These are the second stage of the mediation models and also include controls for partisanship, ideology, race, gender, and education (coefficients not shown). For full models with controls, please see Table A3.10 in the Appendix.

we use two alternate measures of anxiety (the number of worries and level of anxiety) and also test anger as an alternative mediator in a separate model. The mediation results in Table 3.3 demonstrate that participants in the treatment condition remembered a greater proportion of immigration stories out of all stories when controlling for the number of immigration stories read and that the treatment biased attention through increasing respondents' level of anxiety. Again, we find no evidence that the treatment condition affected attention through anger.[18] Furthermore, as in the case of information seeking, this heightened attention to immigration stories was driven by threatening immigration stories. Inducing anxiety about immigration not only caused respondents to seek out more threatening information, but anxiety also increased the salience of threatening information over nonthreatening information. Anxiety may increase the desire for information, but these findings demonstrate that anxious citizens seek and remember news that highlights threatening information about immigration, suggesting that anti-immigration activists are well-served by tapping into and increasing anxiety over immigration.

ENGAGEMENT WITH INFORMATION

Respondents in the treatment condition spent a larger proportion of their time on threatening immigration stories than on nonthreatening immigration stories and were more likely to pay attention to those stories, but what these respondents thought about the information they read is an open question. Although anxiety may increase the potential for persuasion, we do not expect that citizens simply receive political information without evaluating it, regardless of whether their information seeking is prompted by anxiety or not. Yet if anxiety prompts information seeking, then, as part of this process, we expect that anxiety should also affect evaluations of the information gathered. We hypothesize that anxiety biases the way that subjects evaluate information, either by promoting agreement with threatening information or by promoting disagreement with nonthreatening information. Engagement is a broader concept than whether one agrees or disagrees. Engagement might include disdain or disinterest ("your study bores me") or perhaps heightened emotion ("that

---

[18] We replicate these mediation models using the Baron and Kenney product of coefficient method in the Appendix and find that, with this alternative method, the treatment condition is mediated through both our measures of anxiety. See Table A3.6 in the Appendix.

article made me so mad!"). We focus on agreement and disagreement with the information because we expect it affects whether information ultimately affects people's attitudes and behavior. We anticipate that anxiety-driven learning has consequences for public opinion and behavior but that people do not simply accept new information as if they are blank slates.

As a way of measuring agreement and disagreement, subjects were asked what they thought about the stories in an open-ended question. We asked, "What did you think about the stories you read?" Three research assistants unaware of our hypotheses coded the responses first by whether they engaged with a nonthreatening or a threatening immigration story, and then by whether their comment expressed agreement, disagreement, or was neutral (an answer could fall into more than one category). This measure is novel in the emotion and politics literature and will help establish whether anxiety changes the way that people evaluate information. Among the 232 respondents who read threatening stories, 9 percent took the opportunity to disagree with a threatening story, and 45 percent expressed agreement. Many respondents took the opportunity to agree with threatening information. For example, one respondent agreed with the crime story: "all our city streets and businesses are threatened by this overflow of illegals from around the world being a menace to our peace and tranquility, I support mass deportation tomorrow." Another respondent wrote, "Shocking report on the 18th Street Gang and the Mexican Mafia. Two thirds of all fugitive felon warrants are for illegal aliens. No wonder the streets are not safe in Tucson, AZ. Our political leaders are sleeping while America burns." Engagement with nonthreatening stories was less common. Among the 200 respondents who read nonthreatening stories, 15 percent argued with them in some way, and 27 percent expressed agreement.

Did anxiety affect the way that participants engaged with information about immigration? We address this question by comparing the conditions on the percentage of respondents who made a statement agreeing/disagreeing with a threatening/nonthreatening story out of the number of respondents who read a threatening/nonthreatening story.[19] That is, comments were only counted for respondents who read a story and then mentioned that story when prompted by the open-ended question.

---

[19] Our research assistants found that it was often difficult to discern which of the negative and positive stories were referenced when participants were asked to share their thoughts on the stories. For example, an answer such as "I agree, immigration is a huge problem. It's harming our economy" could be referencing just one or both of the negative immigration stories. We rely on a simple dichotomous measure because of this ambiguity.

Neutral comments, in which respondents simply restated the premise of the news story or made unrelated comments, are excluded from our analyses because they do not offer an evaluation of the information.[20] Respondents in the treatment condition were more likely to agree with threatening stories than respondents in the control condition. Among respondents who read a threatening story, 47 percent of respondents in the treatment condition expressed agreement compared to 33 percent of those in the control condition ($\chi^2 = 5.50$, p<.02). Few subjects in either condition argued with threatening stories about immigrations: of those respondents who read a threatening story, only 10 percent of respondents in the treatment condition and 8 percent of subjects in the control condition expressed disagreement (n.s.).

In contrast to their engagement with threatening stories, fewer respondents expressed agreement with nonthreatening stories, implying that these subjects found the threatening stories more memorable and convincing. There are no significant differences between the conditions in the percentage that either agrees with or argues against the nonthreatening stories. Sixteen percent of respondents in the control condition who remembered a nonthreatening story argued against the content of it, whereas 15 percent of treatment subjects argued against the nonthreatening stories. Although 28 percent of respondents in the control condition agreed with a nonthreatening story, this did not differ significantly from the 24 percent of respondents in the treatment condition who behaved similarly. Overall, respondents in the treatment condition evaluated information differently than did respondents in the control condition. Anxious respondents were more likely to embrace the threatening messages about immigration than were those in the control condition, yet they were no more likely to argue against nonthreatening information.

Respondents in the treatment condition were more likely to agree with threatening information, but this might be driven by their higher propensity to read threatening stories. We address this possible confound with multinomial logistic regressions, in which we include the number of threatening (nonthreatening) stories read as a covariate in Table 3.4. We use multinomial logit models because the analysis includes a nominal

---

[20] We also exclude the seven respondents who express both agreement and disagreement with the same story so that the participants are consistent in these models and in the multinomial logistic regression, where their inclusion would create a fifth category on the dependent variable with few observations. Their exclusion does not affect the results.

TABLE 3.4: *Anxiety increases agreement with threatening immigration news.*

	Agree with Threatening Stories vs. No Engagement		Argue against Threatening Stories vs. No Engagement		Agree with Nonthreatening Stories vs. No Engagement		Argue against Nonthreatening Stories vs. No Engagement	
	Model 1	Model 2	Model 1	Model 2	Model 1	Model 2	Model 1	Model 2
	Coef. (s.e)	Coef. (s.e)	Coef. (s.e)	Coef. (s.e)	Coef. (s.e)	Coef. (s.e)	Coef. (s.e)	Coef. (s.e)
Anxiety treatment	**0.57** (0.24)	**0.60** (0.25)	0.31 (0.44)	0.35 (0.45)	−0.43 (0.31)	−0.49 (0.33)	−0.26 (0.40)	−0.34 (0.43)
Number of threatening (nonthreatening) stories read		**1.05** (0.16)		**1.32** (0.33)		**1.47** (0.23)		**1.77** (0.36)
Constant	**−1.19** (0.17)	**−2.42** (0.29)	**−2.56** (0.31)	**−4.21** (0.62)	**−1.56** (0.20)	**−3.30** (0.41)	**−2.28** (0.27)	**−4.51** (0.67)
N	383	383	383	383	378	378	378	378
Pseudo R²	.01	.11	.01	.11	.01	.18	.01	.18

Source: Immigration KN Study 2007.

Model specification: Multinomial logit. Coefficients in bold indicate p<.05, based on a two-tailed test. Dependent variables indicate respondents' engagement with the stories: 0 (did not mention, neither agree nor disagree), 1 (agree with threatening [nonthreatening] story, no disagreement), 2 (argue against threatening [nonthreatening] story, no agreement). Respondents who both agreed and disagreed with stories were excluded (n = 7). The treatment variable is 0 for respondents in the control condition and 1 for respondents in the treatment condition. Number of relevant stories read is a count of how many threatening or nonthreatening stories respondent read during the information search. Models include controls for partisanship, ideology, race, gender, and education (coefficients not shown). Please see Table A3.8 in the Appendix for full models with controls.

dependent variable with more than two categories.[21] We use a slightly different engagement measure in these models that captures whether a respondent engaged with immigration stories at all and, if so, in what direction. Subjects were categorized for threatening and nonthreatening stories separately as: (1) not evaluating the story (either because they did not read immigration stories or because they did not mention these stories), (2) agreeing with the story, or (3) arguing against the story. Each respondent received a score for engagement with threatening stories and a score for engagement with nonthreatening stories. If a respondent expressed both agreement and disagreement with the same story, they were dropped from the analysis.[22] We use "not evaluating" as the baseline category. The models demonstrate that the treatment condition had a significant effect on agreement with threatening information, even controlling for the number of threatening stories read. As in the bivariate analysis, anxiety did not affect engagement with nonthreatening stories or disagreement with threatening stories.

THE ROLE OF PARTISANSHIP

Partisanship acts as a filter and a "perceptual screen" through which citizens process political information (Bartels 2002; Campbell et al. 1960; Zaller 1992). Through processes like selective exposure, selective attention, and engagement, individuals can take in new information that serves to reinforce their existing opinions (Klapper 1960, 64). But what about anxious partisans? Do anxious partisans cope with anxiety in a similar manner? Do anxious Democrats and Republicans engage with threatening information in the same ways? Neuman et al. (2007) suggest that as anxiety increases, individuals will rely less on existing convictions and use more mental effort to weigh the costs and benefits of alternative policies. Provided that people become anxious about a political issue, long-standing political identities should matter less than when anxiety is low. An implication of this line of thought is that once people are anxious,

[21] We have also modeled these effects using four separate logit models in which the dependent variable was whether a respondent agreed (disagreed) with a threatening (nonthreatening) story and find identical results. In these logit models, we exclude all respondents who did not read a threatening (nonthreatening) story. We include these models the Appendix (A3.8).

[22] One respondent both agreed and disagreed with the same threatening story, and six respondents both agreed and disagreed with the nonthreatening stories; these respondents were excluded from this analysis.

they process information in an unbiased manor, taking information on its face. Yet little previous anxiety work considers whether partisanship shapes what individuals remember and accept.

Both Democrats and Republicans became anxious about immigration as a result of the worries-listing treatment. To test whether the treatment affected Democrats and Republicans, we model anxiety (the 0–2 scale coded by research assistants) as a function of the treatment condition, partisan group, and the interaction between the two. We find that the effect of the treatment conditional on being a Democrat is .50 (.10), and the effect of the treatment conditional of being a Republican is .58 (.11), suggesting that both Democrats and Republicans experienced similar increases in their levels of worry.[23] The thought-listing exercise generated anxiety in Democrats and Republicans, but did anxious partisans behave similarly? In this section, we trace the ways that partisanship enters the information-seeking process. Although Republicans and Democrats seek the same amount of immigration information, anxious Republicans are more likely to remember and agree with threatening immigration information than are anxious Democrats. Republicans are not necessarily seeking more threatening news, but, during information processing, they pay closer attention to and engage more positively with news that portrays immigration in a hostile way. This threatening information is then likely to be utilized in deciding which political elites to trust to handle immigration, as well as what policies to support. Although both Republicans and Democrats worry about immigration, in coping with that anxiety, their political habits of partisanship do not disappear but rather serve as a force shaping their engagement with political information.

Figure 3.2 shows the effect of the thought-listing treatment on the proportion of stories that respondents read, broken down by the partisanship of the respondent. Independents who indicated that they "leaned" toward one of the major parties are included as Democrats or Republicans, depending on which party they leaned toward, since leaners tend to act like partisans (Keith et al. 1992). The twenty-eight Independents (7 percent of the sample) who did not lean toward either party are excluded. Democrats and Republicans did not differ in their information seeking. Both Republicans and Democrats in the treatment condition read 72 percent of all their stories about immigration. For Democrats, listing their worries about immigration boosted the proportion of all stories that were threatening immigration stories by 11 percentage points over

---

[23] Please see these interaction models in Table A3.11 in the Appendix.

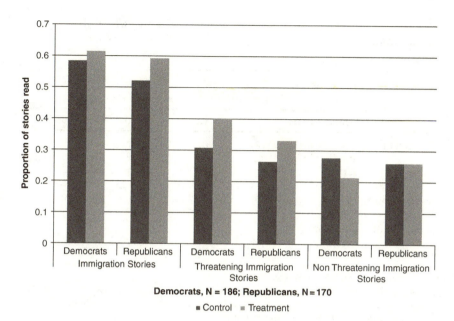

FIGURE 3.2: Anxiety treatment affects Republicans and Democrats similarly on selective exposure

the control condition ($M_{control}$ = .36 vs. M_{treat} = .47). For Republicans, listing their worries increased attention to threatening stories by 9 percentage points ($M_{control}$ = .31 vs. M_{treat} = .40). Partisans do not seek different types of information when made anxious about immigration, but this is just the first step of information processing.

In Table 3.5, we test how partisanship affects what partisans remember of what they read. Listing their immigration worries led Republicans and Democrats to seek out similar amounts of information, but Table 3.5 reveals that Republicans systematically remember more threatening stories than did Democrats.[24] Worrying about immigration increased the proportion of stories that Republicans remember by 22 percent (se = .07), whereas the treatment had no significant effect on Democrats' memory of threatening stories, a difference that is statistically distinguishable and substantively large (χ^2 = 4.03, PR<.05). In an

---

[24] We test whether the effect of the treatment differs for Republicans and Democrats by running a simultaneous equation model of the effect of the treatment on the proportion of stories remembered separately for Democrats and Republicans. After estimating the simultaneous equation model, we run Wald tests using the "test" command in Stata.

TABLE 3.5: *Treatment increases memory of threatening stories for Republicans*

Proportion Remembered

	Immigration Stories		Threatening Immigration Stories		Nonthreatening Immigration Stories	
	Dems	Reps	Dems	Reps	Dems	Reps
Treatment	0.03	0.17	0.02	0.22	0.01	−0.06
	(0.08)	(0.08)	(0.08)	(0.07)	(0.07)	(0.06)
Constant	0.57	0.44	0.35	0.20	0.23	0.25
	(0.05)	(0.06)	(0.05)	(0.04)	(0.05)	(0.04)
Observations	186	170	186	170	186	170
R^2	0.00	0.03	0.00	0.07	0.00	0.01
Wald test of coefficients						
χ^2	1.52		4.03		0.67	
PR<	0.22		0.04		0.41	

Source: Immigration KN Study 2007.
Model specification: OLS. Coefficients in bold indicate $p<.05$, based on a two-tailed test. The dependent variables are the proportion of all stories read that were about immigration, the proportion of all stories read that were threatening about immigration, and the proportion of all stories read that were nonthreatening about immigration. If a respondent did not read any stories, they are set to 0. Wald tests run after the estimation of the models using the "test" command in Stata.

attempt to cope with immigration anxiety, partisans of both parties seek and read immigration stories, but it is anxious Republicans who retain stories that portray immigration negatively. Democrats and Republicans do not differ in their memory for nonthreatening stories. Whether anxious Republicans selectively attend to threatening stories in a motivated way or in a less conscious manner is not clear. Staying consistent with the party's immigration stance could serve to regulate emotion, but it is also possible that the increased attention is a function of beliefs about the information's efficacy in lowering anxiety rather than motivated reasoning.

Partisanship also colors respondents' engagement with information. Overall, we find that the treatment condition increases agreement with threatening immigration stories through increasing anxiety. Table 3.6 shows that it is Republicans who respond to the anxiety treatment by being more likely to agree with threatening stories, whereas Democrats are not moved by the treatment to engage with threatening stories, either to agree with or argue against them. The models in Table 3.6 are logistic regression models of the effect of the treatment on whether a respondent

TABLE 3.6: *Treatment condition increases agreement with threatening stories among Republicans*

	Agree with Threatening Stories		Agree with Nonthreatening Stories		Argue against Threatening Stories		Argue against Nonthreatening Stories	
	Dems	Reps	Dems	Reps	Dems	Reps	Dems	Reps
Treatment	0.08	0.70	0.03	−0.12	0.37	−0.29	0.33	−0.68
	(0.25)	(0.25)	(0.24)	(0.27)	(0.37)	(0.33)	(0.40)	(0.28)
Constant	−0.69	−0.97	−1.08	−1.01	−1.77	−1.38	−2.06	−0.85
	(0.17)	(0.17)	(0.15)	(0.19)	(0.24)	(0.25)	(0.33)	(0.19)
Observations	186	170	186	170	186	170	186	170
Wald tests of coefficients								
χ^2	3.43		0.18		1.99		4.40	
PR<	0.06		0.67		0.16		0.04	

Source: Immigration KN Study 2007.
Model specification: Logit. Coefficients in bold indicate $p<.05$, based on a two-tailed test. Dependent variables indicate respondents' engagement with the stories: 0 (did not agree/disagree), 1 (agree with (non)threatening story). The treatment variable is 0 for respondents in the control condition and 1 for respondents in the treatment condition. Wald tests run after the estimation of the models using the "test" command in Stata.

agreed with or argued against the stories that they read.[25] Anxious Republicans are not only more likely to remember the immigration stories about crime and ill effects on the economy but also more likely to express agreement with them. Listing anxieties about immigration also leads Republicans to be less likely to argue against nonthreatening stories than in the control condition. Democrats in the control condition agreed with threatening stories 25 percent of the time, compared to 27 percent in the treatment condition. In contrast, Republicans agree with threatening stories only 17 percent of the time in the control condition but 40 percent of the time in the treatment condition. Republicans are also less likely than Democrats to be moved to argue against the nonthreatening immigration stories in the treatment condition. In fact, fewer Republicans engage with the nonthreatening stories, arguing against 17 percent of the stories in the control condition and 8 percent in the treatment condition. We speculate

[25] We test whether the effect of the treatment differs for Republicans and Democrats by running a simultaneous equation model of the effect of the treatment on probability of agreeing with or arguing against a (non)threatening story separately for Democrats and Republicans. After estimating the simultaneous equation model, we run Wald tests using the "test" command in Stata.

that Republican respondents shifted their energy from arguing against the nonthreatening stories toward engaging with the threatening stories.

Although partisanship is absent in the first stage of information processing, it emerges as a driver in attention and engagement. Thus, ultimately, Republicans focused on immigration worries bring a more threatening set of considerations about immigration into attitude formation and behavior than do Democrats.

CONCLUSION

To trace the causal impact of anxiety on information processing, we used an experiment in which we manipulated anxiety about immigration and provided subjects with a mock news website. We measured information processing at three stages: first, we track subjects' information seeking by monitoring which stories they read. Then, we measured attention by asking subjects what they remember; and, finally, we measured engagement by asking what they thought about the stories.

Two major findings arise from this study that hold implications for anxiety in politics. First, anxiety trigged biased learning about immigration. We find that anxiety triggers learning about immigration, as suggested by previous scholars, but anxiety also biases the type of information that people prefer. Individuals made anxious about immigration are attracted to threatening information, and this bias is apparent in information seeking, attention, and engagement. Second, attention to threatening information was not costless; when citizens turn their attention toward the object of their anxiety, they are less able to devote time to other issues. Emotional people search for information differently than do those people not concerned about immigration. People do not pay attention to the same news, and, when they pay attention to news, they have different experiences. This is not a new argument – prominent models of opinion formation and change such as Petty and Cacioppo's Elaboration Likelihood Model (ELM) (1986) and Zaller's Receive, Accept, Sample (RAS) (1992) models highlight individual differences in response to persuasive messages. However, the emotion and politics literature rarely traces the effect of emotion through various stages of information processing in a way that makes the work relevant to opinion change. For example, in relation to the RAS model, our measure of exposure is analogous to reception, whereas both attention (do respondents remember the information?) and evaluation (do they agree with it?) suggest individual differences in acceptance. When people remember and agree with information, we think that the information will be more likely to become a relevant consideration for use down the road.

Immigration KN Study 2007 is one of the first studies to incorporate the emotionally charged nature of the contemporary news environment – where immigration coverage includes nonthreatening, neutral, and (most often) threatening stories (Simon and Alexander 1993). In a mock news environment, we track the information that anxious citizens gravitate toward rather than relying on self-reports. Given the opportunity to choose among non-immigration stories, nonthreatening immigration stories, and threatening immigration stories, anxious people systematically favor threat. We examine learning as a three-step process: information seeking, attention, and engagement. Knowing what anxious people read is just one step in understanding how anxiety affects politics. We also measure what they remember and what they think about the information, finding that they favor threatening information at each stage. We show one mechanism by which citizens may form and reinforce anti-immigration attitudes – through a focus on threatening news.

Many studies show that anxiety leads people to seek out information. Our goal was to take a closer look at the valence of that anxiety-driven learning when people are given the choice of threatening, nonthreatening, and irrelevant news. We found that anxious people were more likely to read and remember threatening information, and they were more likely to agree with threatening information. We find that anxiety affects how individuals evaluate the news that they consume; that is, people do not automatically accept information that they encounter. Although anxious people were no more likely to argue against nonthreatening information in this study, they were more likely to agree with threatening information.

Previous research has focused on the potential of anxiety to increase the amount of information that citizens seek. Consequently, anxiety has increasingly been viewed as normatively positive. Our research points to a second political implication: that anxiety biases information processing and does so differentially by the partisanship of the respondent. We find that anxiety does not encourage well-rounded information seeking but instead leads citizens to embrace information that portrays immigration and immigrants in a threatening light. Regardless of partisanship, anxious people were more likely to seek out threatening information, but Republican respondents were especially likely to remember and agree with alarming stories about immigrants. What is striking about anxiety-driven learning in this study is that the bias emerges in all stages of information processing and systematically favors threatening information. Anxious information seekers come away with an unbalanced set of considerations that they then may bring to bear on their political attitudes and behaviors. In the next two chapters, we explore how anxiety conditions who citizens trust to ameliorate threats and just what types of policies these citizens support to help protect them.

4

Don't Worry, Be Trusting?

The Effect of Anxiety on Political Trust

When I am afraid, I will trust in you. In God, whose word I praise, in God I trust; I will not be afraid. What can mortal man do to me?

Psalms 56

In this chapter, we explore the effects of anxiety on political trust. We argue that one method that citizens use to cope with the uncertainty and negative affect that underlie political anxiety is to turn toward political actors who can provide information and advocate policies that will protect them from threats. Higher levels of distress make people less confident in their preferences and political choices (Druckman and McDermott 2008; Loewenstein et al. 2001), making trust in external actors more appealing. Particularly when those actors possess some expertise based on their training, office, or access to information, they are especially appealing. By putting trust in political actors who are perceived to be knowledgeable and expert, citizens motivated to lower anxiety can start to feel better. Like the Biblical Israelites, Americans who are afraid want to put their trust in actors who can effectively protect them, but, rather than turning solely to the Lord, modern citizens might choose to put their trust in government experts.

We use public health and immigration as two cases where anxiety may influence citizens' trust in a variety of public actors. By focusing on which actors citizens turn toward when anxiety is high, we explore whether anxiety-driven trust is targeted or diffuse and to what extent partisanship plays a role. We argue that anxiety may either increase or decrease trust, depending on whether the political actor is seen as responsible for the anxiety. We also argue that anxiety-driven trust is targeted. Anxious citizens do not simply become more trusting in the political system as a whole; they selectively trust in expert actors, those with relevant power and experience to alleviate threats. Who those relevant actors are depends on the threat. When threats come from outside the government, anxious citizens may become more trusting of a host of political actors with relevant expertise. When threats are perceived to originate from government failings, though, the political context may be more polarized, and partisanship may shape which actors are seen as relevant. When threats come from government action (or inaction), citizens may then turn toward actors who are relevant to or "own" the policy area (Petrocik 1996) because they are seen as the party most competent to execute policies to ease these threats.

Anxiety increases sensitivity to risk (Lerner and Keltner 2000; Renshon and Lerner 2012), so, in order to effectively lower anxiety through trust, individuals need to put trust in the actors perceived as most effective at neutralizing threats. Egan (2013) finds that voters perceive issue-owning parties as more competent at making policy. They also prefer politicians who definitely deliver policy, even if that policy is extreme, over politicians who promise but cannot deliver more attractive policies. Together, this literature suggests that in policy domains where the parties disagree and one party holds the advantage, anxious citizens may see the owning party and its members as more trustworthy, despite their own policy preferences or political identities.

The next section explains our hypotheses regarding anxiety-driven trust in two issue areas: public health and immigration. We focus on public health and immigration as the policy areas for these studies because both are topics that can cause a great deal of anxiety in the mass public, but they differ in important ways. Both evoke uncertainty. Public health scares pose threats to citizens' physical well-being, whereas immigration raises threats to cultural and economic security. Although the source of the anxiety may differ across these policy areas, these policy areas both necessitate coordinated government action in order to attenuate the threats that accompany them and thus should affect citizens' level of trust in the government.

We then present four studies that manipulate anxiety in order to understand the relationship between anxiety and trust. The first study focused on the 2009 H1N1 influenza outbreak. The second study triggered anxiety through a fictionalized account of a smallpox outbreak. Our final two studies in this chapter concern immigration, and we trigger anxiety with a campaign advertisement. Across our anxiety manipulations and measures, we find support for our argument that anxiety can lead people to trust (and distrust) depending on the nature of the anxiety and the relevance/expertise of the actors.

ANXIETY AND TRUST

We expect that anxiety may either increase or decrease trust, conditional on (1) the origin of the threat (i.e., internal or external to government) and (2) the expertise and relevance of the actor. Threats that originate from outside the government's control and responsibility (i.e., disease outbreaks, terrorism) should, through increasing anxiety, increase citizens' trust in governmental actors to communicate about and handle those threats. In the aftermath of 9/11, trust in the federal government increased substantially to the highest levels since the 1960s (Chanley 2002). More generally, external threats increase the public's support for the president (Berinsky 2009; Brody 1991; Merolla, Ramos, and Zechmeister 2007; Mueller 1973), as well as for the whole political system (Hetherington and Rudolph 2008; Jost et al. 2008; Jost and van der Toorn 2011).[1] System justification theory argues that one method that people have for combating negative affect is to legitimize and promote existing social arrangements (Jost and Banaji 1994; Jost et al. 2008), including the government in which they reside. Threats to the societal status quo are met by defensive reactions by citizens, who throw support behind societal and governmental institutions even when those institutions do not directly benefit them and may, under some circumstances, actually harm their self-interest (Jost, Banaji, and Nosek 2004). Terror management theory also makes similar predictions when the source of the anxiety is death – that citizens will turn to political figures who can return a feeling of security (Landau et al. 2004). As one example, after the Three Mile Island nuclear accident, nearby residents who trusted in local authorities perceived less danger from the reactor as well as less harm to their health, and, in turn, felt less emotional distress four years after the incident (Goldsteen, Goldsteen, and Schorr 1992).

---

[1] We recognize that the attribution of blame for threats is an ongoing political process and that although the 9/11 attacks were not primarily blamed on government policy by the mass media or other political elites, the 9/11 Commission report laid blame on the U.S. government for not recognizing the plot earlier (National Commission on Terrorist Attacks upon the United States 2004). Yet, we argue that governments are less likely to be blamed for terrorist attacks or public health outbreaks and will be held less responsible for these types of events than for issues like economic policy or immigration policy, which are more clearly government responsibilities.

Anxiety that comes from internal threats – those threats that can be framed as a government shortfall or failure (i.e., immigration, the economy) – should decrease trust in those political actors considered responsible for the shortfall (Fiorina 1981; Key 1966). Hetherington and Rudolph (2008) show that when the public focuses on domestic threats such as the economy and crime, trust in government declines because people attribute these threats to poor government performance. Smallpox and H1N1 are more similar to an external threat to the nation, whereas immigration is an internal threat, so we expect that inducing anxiety about public health should increase trust, whereas inducing anxiety about immigration should decrease trust in those actors considered responsible for the failure.[2] We expect, though, that immigration anxiety should increase trust in actors deemed expert to fixing the problem, actors that come from the party that "owns" immigration – the Republican Party.

Previous public health work suggests that, during health crises, the public trusts individuals seen as expert and authoritative to provide health information, such as the director of the U.S. Centers for Disease Control and Prevention (CDC), while trusting in political appointees less. Over several studies, the director of the Centers for Disease Control and Prevention is rated as the most trustworthy source of information during potential health crises (Blendon et al. 2002, 2009). In a survey of reactions to the 2001 anthrax attacks, Blendon and colleagues (2002) found that no national figure was trusted by a majority of the public as a reliable source of information during a bioterrorism attack but that respondents had more trust in federal officials with a medical background (director of the Centers for Disease Control and Prevention, Surgeon General, President of the American Medical Association) than those without (Secretary of Health and Human Services [HHS], Department of Homeland Security [DHS], and Director of the FBI). Similarly, the 2002 Health Style survey found that, in the case of a bioterrorism attack, 78 percent of respondents would trust the Centers for Disease Control and Prevention for information and 68 percent would trust the Surgeon General. By comparison, only 48 percent would trust the Secretary of HHS, and 41 percent would trust the Homeland Security Director (Pollard 2003). In a 2009 poll by the Centers for Disease Control and Prevention and the Harvard

---

[2] We use "internal" and "external" to capture the perceived origin of the threat – *external threats* are exogenous to the political system, whereas *internal threats* are due to government action or inaction (at least in part). This distinction is separate from the unframed vs. framed threats framework we introduced in Chapter 2, although we expect that unframed threats (threats that involve imminent death and bodily destruction) are external in all but the most extreme circumstances. On the other hand, framed threats, meaning those threats that have a more subjective quality and are contested, have either internal or external causes.

School of Public Health, 78 percent of respondents said that they would trust the director of the Centers for Disease Control and Prevention "somewhat" or "a lot" during an anthrax attack, whereas 69 percent and 65 percent rated the secretary of HHS and President Obama as trustworthy, respectively. Additionally, citizens trust their own clinician as an example of what medical steps to take. In a poll about a potential smallpox outbreak taken in October 2002, 78 percent of the sample indicated that they would get a smallpox vaccination if their own doctor got vaccinated, but only 21 percent said that they would get vaccinated if most doctors refused the vaccination (Blendon et al. 2003).

Policy expertise in the area of public health is relatively straightforward – it is rational to turn toward medical professionals for accurate, useful health information. But how should anxious citizens decide who to trust with immigration? Here, the idea of an expert isn't as clear. Trusted figures are shaped by issue ownership and partisan dynamics. Over a forty-year timespan, Egan (2013) shows that the American public ranks the Republican Party as better able to handle immigration than the Democratic Party by margins as big as 15 percentage points. This issue advantage comes not solely from agreement on policy grounds, but rather a belief that Republicans are more able to implement their immigration policies. Given this advantage, anxious citizens may cope with anxiety about immigration by increasing their trust in Republican actors, even if they themselves are Democrats.

HYPOTHESES

First, we expect that anxiety increases trust in actors and agencies that are relevant and/or expert when a threat is external (public health). When a threat is internal (meaning that government bears at least some responsibility), we expect that anxiety leads to increased trust in relevant and/or expert actors as well. We also hypothesize that anxiety decreases trust in those perceived to be responsible for the problem.

Second, we expect that partisanship shapes relevance in the immigration studies due to the Republican Party's long-standing advantage on the issue. We hypothesize that anxious people will put their trust in Republicans.

AN H1N1 OUTBREAK

To test the hypothesis that health anxiety should increase support for expert actors, we use Public Health – H1N1 Study 2010, which took place in a lab with an undergraduate sample (see Chapter 2, Table 2.3 for sample characteristics). Respondents were randomly assigned to either a treatment condition that induced worry over H1N1 or a control condition. This study relies on the same bottom-up anxiety manipulation technique that we used in Immigration KN Study 2007. In order to evoke anxiety about H1N1, respondents in the treatment condition read the prompt, "First, we'd like you to take a moment to reflect on the H1N1 virus (swine flu). What makes you feel worried about the H1N1 virus (swine flu)? Please describe how you felt as vividly and in as much detail as possible." In the control condition, respondents were given the following prompt: "First, we'd like you to take a moment to reflect on the H1N1 virus (swine flu). What comes to mind when you think about the H1N1 virus (swine flu)? Please list everything that comes to mind."

Respondents had unlimited time to complete the thought listing and were provided a text box to type as much as they wished. By evoking emotions via an open-ended question, we allowed subjects to tell us what makes them worried rather than assuming that an emotional stimulus would have uniform effects on all subjects within the treatment group. Our stimulus holds the salience of H1N1 constant across the two conditions. Respondents in both the control condition and the experimental condition were asked to consider H1N1, whereas only those in the anxiety condition were asked to worry about H1N1.

We had a research assistant unaware of our hypotheses code the number and types of worries that respondents mentioned in both the control and treatment conditions. The treatment condition did not simply increase cognition by causing subjects to think more. Respondents in the treatment condition wrote an average of 54 words, compared to 52 words in the control condition ($F(1, 154)$, $p<.78$). Rather, the treatment condition increased worries about the H1N1 virus. On average, respondents mentioned 4 worries, with a range of 1 to 10 worries. Figure 4.1 displays the number of mentions by respondents about two different topics – worries related to the H1N1 vaccine (lack of access, possible side effects) and mentions that the H1N1 pandemic was "overhyped." Respondents in the treatment condition were more likely to mention the H1N1 vaccine than were control respondents ($M_{control} = .37$ mentions vs. $M_{treatment} = .55$, $F(1, 154) = 2.95$, $p<.08$)[3] and less likely to mention that H1N1 was

---

[3] These statistics come from ANOVA models predicting the number of worries by treatment condition.

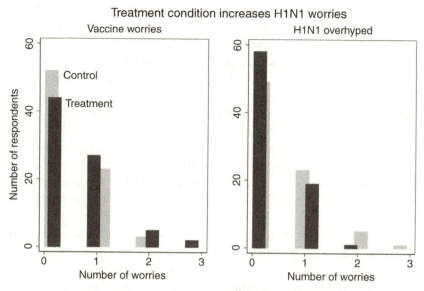

FIGURE 4.1: H1N1 treatment's effect on specific worries
Source: Public Health – H1N1 Study 2010.

overhyped than were their counterparts in the control condition ($M_{control}$ = .46 vs. $M_{treatment}$ = .27, $F(1, 154)$ = 4.21, p<.04). However, there was some buffering against anxiety as well. Respondents in the treatment condition were more likely than the control condition to mention that H1N1 was no longer a problem as of March 2010 ($M_{control}$ = .14 vs. $M_{treatment}$ = .61, $F(1, 154)$ = 28.21, p<.01). By making respondents conjure their anxiety about H1N1, some respondents resisted the feeling, making this is a more difficult test of the hypothesis.

We expect that anxiety will increase trust in "expert" agencies and actors to provide information about H1N1. Multiple federal agencies, as well as state departments of health, produce fliers, commercials, and other communications during flu season to provide the public with information on how to prevent and treat the flu. Barack Obama declared the H1N1 virus a national emergency in October 2009 and later urged people to get vaccinated. In a November 2009 CDC survey of individuals who had traveled in the past year, 70 percent of respondents mentioned seeing posters, billboards, and other ads about flu prevention (Centers for Disease Control and Health 2009). Poll respondents also reported seeking information about the flu from a variety of sources – 16 percent said that they visited the Centers for Disease Control and Prevention's website, 9 percent sought information from the Department of HHS, 16 percent sought information from local or state health departments, and 20 percent from health websites like WebMD. Individuals also receive information and discuss the flu on an interpersonal level – with friends, family, and their doctors. Sixty-four percent of the Centers for Disease Control and Prevention poll respondents said that they discussed flu prevention measures such as hand washing with friends and family.

Subjects in our study answered two questions about their confidence in the government's ability to handle an H1N1 outbreak: (1) confidence in the "federal government's" ability to handle the outbreak and (2) confidence in the president. Subjects rated their confidence as (1) Not too confident, (2) Somewhat confident, or (3) Very confident. We rescaled these answers to range from 0 to 1, with higher values indicating more confidence. On average, confidence is relatively high in both actors, but subjects are more confident in the federal government's ability to handle an outbreak than in the president's ability ($M_{fed} = .74$ vs. $M_{pres} = .67$, $t = 3.48$, $p<.01$). Turning to differences based on experimental conditions, we find subjects in the treatment condition had more confidence in the federal government compared to the control condition, but there were no differences in their confidence in the president. Anxiety over the H1N1 flu significantly increased ratings of the federal government's ability to handle a health crisis ($M_{control} = .70$ vs. $M_{treatment} = .77$, $F(1, 154)$, $p<.06$) but did not affect ratings of Obama ($M_{control} = .63$ vs. $M_{treatment} .71$, $F(1, 154)$, $p<.12$). Ratings of the "federal government" may be driven in part by ratings of specific health agencies like the Centers for Disease Control and Prevention, whereas the president has no professional health expertise. It is also possible that President Obama's partisanship made him a less attractive outlet for anxiety-driven trust.

To test whether anxiety over the H1N1 flu translated into trust in a variety of specific government and nongovernmental information sources, we asked subjects to rate their trustworthiness to provide H1N1 information. Respondents were asked if they trusted the following (randomly ordered) groups/individuals: (1) Not at all, (2) Not very much, (3) Somewhat, or (4) A great deal as a source of information about the H1N1 flu. The groups/individuals were (1) Your personal doctor, (2) The Centers for Disease Control and Prevention (CDC), (3) The Food and Drug Administration (FDA), (4) Surgeon General Regina Benjamin, (5) The American Medical Association (AMA), (5) The Department of Homeland Security (DHS), (7) The Department of Health and Human Services (HHS), (8) Friends or family members employed in healthcare, (9) Websites from health organizations like WebMD, and (10) President

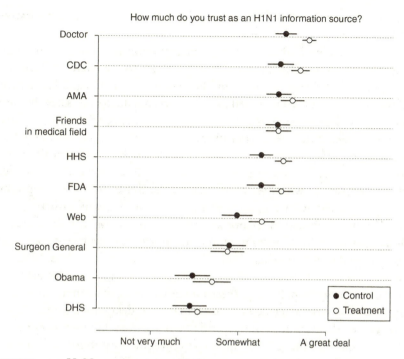

FIGURE 4.2: H1N1 anxiety treatment increases trust in expert actors
Source: Public Health – H1N1 Study 2010.

Barack Obama. We rescaled the trust measure to range between 0 and 1, with higher scores indicating more trust.

Figure 4.2 shows respondents' average ratings of the ten groups and individuals in the control condition and the treatment condition. The white circles represent respondents in the treatment condition, and the black circles represent control respondents. Consistent with previous work (Blendon et al. 2002, 2003), respondents differentiated between actors whom they viewed as trustworthy in a health crisis and those who may be less useful in providing information. On average, respondents rated the Centers for Disease Control and Prevention, the AMA, and their personal doctor as the sources they would trust most to provide H1N1 information. Fifty-nine percent of respondents answered that they trusted their doctor "a great deal," 58 percent answered "a great deal" for the Centers for Disease Control and Prevention, and 52 percent trusted the AMA "a great deal." In contrast, only 18 percent of respondents trusted President Obama "a great deal," and 12 percent would turn to the DHS. Although the president did make public remarks about H1N1 preparedness and the production of vaccines in September 2009, citizens did not view him as an authoritative figure in providing health information.

Figure 4.2 reveals that the treatment condition led respondents to be more trusting of the three federal agencies most closely related to health – the Centers for Disease Control and Prevention, the FDA, and HHS – for information about the flu as well as one's personal doctor. It is not the case that anxiety simply increases support of government agencies, though; there are no significant differences in ratings of DHS, which is considerably less related to infectious disease information. Additionally, trust in health web-sites also increases when respondents were asked to worry about the flu, which is consistent with the finding that web searches about flu symptoms increase in areas with high concentrations of flu cases (Ginsberg et al. 2008). Finally, anxiety does not seem to increase trust in individuals in the same ways as it increases trust in institutions – the treatment condition did not make respondents think that President Obama, the Surgeon General, or even friends in the medical fields were more trustworthy as source of information. Perhaps these individuals are considered to have less expertise than federal agencies or less capacity to deal with a crisis.

Together, the trust and confidence findings suggest that worry over health risks may improve the standing of "expert" federal institutions in the minds of Americans but may not increase ratings of or confidence in partisan actors, even when those individuals have publicly taken stances on the health issue.

A SMALLPOX OUTBREAK

To further test the hypothesis that anxiety may increase trust in those with expertise, we designed Public Health – Smallpox YG/P Study 2011, a web-based experiment with a different health issue and a broader array of political actors. This study had the advantage of a nationally representa-tive sample recruited from YouGov/Polimetrix's online panel of respon-dents in Spring 2011 (see Chapter 2, Table 2.3 for sample characteristics). In this study, we triggered anxiety over a (fictional) smallpox outbreak in Cleveland, Ohio. We used smallpox as our public health threat because it is noncyclical, serious, and carries with it a grave danger of death. Few people have immunity to this highly contagious disease, so the risk of contraction and serious complications would be high in the event of an outbreak. Smallpox is an eradicated disease, but there was an increase in attention to the disease in 2003 because of concerns that Iraq had biological weapons that could be deployed against soldiers or citizens during an American invasion. In a survey of 1,000 respondents in Fall 2002, 64 percent said that a smallpox attack was likely if the United States invaded Iraq. Thirty percent of respondents believed (falsely) that there had been a case of smallpox in the United States in past 5 years, and 63 percent falsely believed that there was an outbreak somewhere in the world. The concern that respondents showed and the false beliefs suggested that we could increase anxiety about this disease in an experimental context (Blendon et al. 2003).

This study used a newspaper story to manipulate respondents' anxiety. Subjects read about either a smallpox outbreak that was currently happening (Smallpox–present), a smallpox outbreak that occurred twenty-five years ago (Smallpox–past), or a control condition in which respondents read a neutral newspaper story that focused on the discovery of a stone bearing an ancient Olmec language. In pre-testing, raters rated the control story as interesting (71 percent of raters said that they would read the story based on the headline) but not emotional (81 percent of raters said that the headline did not make them worried at all). Respondents were randomly assigned to either the Smallpox–present, Smallpox–past, or the control group. All the newspaper stories were of approximately the same length and were in the font style and under the banner of The *New York Times*.[4]

After reading one of the newspaper stories, respondents were asked to rate how anxious, angry, sad, and excited they felt on a 9-point scale from "not at all" to "very strongly," which we rescaled to vary between 0 and 1. Figure 4.3 shows the average level of anxiety across our three experimental conditions. Our experimental treatments succeeded in increasing respondents' negative emotions (including anger and sadness) and most powerfully increased respondents' anxiety. Control condition respondents had an average level of anxiety of .17 on the 0 to 1 scale, whereas the smallpox–past condition increased anxiety by .18 (se = .03, p<.01) and the smallpox–present condition increased anxiety by .36 (se = .03, p<.01). Our most threatening condition, the smallpox–present condition, increased anxiety over the control condition significantly more than the smallpox–past condition ($F_{(1, 573)} = 29.0$, p<.01).[5] We are

---

[4] The treatments were somewhat unbalanced on the number of Latinos per condition (p<.08) and education (p<.05). The subsequent mediation analyses will account for demographics to account for some of the imbalance as well as to satisfy the assumptions underlying the models (Imai et al. 2011). We also weight all models with the post-stratification weights provided by YouGov/Polimetrix.

[5] The present outbreak condition also increased respondents' anger significantly over the control condition by .28 (se = .03, p<.01) as well as the past outbreak condition by .13 (se = .03, p<.01). Respondents in the present outbreak condition were also significantly more sad ($M_{control}$ = .40, p<.01, past: .12, p<.01) and less excited (control: –.15, p<.01, past: –.09, p<.01) than respondents in other conditions. Although the present outbreak

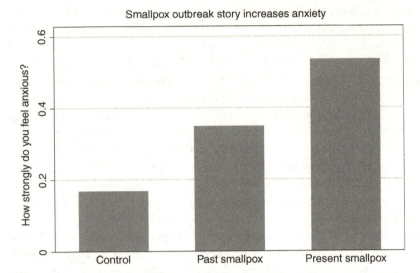

FIGURE 4.3: Smallpox treatment condition increases anxiety
Source: Public Health – Smallpox YG/P Study 2011.

confident that this manipulation roused respondents' anxieties about
smallpox and tested the effect of anxiety on trust (see Chapter 2 for further
study details and a manipulation check).[6,7]

story increased a number of negative emotions, its effect on anxiety was of similar
magnitude to its effect on sadness (χ^2 = 1.88, p<.17) and significantly larger than its effect
on excitement (χ^2 = 176.4, p<.01) and anger (χ^2 = 5.51, p<.02).

[6] YouGov/Polimetrix maintains a panel of respondents, which it recruits through a polling
website, Polling Point. Once individuals agree to become part of the YouGov/Polimetrix
panel, they provide demographic information and are offered opportunities to participate in
surveys. Since recruitment into the panel is voluntary, this means that the larger panel is an
opt-in sample that may be unrepresentative of the larger population. Opt-in Internet samples
tend to be more interested in politics as well as composed of more white respondents than the
general public (YouGov/Polimetrix 2006). In order to draw a nationally representative
sample from a larger, nonrepresentative sample, YouGov/Polimetrix uses a method called
sample matching. It draws a random sample from the American Community Study run by
the Census Bureau and then matches a respondent in the opt-in panel who is the closest to
the Census respondent based on the joint distribution of age, race, gender, and education, as
well as on imputed values of partisanship and ideology. The purpose of the matching is to
find an available respondent who is as similar as possible to the selected member of the target
sample, which results in a sample of respondents who have the same characteristics as the
target sample. By matching respondents in the YouGov/Polimetrix panel to those in the
larger target population, YouGov/Polimetrix samples reflect the population. Hill et al.
(2007) argue that the sample matching technique produces samples similar to RDD phone
samples, thus increasing the external validity of the study.

[7] The experimental conditions were balanced on gender (p<.81); age (p<.25); the percentage
of white respondents (p<.64), blacks (p<.25), and Asians (p<.17); respondents' interest in

We expect that health anxiety should motivate citizens to trust actors they deem expert and relevant in ameliorating threats. We asked respondents to rate how much they trusted each actor as a source of information about smallpox: (1) Not at all, (2) Not very much, (3) Somewhat, or (4) A great deal. We included actors who varied in how expert they were in areas of health. The groups/individuals were: (1) Your personal doctor, (2) The Centers for Disease Control and Prevention, (3) The FDA, (4) Surgeon General Regina Benjamin, (5) The DHS, (6) HHS, (7) Friends or family members employed in healthcare, (8) Websites from health organizations like WebMD, (9) President Barack Obama, (10) The Internal Revenue Service (IRS), (11) Federal Reserve Chair Ben Bernanke, and (12) Oprah Winfrey. We also varied how we described Surgeon General Regina Benjamin: (1) as an expert in infectious disease, (2) as having a medical background, or (3) as being a political appointee.

Figure 4.4 displays the percent of respondents in the smallpox–past treatment and the smallpox–present treatment who trust each actor "a great deal," the highest level of trust on our scale. We present just the two treatment conditions here for clarity. Respondents ranked the IRS and the Fed chairmen as the least trustworthy and the Centers for Disease Control and Prevention and one's personal doctor as the most trustworthy. Respondents were also highly trusting of their friends in the medical field and the AMA. Although only five respondents (.8 percent) said that they trusted the IRS "a great deal" on health issues, 48 percent gave the Centers for Disease Control and Prevention and 56 percent gave their doctor the highest level of trust. Consistent with Public Health – H1N1 Study 2010, respondents in our most threatening experimental condition are *more* trusting of actors than in the less threatening smallpox–past condition.

The increase in trust in the present outbreak condition was statistically significant at conventional levels for respondents' ratings of the DHS, the FDA, HHS, and the Centers for Disease Control and Prevention. Subjects increased trust in DHS by 6 percentage points ($\chi^2 = 7.10$, p<.01). In this instance, turning toward an agency designed to handle terrorism is logical because the news story mentioned smallpox's possible use for bioterrorism. The increases in trust in the health agencies were of even larger magnitudes. Respondents in the present outbreak condition were 9 percentage points more likely to highly trust the FDA (Past = 8 percent vs. Present = 17 percent,

the news (p<.62); and health status (p<.27), as well as on political identities (Partisanship p<.53, Ideology p<.89). These probabilities were derived from a χ^2 test comparing the distribution of respondents' demographics by experimental condition.

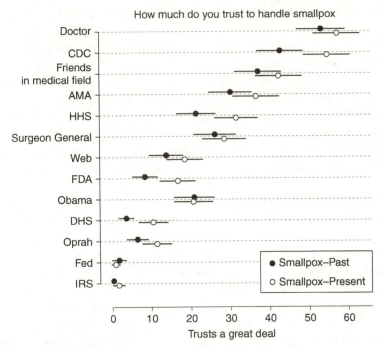

FIGURE 4.4: Smallpox anxiety treatment increases trust in experts
Source: Public Health Smallpox YG/P 2011.

χ^2 = 5.49, p<.02), 10 percentage points more trusting of HHS (Past = 21 percent vs. Present = 31 percent, χ^2 = 4.60, p<.03), and 12 percentage points more trusting of the Centers for Disease Control and Prevention (Past = 43 percent vs. Present = 55 percent, χ^2 = 7.10, p<.01). As expected, as one way of lowering anxiety, respondents turn toward actors who can provide useful information and help alleviate the uncertainty and negative affect that accompanies anxiety.

Mediation

We attribute the difference in trust between the present outbreak condition and the other conditions to different levels of anxiety generated by the newspaper story. In order to test this causal mechanism directly, we use a mediation model that accounts for the level of anxiety expressed by each individual. We also include respondents' level of anger in the mediation models and check that the treatment condition influences trust through anxiety rather than through anger. By using the level of anxiety expressed, we can test whether anxiety is mediating the relationship between the experimental manipulation and trust.

Table 4.1 demonstrates that the treatment condition led respondents to be more trusting of various political actors by increasing anxiety. Table 4.1 shows the effect of being in the present outbreak condition or the past outbreak condition (compared to the control condition) on the level of trust in each of the twelve actors respondents rated. We have modeled separately the effect of anxiety on trust in the Surgeon General when she is described as having medical expertise and when she is described as a political appointee. To satisfy the statistical assumptions underlying this model (Imai, Keele, and Tingley 2010b), we also include pretreatment variables (gender, education, race, health status, age, news interest, ideology, and partisanship) that may be related to trust in government, as well as anxiety in both the models predicting the mediator and the models predicting the outcomes of interest.[8] Models showing all the demographic controls and the mediation coefficients are in Table A4.1 in the Appendix.

The models in Table 4.1 are the second stage of the mediation models.[9] Consistent with our theory, the threatening newspaper stories affected trust through increasing respondents' level of anxiety, not through simply making the disease salient or providing information. These full models account for the role of demographics as well and tell a consistent story. To the extent that respondents became anxious through reading a newspaper story about a current threatening public health crisis, they became increasingly trusting in a host of actors with relevant information ranging from the DHS to health websites. Anxious respondents also become more trusting in the Surgeon General when she is described as being an expert (p<.10) but not when she is described as a political actor. Surprisingly, the mediation models also reveal that anxiety also boosts trust in the IRS, an agency clearly unrelated to health issues. All together, these two studies provide evidence that anxious citizens are significantly more trusting of federal agencies to provide useful health information in times of health crises when those crises are not framed as the government's fault.

---

[8] We include anger only in the second-stage model that predicts information seeking as a function of emotions and the treatment. Including anger as a predictor of fear would imply that anger was a cause of fear and would thus be a post-treatment confounder, which would violate the sequential ignorability assumption that underlies these mediation models.

[9] We do not include the first-stage models because they replicate the manipulation check findings from Chapter 2 by showing that the smallpox–present story increases respondents' anxiety compared to the control condition. For the formal manipulation check, see Table A5.2 in the Appendix.

TABLE 4.1: *Smallpox anxiety increases trust in public health experts*

	IRS	Fed Reserve Chair	Oprah	DHS	Obama	Websites	HHS
Smallpox– present	−0.04	−0.03	−0.08	−0.06	0.00	−0.04	−0.02
	(0.03)	(0.03)	(0.04)	(0.04)	(0.04)	(0.04)	(0.04)
Smallpox–past	−0.08	−0.08	−0.09	−0.10	−0.03	−0.05	−0.03
	(0.03)	(0.03)	(0.04)	(0.04)	(0.04)	(0.03)	(0.03)
Anxiety	0.16	0.10	0.21	0.30	0.13	0.19	0.26
	(0.05)	(0.05)	(0.06)	(0.05)	(0.05)	(0.06)	(0.05)
Anger	−0.02	0.07	−0.06	−0.07	−0.14	−0.02	−0.19
	(0.05)	(0.06)	(0.06)	(0.06)	(0.05)	(0.05)	(0.05)
Constant	0.27	0.29	0.41	0.31	0.53	0.52	0.73
	(0.07)	(0.07)	(0.10)	(0.09)	(0.09)	(0.08)	(0.09)
N	554	551	555	551	553	552	554
R^2	0.17	0.17	0.22	0.18	0.52	0.08	0.24

	FDA	AMA	CDC	Friends and Family in the Medical Field	Personal Doctor	Surgeon General (Expert Framing)	Surgeon General (Political Framing)
Smallpox– present	0.00	−0.01	0.01	0.02	0.00	−0.02	0.11
	(0.04)	(0.04)	(0.04)	(0.03)	(0.03)	(0.07)	(0.09)
Smallpox– past	−0.04	−0.03	0.00	−0.02	−0.03	0.00	0.01
	(0.04)	(0.03)	(0.03)	(0.03)	(0.03)	(0.06)	(0.08)
Anxiety	0.15	0.14	0.16	0.07	0.06	0.19	−0.01
	(0.06)	(0.04)	(0.05)	(0.04)	(0.04)	(0.09)	(0.12)
Anger	−0.09	−0.18	−0.13	−0.06	−0.03	−0.20	−0.09
	(0.06)	(0.05)	(0.05)	(0.05)	(0.04)	(0.10)	(0.12)
Constant	0.44	0.55	0.66	0.69	0.64	0.08	0.34
	(0.09)	(0.09)	(0.08)	(0.07)	(0.07)	(0.16)	(0.21)
N	553	554	551	553	553	370	183
R^2	0.11	0.13	0.18	0.04	0.09	0.23	0.19

Source: Public Health – Smallpox YG/P Study 2011.
Model specification: OLS mediation models. Coefficients in bold indicate p<.05, based on a two-tailed test. Dependent variables indicate how much respondents trust each actor from "not at all" (0) to "very much" 1. OLS with mediation effect calculated using algorithm in Imai, Keele, and Tingley (2010). Models showing full demographic controls and mediation coefficients can be found in Table A4.1 in the Appendix.

AN IMMIGRANT THREAT?

To test anxiety's effect on trust and attitudes in a policy area where threats can be perceived as internal – that is, attributable to government inaction or policy failures – we use the issue of immigration. To create an environment similar to how many citizens receive campaign information, subjects were recruited and participated in the experiment online. We recruited 174 subjects through Amazon's Mechanical Turk to participate in a study on political advertising (Immigration MT Study 2011; see Chapter 2, Table 2.3 for sample characteristics). Once respondents agreed to take the survey, they were directed to a website that randomly assigned them to watch either the control condition ad (threatening verbal information, neutral imagery, no music) or the treatment condition ad (threatening verbal information, imagery, and music)[10] and then answer a series of questions on their level of trust in various political actors to handle immigration and attitudes about illegal immigrants' access to state services.

In the smallpox and H1N1 studies, anxiety served to increase trust in a variety of sources to provide information. Anxiety did not systematically lower trust. We expect that anxiety will increase trust most strongly in the party that owns the policy area. To test how partisanship moderates the effect of anxiety, we asked respondents to rate their trust in six (randomly ordered) political figures to "handle" immigration who vary on their partisan affiliations and position on immigration reform: (1) President Barack Obama, (2) The Democratic Party, (3) The Republican Party, (4) Citizen groups like the Minutemen, (5) Arizona governor Jan Brewer, and (6) U.S. Customs and Border Control. The trust variable was scaled from 1 (do not trust at all) to 4 (trust a great deal). Note that the trust variable in the immigration study differs from the public health studies; this is a measure of how much respondents trust these actors to implement policy (i.e., handle immigration) rather than provide information.

---

[10] A randomization check showed that the conditions were balanced on age, gender, race, education, partisanship, and ideology. Using a logit model to predict whether a respondent was assigned to the treatment condition, we found no significant effects for age ($p<.89$); gender ($p<.21$); whether a respondent was white ($p<.99$), Latino ($p<.73$), African American ($p<.35$); education level ($p<.85$), partisanship ($p<.34$), or ideology ($p<.16$).

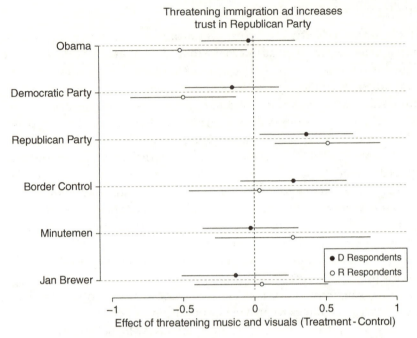

FIGURE 4.5: Immigration treatment condition both increases and decreases trust
Source: Immigration MT Study 2011.

On average, U.S. Customs and Border Control was the most trusted actor (M = 2.77, sd = .90) with broad trust across partisan respondents (M_{Dem} = 2.77, M_{Ind} = 2.53, M_{Rep} = 2.92). For the other, more political actors, partisanship significantly shaped the level of trust. On average, Democrats were the most trusting of Obama (M = 2.96, sd = .84) and the Democratic Party (M = 2.77, sd = .79) to handle immigration, whereas Republicans were most trusting of the Republican Party (M = 2.92, sd = .70), Republican governor Brewer (M = 2.98, sd = .92), and the Minutemen (M = 2.68, sd = .94). We expect that partisanship should also moderate the effect of anxiety on these trust judgments.

We expect that who citizens trust to handle immigration depends, in part, on their own partisan identity, as well as on which party "owns" the issue. To test the hypothesis that anxiety may increase trust in political actors seen as expert, Figure 4.5 shows the differences in mean trust judgments and 90 percent confidence intervals around the differences between the treatment and control conditions. Independent "leaners" are grouped with the party that they lean toward. The black circles represent Democratic respondents, and the white circles represent Republican respondents. If the differences are to the right of the dotted vertical line, the treatment condition increased trust, and if the differences are to the left of the dotted line, exposure to the threatening music and images decreased trust. What the figure reveals is that exposure to an emotionally evocative immigration ad affects respondents in a variety of ways. The treatment condition did not significantly affect trust in the Border Patrol, Governor Brewer, or the Minutemen. Democrats distrust Brewer and the Minutemen, whereas Republicans consistently trust them to handle immigration policy, regardless of the emotional content of the immigration ad that they saw. The evocative immigration ad did significantly affect respondents' trust evaluations in the three actors most visibly responsible for federal immigration policy – the political parties and the president. Consistent with our expectation that partisanship moderates the effect of the treatment, Republicans faced with an anxiety-provoking immigration ad are significantly *less* trusting of Obama by .43 (se = .25, p<.09), less trusting of the Democratic Party by .45 (se = .19, p<.03), and significantly *more* trusting of the Republican Party by .47 (se = .20, p<.02) than are Republicans who saw the less evocative ad.[11] Democrats faced with an evocative immigration ad did not significantly increase trust in political actors from their side of the political spectrum, but their trust in the *Republican* Party increased by .37 (se = .17, p<.03), consistent with the issue ownership hypothesis.

When ads focused on the concerns most likely to be expressed by conservatives and Republicans, the resulting anxiety boosts trust in the Republican Party and decreases trust in the Democratic Party and the president. There are two possible explanations for this finding. Our ads focused on the dire consequences of immigration, a theme that is more common in Republican immigration rhetoric. Additionally, threat and anxiety tend to increase support for restrictive immigration policies (Citrin et al. 1997), policies that are more consistent with the Republican Party's position on immigration. A second possible explanation is that

---

[11] These coefficients and standard errors come from separate OLS models that model the effect of being in the treatment condition on trust judgments of the political actors, controlling for ideology. Each model was done separately for Democratic and Republican respondents.

anxiety may prompt the desire for certainty (Starcevic and Berle 2006), and the Republican Party's stance on immigration is clearer than the Democrats' and so the party may be viewed as more able to implement its policy (Egan 2013).

THREATS VS. POLICIES IN RESPONSE TO IMMIGRATION ANXIETY

If anxiety motivates people to reduce uncertainty and find "experts" who can lower their level of discomfort, we expect that citizens will seek out political actors with policy solutions rather than actors who simply refer to immigration as problematic. To test this proposition, we use Immigration KN Study 2011, a nationally representative sample gathered through Knowledge Networks (KN). The 1,053 respondents were recruited from the KN panel (see Chapter 2, Table 2.2 for sample characteristics). We weight all models using the post-stratification weights provided by KN.

In the study, we made immigration salient through having respondents watch a campaign ad about the perils of illegal immigration. After respondents watched the ad, which featured evocative imagery about immigration, we asked them to rate how worried and angry they felt on a scale from 1 (not at all) to 8 (extremely). Respondents were then asked to rate how much they trusted seven different relevant political actors to handle the issue of immigration: (1) President Obama, (2) The Democratic Party, (3) The Republican Party, (4) Arizona's Republican governor Jan Brewer, (5) The Department of Homeland Security, (6) The Minutemen, and (7) A citizens group dedicated to the issue of immigration. When rating each actor, respondents went to a separate screen that showed a picture of the actor paired with either a policy position (based on that actor's actual policy position as expressed through speeches or party platform) or a threatening message, also taken directly from the actor.

Each actor's position was randomly assigned to either offer a policy solution to the issue of illegal immigration or simply to focus on the threat of illegal immigration. This design allows us to differentiate whether anxious citizens trust expert actors to handle immigration because of their policy positions or simply based on threatening rhetoric. This table shows examples from the Democratic Party's message.

Threat Message	Policy Message
"We cannot ignore the nearly 12 million immigrants currently living in the United States illegally. The exploitation of undocumented immigrant workers threatens to drive down wages, benefits and working conditions for middle-class workers and low-income Americans striving to earn a middle-class standard of living."	"We cannot ignore the nearly 12 million immigrants currently living in the United States illegally. The exploitation of undocumented immigrant workers threatens to drive down wages for Americans. We support comprehensive reform grounded in the principles of responsibility. Employers who exploit undocumented workers undermine American workers, and they have to be held accountable."

Although both statements outline a major problem with undocumented immigration, the threat message continues to focus on one threat of immigration (i.e., exploitation) whereas the policy message offers a solution (i.e., comprehensive reform). All policy and threatening messages match the ideology and real positions of the actual actors. For the fictional citizen interest group, we randomly assigned respondents to either read a liberal policy message or a more conservative policy message. Each respondent rated their trust in seven actors: six were real (three offering threatening messages and three offering policy messages), and the seventh was a fictional citizen interest group paired with either a liberal or a conservative policy solution.[12] Each respondent received a mix of liberal and conservative figures offering policy messages. Respondents rated how much they trusted each actor on a 4-point scale from (1) "not at all" to (4) "a great deal."

Current work on trust related to dealing with immigration is limited, but polling suggests a strong role for partisanship. Forty-five percent of Americans trust Republicans to do a better job of handling illegal immigration, whereas 43 percent trust Democrats more (Associated Press/GfK Poll 2010). People appear to evaluate President Obama's performance on immigration through a partisan lens. Only 8 percent of Republicans

---

[12] Respondents were divided into two groups. In the first group, respondents read threatening messages from Obama, the DHS, and the Republicans and a solution message from Brewer, the Minutemen, and the Democrats. They received the liberal solution from "Citizens Concerned about Immigration." The second group read a threatening message from Brewer, the Minutemen, and the Democratic Party, and a solution message from Obama, DHS, and the Republicans. They read a conservative message from the interest group.

approve of President Obama's handling of immigration policy, whereas 37 percent of Democrats approve (Pew Research Center for the People and the Press 2010a). Republicans are far more likely to approve of the Minutemen. According to a 2006 Pew Survey, 49 percent of Republicans approve, 12 percent disapprove, and 37 percent have never heard of the Minutemen. This is in contrast to the 25 percent of Democrats who approve, 28 percent who disapprove, and 44 percent who have never heard of the Minutemen (Pew Research Center for the People and the Press 2006a).

On average, Arizona's governor Jan Brewer garnered the highest level of trust in this sample ($M = 2.83$, sd $= 1.02$), and Obama had the lowest level of trust ($M = 2.27$, sd $= 1.02$). However, both of these averages belie significant polarization by party. Republicans were significantly more trusting of Brewer than were Democrats ($M_{Rep} = 3.29$ vs. $M_{Dem} = 2.42$, $t = 14.9$, p<.01) and significantly less trusting of Obama ($M_{Rep} = 1.64$ vs. $M_{Dem} = 2.89$, $t = 23.1$, p<.01). The DHS rated as the second most trusted actor with an average level of trust of 2.63 (sd $= .84$).

We expect that anxiety will increase trust in actors deemed expert in helping to protect the public and solve the immigration problem. Who those experts are deemed to be may be a function of the partisan identities of the rater and the actor. We test the effect of respondents' anxiety on their evaluation of how trustworthy each of the seven actors is, using ordinary least squares (OLS) controlling for respondents' partisanship, ideology, gender, highest level of schooling completed, and whether the respondent identifies as black or Latino. All independent variables are scaled from 0 to 1, with higher values indicating respondents are female, more conservative, Republican, have a higher level of education, and that the respondent is black or Latino. The models in Table 4.2 also include an indicator of whether the respondent read the threat or the policy message and respondents' level of immigration anger, a common emotion in studies of immigration.

Immigration anxiety increased support for a range of actors who offer restrictionist immigration policies. Anxiety over immigration significantly increased trust in the Republican Party, Brewer, and the militia group the Minutemen between 12 and 25 percent on the trust scale. In contrast, immigration anxiety did not significantly affect trust in the actors with more liberal immigration positions – Obama and the Democrats or the DHS, an agency presently headed by Democrats. However, respondents angry about immigration were significantly less trusting in Democratic actors, a finding consistent with previous work that shows that even

TABLE 4.2: *Anxiety increases trust while anger decreases trust*

	Obama	Democrats	Republicans	Brewer	DHS	Minutemen	Citizens Group
Threat	0.07	**-0.19**	-0.11	**-0.15**	**-0.13**	**-0.14**	**-0.28**
	(0.06)	(0.06)	(0.07)	(0.07)	(0.07)	(0.07)	(0.08)
Anxiety	-0.21	0.09	**0.48**	**1.04**	0.24	**0.75**	0.07
	(0.15)	(0.14)	(0.20)	(0.18)	(0.17)	(0.17)	(0.21)
Anger	**-0.41**	**-0.29**	0.04	0.12	**-0.32**	**0.32**	0.12
	(0.14)	(0.13)	(0.17)	(0.17)	(0.15)	(0.16)	(0.20)
PID	**-1.23**	**-1.18**	**0.82**	**0.63**	-0.19	**0.65**	0.10
	(0.14)	(0.13)	(0.13)	(0.13)	(0.14)	(0.13)	(0.15)
Ideology	**-0.70**	**-0.53**	**0.41**	**0.55**	-0.22	0.23	-0.12
	(0.17)	(0.17)	(0.18)	(0.16)	(0.16)	(0.16)	(0.20)
Female	0.04	0.04	0.01	0.05	0.12	0.10	**0.17**
	(0.06)	(0.06)	(0.07)	(0.07)	(0.07)	(0.07)	(0.08)
Education	0.26	-0.39	-0.03	-0.17	-0.13	**-0.40**	-0.13
	(0.22)	(0.20)	(0.25)	(0.23)	(0.22)	(0.21)	(0.28)
Black	**0.49**	**0.23**	0.05	-0.01	0.08	0.11	0.20
	(0.11)	(0.11)	(0.12)	(0.12)	(0.10)	(0.11)	(0.13)
Latino	**0.25**	0.09	-0.19	**-0.42**	-0.12	-0.15	-0.09
	(0.12)	(0.11)	(0.12)	(0.13)	(0.12)	(0.11)	(0.14)
Constant	3.25	3.60	1.63	1.80	2.98	1.77	2.52
	(0.19)	(0.19)	(0.22)	(0.21)	(0.20)	(0.20)	(0.26)
N	954	952	955	953	954	951	953
R²	0.46	0.36	0.22	0.33	0.04	0.26	0.04

(Variable labels in the Citizens Group column: Liberal policy, Anxiety, Angry, PID, Ideology, Female, Education, Black, Latino, Constant, N, R².)

Source: Immigration KN Study 2011.
Model specification: OLS. Coefficients in bold indicate p<.05, based on a two-tailed test. Dependent variables indicate how much respondents trust each actor from "not at all" (0) to "very much" 1. Anger and anxiety were measured directly after watching an immigration ad with two questions: How worried do you feel right now? How angry do you feel right now? Answers were given on a 9-point scale recoded to range from 0 (Do not feel this emotion at all) to 1 (Feel very strongly).

incidental anger can decrease trust in actors whom the rater does not personally know (Dunn and Schweitzer 2005). The policy message offered by the elite mattered as well. In four of the six models, actors paired with a threatening message were significantly less trusted than the same actors offering a policy solution by between .13 and .19 (p<.05). This suggests that citizens want a resolution to a policy problem rather than just threatening rhetoric.

In Table 4.3, we model the effect of respondents' anxiety on trust by the partisanship of the respondent and find broadly consistent results. The Republican Party, advantaged by the priority that it puts on immigration issues (Egan 2013), gains support from a public made anxious about immigration. Among Democratic respondents, anxiety over immigration does not increase trust in Democratic actors but does significantly enhance trust in the Republican Party by .62 (15 percent of the scale), Brewer by 1.04 (26 percent of the scale), and the Minutemen by .97 (24 percent of the scale). Anxiety does not simply move people toward the other party though; immigration anxiety has no effect on Democratic trust among Republican respondents. Rather, immigration anxiety triggers support for actors with more conservative immigration positions (Brader, Valentino, and Suhay 2008; Groenendyk, Brader, and Valentino 2011).[13] Overall, this study demonstrates that the uncertainty underlying immigration anxiety may be a boon for trust in Republican actors, even among citizens who may not normally support them.

CONCLUSION

Previous research has demonstrated that threat and its accompanying anxiety can increase institutional trust. Our research is consistent with this work: anxiety increased trust in a variety of governmental and non-governmental sources to provide information. By measuring trust in a variety of sources, this research also suggests that anxious individuals are not indiscriminately more trusting. For instance, in the health studies, anxiety increased trust in potentially relevant government actors

---

[13] Anger is a common emotion in the area of immigration; we show that it affects trust in a variety of actors. Although anxiety increases trust, immigration anger decreases trust in Obama by .49, the Democratic Party by .46, and the DHS by .59 among Republicans. To the extent that citizens are certain about who the cause of the immigration problem is and who to blame, their anger decreases trust in those actors (Lerner and Keltner 2000). For Republicans, those actors are the Democrats running the government at the time of the study.

TABLE 4.3: *Anxiety and anger's effect on trust by partisan identification (PID)*

	Obama		Democrats		Republicans		Brewer	
	Dem respondents	Rep respondents	Dem	Rep	Dem	Rep	Dem	Rep
Threat	0.08	0.03	−0.20	−0.19	−0.08	−0.13	−0.08	−0.24
	(0.09)	(0.09)	(0.09)	(0.09)	(0.10)	(0.09)	(0.10)	(0.09)
Anxiety	−0.38	−0.14	−0.02	0.05	0.62	0.36	1.04	0.97
	(0.21)	(0.21)	(0.19)	(0.22)	(0.21)	(0.33)	(0.23)	(0.30)
Anger	−0.27	−0.49	−0.10	−0.46	−0.08	0.11	0.13	0.02
	(0.21)	(0.21)	(0.17)	(0.21)	(0.19)	(0.30)	(0.23)	(0.26)
Ideology	−0.59	−1.17	−0.38	−1.28	0.53	0.52	0.58	0.51
	(0.23)	(0.20)	(0.22)	(0.23)	(0.25)	(0.26)	(0.22)	(0.22)
Female	0.03	−0.01	0.02	0.00	0.06	−0.04	0.15	−0.05
	(0.09)	(0.08)	(0.09)	(0.09)	(0.10)	(0.09)	(0.10)	(0.09)
Education	0.46	0.24	−0.39	−0.09	−0.19	0.18	−0.56	0.15
	(0.33)	(0.32)	(0.28)	(0.31)	(0.33)	(0.38)	(0.34)	(0.31)
Black	0.58	0.80	0.34	0.31	−0.03	−0.37	−0.09	−0.47
	(0.12)	(0.27)	(0.12)	(0.39)	(0.13)	(0.25)	(0.12)	(0.29)
Latino	0.21	0.29	0.12	−0.01	−0.28	−0.07	−0.60	−0.15
	(0.13)	(0.23)	(0.11)	(0.22)	(0.14)	(0.23)	(0.19)	(0.19)
Constant	2.89	2.60	3.30	3.08	1.81	2.15	2.10	2.34
	(0.30)	(0.28)	(0.27)	(0.29)	(0.32)	(0.36)	(0.30)	(0.31)
N	487	448	487	447	488	449	487	448
R^2	0.16	0.19	0.07	0.15	0.08	0.06	0.23	0.21

	DHS		Minutemen			Citizens group	
	Dem respondents	Rep respondents	Dem	Rep		Dem	Rep
Threat	-0.11	-0.11	-0.10	-0.20	Liberal policy	0.33	-1.04
	(0.09)	(0.10)	(0.10)	(0.09)		(0.11)	(0.10)
Anxiety	0.17	0.22	0.97	0.56	Anxiety	0.13	0.33
	(0.19)	(0.25)	(0.22)	(0.28)		(0.24)	(0.35)
Anger	-0.13	-0.59	0.17	0.48	Angry	0.10	-0.11
	(0.19)	(0.23)	(0.21)	(0.25)		(0.23)	(0.33)
Ideology	0.23	-0.93	0.25	0.16	Ideology	-0.26	0.13
	(0.22)	(0.21)	(0.22)	(0.22)		(0.26)	(0.30)
Female	0.15	0.02	0.19	0.00	Female	0.27	0.07
	(0.09)	(0.10)	(0.10)	(0.09)		(0.11)	(0.10)
Education	0.09	-0.12	-0.80	0.17	Education	-0.09	-0.07
	(0.30)	(0.36)	(0.30)	(0.35)		(0.42)	(0.38)
Black	0.13	-0.22	-0.02	0.17	Black	0.18	0.12
	(0.10)	(0.32)	(0.12)	(0.20)		(0.13)	(0.31)
Latino	-0.07	-0.25	-0.35	0.10	Latino	-0.19	0.08
	(0.16)	(0.18)	(0.13)	(0.18)		(0.18)	(0.22)
Constant	2.53	3.53	2.09	2.03	Constant	2.20	2.86
	(0.28)	(0.31)	(0.28)	(0.30)		(0.39)	(0.38)
N	487	449	486	447	N	486	448
R^2	0.30	0.09	0.20	0.14	R^2	0.07	0.26

Source: Immigration KN Study 2011.

Model specification: OLS. Coefficients in bold indicate $p<.05$, based on a two-tailed test. Dependent variables indicate how much respondents trust each actor from "not at all" (0) to "very much" 1. Anger and anxiety are indices that indicate how strongly the respondent felt after watching an immigration ad on a 9-point scale recoded to range from 0 (not at all) to 1 (very strongly).

(e.g., Centers for Disease Control and Prevention, HHS) and generally not in less relevant government agencies (e.g., the Chair of the Federal Reserve Board).

In the immigration studies, we find that anxiety-driven trust has a partisan dimension. Democrats and Republicans are both more likely to trust fellow partisans to handle immigration. However, anxiety causes both Democrats and Republicans to become more trusting of the Republican Party. Although anxiety causes Republicans to become less trusting of Democrats and President Obama, it does not affect trust in these actors among Democrats. We used an explicitly partisan issue in this study to contrast the comparatively apolitical threats of smallpox and H1N1 and found that Democratic elites have little to gain in terms of increasing trust by stoking fears about immigrants taking social services or affecting the economy.

5

The Politics of Anxiety

Anxiety's Role in Public Opinion

> *This is a time when we're faced, not with a nation that is – that is extraordinarily secure in a very, very calm world. We're facing a very dangerous world.*
>
> Mitt Romney, 2011, New Hampshire GOP Primary Debate

Politicians regularly sound alarm bells. To listen to contemporary political debates, immigrants are taking hard-working Americans' jobs, terrorists are getting past our defenses, and we are irreversibly destroying our environment for future generations. It is a very dangerous world. If we think back to two of the most memorable presidential advertisements, LBJ's 1964 Daisy ad and the 1988 Willie Horton ad, both have strong elements of fear. The Daisy ad confronts viewers with a nuclear war while the Willie Horton ad warns of a world where lax law enforcement allows dangerous criminals out on weekend passes. Both ads are designed to scare viewers and urge them to choose the safer option. Our purpose here is not to evaluate the veracity of any particular threats but to evaluate how people react to political alarms. In previous chapters, we explored the effects of anxiety on learning and trust and found that anxiety biases learning and the kinds of leaders that we trust in systematic ways. So far, we have not addressed the basic public opinion question – what sorts of policies do anxious people support? This final empirical chapter is devoted to the attitudinal consequences of anxiety.

We argue that anxiety can trigger support for protective measures. In each section, we draw specific hypotheses about how protection is manifest across the four policy areas: public health, immigration, terrorism, and climate change. Policies can be considered protective based on the quality of the policy, because political leaders frame them as such, or because few opposing policies effectively challenge them. These four cases provide examples of policy areas with clear best protective practices (public health) and where elite frames shape views of what constitutes protection (immigration, terrorism, climate change). These policies also vary in their connection to partisan politics. How to tackle disease outbreaks is less contentious on partisan grounds than is the best way to stem illegal immigration flows or prevent future terrorist attacks, where "best practices" tend to depend on the party advocating the policy. In three of the policy areas (immigration, terrorism, climate change), one party's ownership creates an advantage for its preferred protective policy.

PURSUING A SAFER WORLD

The idea that people use their political attitudes to cope with feelings of threat and anxiety has been explored from a variety of research traditions. Various theories suggest that the need to manage uncertainty, ambiguity, and anxiety leads individuals to embrace attitudes, leaders, and ideologies that create balance. For example, *protection motivation theory* (PMT) (Rogers 1975) argues that individuals desire protection, which "arises from the cognitive appraisal of a depicted event as noxious and likely to occur, along with the belief that a response can effectively prevent the occurrence of the aversive event" (99). PMT takes a broad view of the threats that might trigger protective instincts, but research typically involves responses to health threats, where protective behaviors are in compliance with the healthy recommendation. PMT draws attention to our need for protection, but it neglects the emotional components of decision making. We argue that it is precisely the feeling of anxiety, rather than the knowledge of threat alone, that leads individuals to want and seek out protection.

Several strands of research in psychology demonstrate that anxious individuals cope with a threatening world by supporting policies and leaders that promise protection. From the literature on emotion comes the insight that anxiety motivates a desire for protection (Jarymowicz and Bar-Tal 2006; Roseman and Evdokas 2004), and we expect that this manifests itself as support for policies and behaviors that are perceived as subduing threats. *Terror management theory* (TMT) posits that threat influences attitudes by invoking a fear of death. According to TMT, we seek to prevent the anxiety that accompanies thoughts of our own mortality by supporting aggressive policies and political leaders who promise protection (Bonanno and Jost 2006; Greenberg et al. 2003; Landau et al. 2004). Another strand of research in psychology focuses on conservative values and ideology. In their theory of the authoritarian personality, Adorno et al. (1950) argue that parental punitiveness creates fear and aggressiveness that encourages individuals to seek certainty and environmental control. This motivation leads people to embrace authority, suppress societal difference, and generally endorse attitudes in line with conservatism. Frenkel-Brunswik (1949) developed a theory of ambiguity intolerance that argued that individuals' discomfort with ambiguous situations created motivations to seek certainty, ultimately leading to an embrace of the familiar, rigidity in thinking, and closed-mindedness. Similarly, in Rokeach's model of dogmatism, individuals' belief systems serve to help individuals understand and stave off threat. When the need to avoid threat predominates, belief systems become more closed in order to allay anxiety (Rokeach 1960). Bringing together these and other theories of political conservatism, Jost et al. (2003, 351) argue that conservatism stems from a wide variety of motives including epistemic motives (dogmatism, ambiguity intolerance, uncertainty avoidance, cognitive complexity), existential motives (self-esteem, terror management, fear, threat, anger, and pessimism), and ideological motives (self-interest, group dominance, and system justification), all related to the psychological need to manage uncertainty and fear.

Although these models predict that citizens embrace conservatism as one way of regulating a variety of anxieties, we suggest that anxiety regulation may lead to a wider range of attitudes, depending on the political context. We expect that citizens will seek out and support policies deemed to be protective whether those policies are conservative, liberal, or nonpartisan. Whether anxious citizens support policies on the right or left depends on whether there are multiple policies offered by elites during times of threat (Zaller 1992) and which party owns the issue (Petrocik 1996). To the extent that elites offer conservative policy solutions with few liberal alternatives or the Republican Party owns the issue, anxious citizens are more likely to embrace conservative policies. To the extent that liberal elites are advantaged during times of threat because of a lack of political opposition or because the Democratic Party owns the issue, then managing anxiety may lead citizens toward liberal protective policies. Whether anxiety is caused by a faltering economy, a fear-mongering politician, or a terrorist attack that triggers our worries about death, the emotion is uncomfortable and triggers defense mechanisms. We seek to relieve anxiety by seeking protection.

On average, anxiety increases risk aversion (Fischhoff et al. 2003), but we argue that anxiety does not always lead to support for cooperative or passive types of protective policies. For example, we argue that terrorism anxiety after 9/11 increased support for hawkish foreign policy. As Lupia and Menning (2009) argue, risk-aversion does not have to imply that citizens prefer no government action in the face of threats because there are risks involved in government inaction as well. In their model, anxious citizens are more likely to support government action right after a fear-provoking stimulus occurs, at a time when anxiety tends to be the highest and elite divergence tends to be minimal (Brody 1991).

When facing life-or-death choices, people tend to be more risk-seeking than with problems involving money or property (Druckman and McDermott 2008), suggesting that when facing anxiety from existential threats, individuals may not prefer policies that are seen as passive. A fundamental feature of prospect theory (Kahneman and Tversky 1979) is that risk tolerance depends on the context of the decision. When facing gains, people are risk averse but when confronting losses, they are risk seeking. Humans are more sensitive to changes that may make situations worse than to stasis or changes that may improve conditions, and they may make different behavioral decisions in contexts that are punishing than in more rewarding ones. McDermott, Fowler, and Smirnov (2008) draw on evolutionary biology and optimal foraging theory to provide insight into why some seemingly riskier policies may be more attractive in highly threatening environments. Animals are most accepting of risk in food foraging when their chance of starvation is high because they may reap higher rewards and avoid starvation even against a higher risk. As McDermott et al. (2008) point out, this flexibility in the survival strategies that animals pursue has parallels in political behavior. The basic inclination to prefer restraint in good times and risk in bad times may explain why citizens are willing to take chances during crisis times (Weyland 1996). Particularly if policies are framed as increasing the individual's or nation's chance to survive and thrive, supporting protective policies that may bring some risk may actually lower public anxiety.

ANXIETY AND THE POLITICAL ENVIRONMENT

Anxiety stimulates the search for a safe environment (Roseman 1984). What policies will help bring about a safe environment is open for political debate, and we expect that public perceptions of what constitutes protective policies are a function of the dimensions of that political debate.

Whether the public accepts anxiety-inspiring messages and what policies they prefer to protect them depend on how competitive the partisan rhetorical environment is (Zaller 1992), whether the policy is "owned" by one of the parties (Petrocik 1996), and whether fear messages are overtly persuasive or not. In all but the most extraordinary times with high threat and an attentive public, the political environment shapes what policies are considered effective and whether the public recognizes and accepts threat. Who sounds alarm bells and offers solutions matters as much as what those policy solutions are. Similarly, when fear messages are overtly persuasive, the message source determines whether appeals are forceful in generating emotion or ineffective.

Partisan rhetoric, as well as the origin of the threatening message, creates different meanings that structure emotional and opinion reactions. As Frijda (1988) argues, "Emotions arise in response to the meaning structures of given situations; different emotions arise in response to different meaning structures" (349). Whether threatening messages are used by nonpartisan sources like the news or deployed directly by interest groups or elites affects which citizens accept the policy prescriptions in these messages or even accept whether they should be scared at all. When citizens encounter fear-inspiring news in a time of compressed political debate, when opposition voices are silent or hushed, they are likely to accept the emotion as well as the policies offered to eliminate that anxiety (Brody 1991; Mueller 1973; Zaller 1992). Even in the face of stronger policy opposition, political anxiety may increase support for protective policies when offered by elites and parties that own those issues (Budge and Farlie 1983; Petrocik 1996).

Persuasive communication, such as campaign ads, can potentially lead to backlashes, especially when the language is intense, forceful, or dogmatic (Dillard and Shen 2005); when the message evokes fear (Brehm and Brehm 1981); and when the message runs up against a motivation to remain consistent with prior attitudes (Kunda 1987). Persuasion may also break down when individuals consider the persuasive communication itself as manipulative. When an individual perceives that the communication threatens her freedom to act, this may lead to an unpleasant motivational state whereby the individual re-establishes control through engaging in the behavior proscribed by the persuasive message, in a process called *reactance* (J. W. Brehm 1966). That is, messages may lead to the exact opposite behavior as intended by the communication. Messages that use forceful and dogmatic language that explicitly pressures listeners to conform to recommendations (Quick and Stephenson 2008) or vivid and graphic imagery (Bushman 1998; Quick and Stephenson 2008) often trigger backlashes. Together, these features suggest that vivid messages may invoke a boomerang effect when they are perceived to threaten individuals' freedom to form their own attitudes. Those people with a stronger stake in the policy area and those with attitudes that normally differ from the policies offered in the persuasive communication should be harder to convince and more likely to not react.

TESTING ANXIETY'S EFFECT ON PROTECTIVE ATTITUDES

We set out to establish the relationship between anxiety and attitudes in multiple policy areas (see Table 5.1 for an overview). These different areas allow us to test the generalizability of our theory. These threats vary in whether they are inherently frightening because they evoke dread and death (e.g., public health scares) or whether they are framed as threatening by political actors. Our substantive areas also vary in terms of the appropriate protective measures. Vaccinations and other healthcare services offer protection in the context of a disease outbreak, whereas more restrictive policies toward immigrants might calm anxiety over

TABLE 5.1: *Overview of studies*

	Nature of Threat	Attitudes	Anxiety Manipulation
Public Health – Smallpox YG/P Study 2011	Unframed	Civil liberties restrictions	Newspaper article
Climate Change PMR Study 2012	Framed	Actions to combat climate change (e.g., talk about the issue, donate)	None; cross-sectional data
Terrorism YG/P Study 2006	Framed	Hawkish foreign policy	Television news
Immigration KN Study 2007	Framed	Denial of services to undocumented immigrants	Bottom-up manipulation (thoughts vs. worries)
Immigration MT Study 2011	Framed	Denial of services to undocumented immigrants	Campaign advertisement

immigration. We also vary the ways in which we manipulate anxiety across these studies. To the extent that we find similar effects across diverse measures and manipulations of anxiety, we are more confident in the link between anxiety and support for protective measures.

HYPOTHESES

Our main hypothesis is that anxiety increases support for public policies deemed effective at offering protection, even when those policies conflict with people's predispositions (partisan or otherwise). We rely on our public health study to demonstrate the connection between anxiety and protective policies in reaction to an unframed threat, and then we turn to framed issues.

Regulating anxiety does not simply lead citizens to the right or the left, but rather toward security; and what makes us secure is defined, in part, by the political context. When events create broad anxiety or when citizens create their own anxiety, citizens across the political spectrum will seek protective policies. When the political environment is constrained to promote a dominant policy, the preferred protective policies are likely to be from the party that "owns" the policy area. Thus, we hypothesize that anxiety can overwhelm the unusually strong impact of partisan identity on attitudes when that anxiety is high and broadly felt. Even on framed issues, when anxiety comes from the bottom up, emotion can undercut partisanship when one party dominates the policy message, either through ownership or through silence from the other party.

A PUBLIC HEALTH CRISIS

We begin with a public health crisis. Public health threats can strike fear into the population, and we expect that this anxiety will lead respondents to seek protection from the diseases that may cause harm to them or their family. In a time of high uncertainty and anxiety, we expect that this desire for protection will increase support for state powers that may lead to quarantine or other civil liberties restrictions. Not only do public health crises provide an objective set of "best practices" designed by health experts to protect the populace, but public health crises tend to scare people at a visceral level rather than one based on dimensions such as power and money, which are more clearly tied to partisan politics. Anxiety over health issues should then be more universal, as should support for protective policies.

We use the case of smallpox to test the effects of anxiety on support for a variety of best practices designed to control smallpox outbreaks and thus keep the population safe. In a 2011 op-ed in the *New York Times*, Secretary of Health and Human Services Kathleen Sebelius warned against destroying the last known samples of smallpox in existence, arguing that weaponized smallpox could bring great destruction to the world community, which has no immunity to the disease. She called for the development of new vaccines, suggesting that preparation and protection in the face of even an eradicated disease are necessary (Sebelius 2011). To combat a smallpox outbreak, both the World Health Organization (WHO) and the U.S. Centers for Disease Control and Prevention (CDC) recommend vaccination; isolation of patients diagnosed with the disease either at home or in a hospital; and decontamination of clothing, bedding, and other personal property through bleach or incineration (Centers for Disease Control and Prevention 2003; World Health Organization 2001). These policies are designed to offer widespread protection yet also entail a number of limitations (albeit temporary ones) on free movement, participation in public life, and the potential loss of property.

Previous survey data demonstrate that in times of health fears, support for these types of restrictive policies increases. In the run-up to the 2003 Iraq war, there was increasing concern that smallpox could be used as a bioweapon, and surveys asked a number of questions about the public's willingness to support particular health policy powers in those circumstances. In a survey of 1,000 respondents in Fall 2002, 73 percent of respondents favored a quarantine for smallpox patients, and 67 percent supported allowing governors to use the National Guard to prevent people from leaving areas with reported cases of smallpox (Meinhardt et al. 2006). In a study of opinions about potential quarantines and compulsory vaccination programs in the event of a smallpox outbreak, fears about personally contracting smallpox increased support for mandatory vaccinations (Taylor-Clark et al. 2005). We use Public Health – Smallpox YG/P Study 2011 in this section, in which subjects read a mock news article about an ancient language (control condition) or about a smallpox outbreak that occurred just last week (present outbreak condition) or twenty-five years ago (past outbreak condition) (see Chapter 2 for study details). We demonstrated in Chapter 2 that respondents in the "present outbreak" condition are significantly more anxious than respondents in the control condition or the "past outbreak" condition.

After reading the news article, we asked respondents how much they supported a number of "emergency powers that have been proposed by state officials to be used in the event of a smallpox outbreak" on a 5-point scale from "strongly oppose" to "strongly favor." The policies are: (1) Requiring hospitals to provide services to people with smallpox, (2) Requiring individuals to be vaccinated against smallpox, (3) Requiring a medical exam to diagnose smallpox, (4) Quarantining those suspected of smallpox, (5) Requiring those with smallpox to be isolated in a special health facility, and (6) Destroying property contaminated by smallpox. The policies vary in terms of the burden they place on people and whether they are directed at the general population or just those afflicted with the disease. These policies reflect those advocated by both the WHO and the Centers for Disease Control and Prevention in the event of a smallpox outbreak.

Consistent with our hypothesis, we found that respondents in the present-outbreak condition (i.e., the most anxiety-inducing) were the most supportive of protective policies. Providing respondents with information about smallpox (past outbreak) did not automatically increase their willingness to forgo civil liberties for others; rather, it was the combination of threatening information and the anxiety created by a current outbreak that increased support for civil liberties restrictions. Respondents in the "past outbreak" condition did not significantly differ from respondents in the control condition in their willingness to allow state power to restrict civil liberties.

Across four of the six civil liberties questions, the present treatment condition significantly increased respondents' willingness to forgo the rights of others in the name of protection.[1] The average level of support for the policies is quite high, and the treatment conditions increases support even further. Overall, respondents were most likely to support requiring hospitals to treat patients suspected of smallpox exposure, but support for that policy did not differ by treatment condition. However, respondents in the present-outbreak condition were significantly more likely to support requiring citizens to have medical exams, vaccines, to be in isolation, and even quarantined than were respondents in the control condition. Interestingly, anxiety had similar effects on those policies that were aimed at the general population and those that only affected those diagnosed with smallpox. Subjects in the treatment condition were more supportive of requiring vaccinations ($M_{control}$ = 2.97 vs. $M_{present-outbreak}$=

---

[1] Table A5.1 in the Appendix shows an ordinary least squares (OLS) model of the effect of the treatment conditions compared to the (excluded) control condition with full controls.

3.24, t = 1.88, p<.06)[2] and requiring medical exams to diagnose smallpox ($M_{control}$ = 2.87 vs. $M_{present-outbreak}$ = 3.15, t = 2.04 p<.05). Anxiety also significantly increased support for both isolation policies by .25 over the control condition ($M_{control}$ = 3.01 vs. $M_{present-outbreak}$ = 3.26, t = 1.84, p<.07) and even the most extreme policy of a forced quarantine by .38 ($M_{control}$ = 3.25 vs. $M_{present-outbreak}$ = 3.63, t = 2.89, p<.05). Only on the questions of isolation and quarantine does exposure to simply information about smallpox in the past-outbreak condition increase support for civil liberties restrictions over the control condition at the same magnitude as the anxiety condition, suggesting that, for most civil liberties, respondents are not willing to forgo others' rights unless presented with an anxiety-producing situation. In general, we find that anxiety prompts people to support a more expansive role for the government to protect them during a health crisis.

To provide further support for our claim that citizens are motivated to support protective policies as a way of coping with anxiety, we look at how the experimental treatments affect attitudes through shaping anxiety. Table A5.3 in the Appendix displays six mediation models that demonstrate that the effect of the present-smallpox condition on attitudes is a function of raising anxiety. Figure 5.1 shows even more clearly how anxiety about a smallpox outbreak made respondents significantly more likely to trade off privacy, free movement, and even property for safety. We measured anxiety in the study by how anxious respondents reported feeling after reading the news stories on a scale from "not at all" (0) to "very" (8). High-anxiety respondents were those in the experimental conditions who were above the mean level of anxiety (mean = 4.3), whereas low-anxiety respondents were those people in the experimental conditions rated below the means. Figure 5.1 shows the average level of support for the smallpox policies for both high-anxiety and low-anxiety respondents with confidence intervals around the mean. Across five of six policies, highly anxious respondents are significantly more supportive, both substantively and statistically. Anxiety heightens respondents' willingness to require others to be vaccinated by 16 percent, willingness to undergo a medical examination by 20 percent, to quarantine suspected smallpox patients by 12 percent, to isolate those with smallpox by

---

[2] These t- and p-values come from an OLS model comparing the effect of the present-outbreak condition and the past-outbreak condition to the control condition. Models are weighted by the post-stratification weights provided by YouGov Polimetrix.

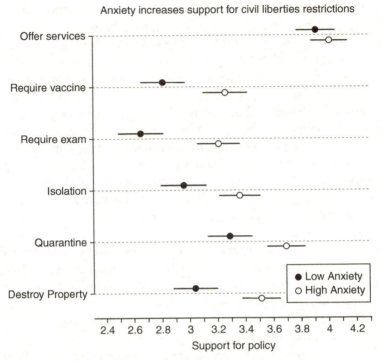

FIGURE 5.1: Smallpox anxiety increases civil liberties restrictions
Source: Public Health Smallpox YG/P 2011.

13 percent, and to destroy property contaminated by smallpox by
15 percent.[3] For four of these policies, increasing anxiety pushed respondents from ambivalence over the policy to support, suggesting that anxiety
may be a powerful force in creating public support for even relatively
costly emergency health measures.

Anxiety increases support for a variety of policies agreed upon by
health organizations. What happens when citizens confront anxiety
about policies where there are no clear "best practices" but rather
competing policies offered by partisan actors? We use the policy areas
of climate change, terrorism, and immigration to explore how the political environment and issue ownership condition anxiety's effect on
attitudes.

---

[3] Please see Table A5.4 in the Appendix for these calculations.

A WARMING PLANET: CLIMATE CHANGE STUDY

First, I worry about climate change. It's the only thing that I believe has the power to fundamentally end the march of civilization as we know it, and make a lot of the other efforts that we're making irrelevant and impossible

Bill Clinton

Climate change is a contentious issue in American politics, and climate change advocates face significant challenges in convincing both elites and the mass public to take action. Advocates of climate change policies must confront the challenges of a public that views the effects of climate change as physically and temporally remote (Nisbet and Myers 2007). Surveys of Americans show that climate change is important among environmental issues, but, as a whole, environmental issues rank much lower than issues such as national security and the economy (Busby 2008; Pew Research Center for the People and the Press 2010b).

The existing research on climate change attitudes focuses on cognition. For example, the public's level of concern over climate change is related to their knowledge about climate change (its causes and impacts), their trust in scientists, and their belief in a scientific consensus on the causes of climate change (Malka, Krosnick, and Langer 2009). Beyond factual knowledge and beliefs, partisanship is becoming increasingly tied to climate change attitudes in the United States. There is a deep and growing partisan divide in the United States when it comes to energy policy. As recently as 2008, partisans were indistinguishable in their support for funding research on alternative energy, but, in recent years, Republicans have distanced themselves from the policy (Pew Research Center for the People and the Press 2011).

On the elite level, the Democratic and Republican parties take significantly different stances both about the occurrence of climate change and how to combat it. The 2012 and 2008 party platforms echo these sentiments. In its 2012 platform, the Republican Party advocated an "all of the above approach" to energy with a call for more domestic production of natural gas and oil and less activist regulation from the Environmental Protection Agency (EPA). The platform did not explicitly mention climate change and called for a devolution of power to states to regulate the environment (Republican National Committee 2012). In contrast, the 2012 Democratic platform affirmed the science of climate change while calling for reducing emissions and increasing alternative energy use. Both parties frame their policies as protective of the environment and the American economy (Democratic National Committee 2012).

Public opinion tracks the elite divergence in views on climate change. In 2006, a Pew Center poll found that a majority of Democrats (81 percent), Republicans (58 percent), and Independents (71 percent) believe that there is solid evidence of global warming. However, only 24 percent of Republicans were willing to say there was solid evidence that this was due to human activity, compared to 54 percent of Democrats and 47 percent of Independents (Pew Research Center for the People and the Press 2006b). By March 2008, the partisan gap on whether climate change was already occurring had grown to more than 30 percentage points, up from an indistinguishable difference in 1998 (Dunlap 2008). An October 2010 Pew poll found a staggering partisan gap between Democrats and Republicans with 79 percent of Democrats and 38 percent of Republicans agreeing with the question, "Is there solid evidence the earth is warming?" Furthermore, 53 percent of Democrats and only 16 percent of Republicans ascribed global warming to human activity (Pew Research Center for the People and the Press 2010b).

Americans are divided over what measures are best suited to protect the environment. According to a 2011 Pew Research Center Survey, 71 percent of Americans believe that the country should do "whatever it takes" to protect the environment. Of course, whatever it takes is ambiguous: for example, the same poll finds that 63 percent of Americans think that the country's energy supply should be addressed by developing alternative sources, such as wind, solar, and hydrogen technology, whereas 29 percent prefer to expand exploration and production of oil, coal, and natural gas. For instance, 47 percent of Democrats and 69 percent of Republicans approve of using nuclear energy to produce electric power. When it comes to building more nuclear power plants in this country, the differences are just as stark, with 34 percent of Democrats in favor and 57 percent of Republicans in favor (CNN 2011). A 2011 Pew Survey found similar partisan differences in support of greater use of nuclear power (30 percent of Democrats vs. 54 percent of Republicans). This survey also showed differences in support for offshore oil and gas drilling (46 percent of Democrats vs. 77 percent of Republicans) and in support for more federal funding for alternative energy research (83 percent of Democrats vs. 53 percent of Republicans) (Pew Research Center for the People and the Press 2011).

The emotional side of the climate change debate has not received much attention, but we expect that anxiety over climate change will trigger support for protective measures. We expect that, in the realm of climate change and the environment, respondents seeking protection will prefer more government regulation of the environment and be supportive of policies to mitigate the negative effects of climate change, which may vary from individual behaviors like buying environmentally friendly products to lobbying for stricter emissions standards. In experimental work, Meijnders, Midden, and Wilke (2001) demonstrate that exposure to fear appeals about the consequences of greenhouse gases increases positive attitudes toward energy-saving lightbulbs and also increases actual purchasing behavior of energy-efficient lightbulbs. We also seek to establish that anxiety is significantly related to climate change attitudes, even after controlling for more established predictors such as knowledge and partisanship.

Even though the mass public is divided by party on the potential effects of climate change and the best policies to ameliorate its effects, it is more trusting of the Democratic Party on environmental issues. Since the 1980s, survey respondents have consistently said that the Democrats do a better job on environmental issues by between 17 and 25 percentage points (Egan 2013). Given this strong, consistent issue advantage for the Democratic Party, we expect that anxious citizens seeking protective policies will be more likely to support policies similar to Democratic positions than Republican positions.

To test our hypothesis, we use the Climate Change PMR Study 2012, a cross-sectional survey of climate change opinions. The survey was conducted online with 251 respondents recruited through Pacific Market Research (see Chapter 2, Table 2.3 for sample characteristics). After reading a story on climate change, we asked all respondents to rate their emotional reactions about climate change on a scale from 0 (did not feel this emotion at all) to 8 (felt the emotion very strongly). To tap anxiety, we asked respondents to rate how worried, anxious, and fearful they felt and combined these into an additive index (Cronbach's alpha = .91) recoded to vary between 0 and 1, with higher values indicating more anxiety. To measure anger, we asked respondents how angry, mad, and furious they felt (Cronbach's alpha = .94), and we also measured sadness by asking how sad, depressed, and grief-stricken respondents felt (alpha = .83). Overall, Democratic respondents were more emotional about climate change than were Republican respondents. The 115 Democrats had an average anxiety score of .57 on the 0–1 scale, compared to .42 for the 50 Republicans (t = 3.56, p<.01). Democrats were also sadder than Republicans ($M_{Democrats}$ = .41 vs. $M_{Republicans}$ = .32, t = 2.28, p<.05) but not significantly more angry ($M_{Democrats}$ = .34 vs. $M_{Republicans}$ = .27, t = 1.55, n.s.). Given these emotional differences by party, we control for respondents' partisanship in models of climate change attitudes.

We expect that anxiety will increase support for protective policies, particularly those advocated by the Democratic Party. To test this hypothesis, we utilize eight different policies that are advocated by experts and partisan actors as potential actions to combat climate change. These measures vary on whether they are more likely to be advocated by Republican leaders or Democratic leaders. For each measure, respondents answered how much they supported or opposed the measure on a 4-point scale rescaled to vary between 0 and 1, where high values indicate stronger support. The eight policies varied in their overall popularity with respondents, with Democratic policies more popular overall with this sample that skewed more heavily Democratic. Forty-five percent of respondents supported or strongly supported equalizing the playing field for energy production by supporting subsidies for alternative energies, a policy more aligned with the Democratic Party, whereas 46 percent supported building more nuclear power plants and 47 percent supporting expanding domestic off-shore drilling, both Republican policies. By contrast, support for two more Democratic Party-oriented policies was quite high. Seventy-three percent of respondents supported signing an international treaty that requires the United States to cut its emissions of carbon dioxide 90 percent by the year 2050, and 79 percent supported requiring electric utilities to produce more electricity from wind, solar, or other renewable energy sources. The remaining Democratic-favored policies were also very popular. Seventy-nine percent supported regulating carbon dioxide (the primary greenhouse gas) as a pollutant, 86 percent supported providing tax rebates for people who purchase energy-efficient vehicles or solar panels, and 90 percent supported funding more research into renewable energy sources, such as solar and wind power.

Because the Climate Change PMR Study 2012 is a cross-sectional survey, we include controls for established predictors of climate change attitudes: partisanship (measured on a 7-point scale with higher values indicating strong Republican, rescaled from 0 to 1), trust in scientists (ranging from "Not at all" to "Completely," on a 4-point scale rescaled between 0 and 1), and knowledge. We measure knowledge in two ways: a felt knowledge measure (a subjective assessment ranging from "Nothing" to "A lot," on a 4-point scale rescaled between 0 and 1) and an objective knowledge scale based on three factual questions about the Kyoto Protocol and contributors to the greenhouse effect (rescaled from 0 to 1 with scores indicating higher knowledge).[4] We use OLS

---

[4] See Appendix for full question wording and scaling information.

models to estimate the effects of anxiety, partisanship, trust in scientists, and knowledge on willingness to take action to combat climate change (see Table 5.2).

Table 5.2 demonstrates the effect of respondents' anxiety about climate change on their support for all climate change policies.[5] As expected, we find that anxiety increases support for policies designed to protect the nation from climate change and significantly increases support for policies advocated by the Democratic Party. Climate change anxiety significantly increased support for signing an international treaty, requiring utilities to use renewable sources, regulating carbon dioxide, providing tax rebates for fuel efficiency, and funding research on renewable resources by between 21 percent and 42 percent of the scale. These findings stand even when controlling for knowledge, trust in science, and partisanship.[6]

In all five models where anxiety significantly increases support for climate change protection, its effects are substantively similar for Democrats and Republicans. Republicans who are already anxious about climate change are significantly more supportive of Democratic policies such as renewables, international treaties, and funding research about renewables than are their Republican counterparts unconcerned about climate change. Republicans at the highest quartile of anxiety ($\geq$.70 on the 0–1 scale), are as supportive of renewables, regulations, rebates, and a treaty as are anxious Democrats.[7] These results suggest that, to the extent that interest groups, ads, or political leaders can increase anxiety about climate change, this emotion can break through the increasing partisan divisions on the issue. For Democratic elites in particular, appealing to Republicans on climate change may increase support for the policies advocated by the party, where it is advantaged.

---

[5] We have also controlled for respondents' anger and sadness in these models and find substantively identical results.

[6] One drawback of this study is that the data is cross-sectional. We controlled for several possible predictors of climate change attitudes, but it is possible that anxiety is correlated with other cognitive variables that we have failed to include and that it is these cognitive factors rather than anxiety that are driving support for more protective policies.

[7] To determine whether anxiety influences Republicans and Democrats differently, we ran the same models from Table 5.2 and included an interaction term of anxiety and partisanship. Across all eight models, the interaction was significant only for tax rebates, where Republicans are significantly more positive toward rebates as a function of anxiety than are Democrats. To calculate when the preference of anxious Democrats and anxious Republicans overlapped, we used the predxcon command in Stata.

TABLE 5.2: *Climate anxiety increases support for Democratic climate policies*

	Nuclear Power Plants	Eliminate Federal Subsidies	Expand Offshore Drilling	Sign International Treaty	Require Utilities/ Renewable	Regulate Carbon Dioxide	Provide Tax Rebates	Fund Research Renewables
Anxiety	-0.05	0.01	-0.03	**0.41**	**0.35**	**0.42**	**0.21**	**0.28**
	(0.14)	(0.14)	(0.14)	(0.11)	(0.10)	(0.11)	(0.10)	(0.09)
Anger	0.10	0.14	-0.03	-0.03	-0.06	-0.11	-0.11	-0.09
	(0.12)	(0.12)	(0.12)	(0.09)	(0.09)	(0.09)	(0.08)	(0.07)
Sadness	-0.12	-0.06	-0.05	0.09	0.10	-0.03	0.08	0.03
	(0.16)	(0.16)	(0.15)	(0.12)	(0.12)	(0.19)	(0.11)	(0.09)
Partisanship	**0.15**	0.11	**0.40**	**-0.19**	**-0.19**	**-0.15**	**-0.11**	**-0.07**
	(0.08)	(0.08)	(0.08)	(0.06)	(0.06)	(0.06)	(0.05)	(0.05)
Trust science	-0.06	-0.01	**0.31**	**-0.55**	**-0.42**	**-0.49**	**-0.33**	**-0.40**
	(0.11)	(0.12)	(0.11)	(0.09)	(0.08)	(0.09)	(0.08)	(0.07)
Felt knowledge	0.08	0.15	0.07	-0.07	-0.10	-0.08	0.00	-0.09
	(0.12)	(0.12)	(0.11)	(0.09)	(0.09)	(0.09)	(0.08)	(0.07)
Knowledge scale	**0.46**	-0.09	0.04	**-0.15**	-0.04	-0.03	0.00	-0.05
	(0.08)	(0.08)	(0.08)	(0.06)	(0.06)	(0.06)	(0.06)	(0.05)
Constant	0.13	0.37	0.18	0.88	0.84	0.88	0.89	1.01
	(0.12)	(0.12)	(0.11)	(0.09)	(0.09)	(0.09)	(0.08)	(0.07)
N	189	189	188	190	189	187	190	190
R^2	0.20	0.03	0.26	0.48	0.41	0.40	0.27	0.36

Source: Climate Change PMR Study 2012.
Model specification: OLS. Bold coefficients are significant at $p<.05$. All variables are scaled from 0 to 1, with higher values indicating higher knowledge, stronger emotion, and more Republican (0 = Strong Dem, 1 = Strong Rep).

A TERRORIST THREAT

We do not create terrorism by fighting the terrorists. We invite terrorism by ignoring them.

George W. Bush

Our next study in this chapter focuses on terrorism. The issue of terrorism has received significant attention in the existing literature on threat and anxiety (Huddy et al. 2005a), and it presents a useful test for our theory regarding protective attitudes. Utilizing the Terrorism YG/P Study 2006, this section shows that when news stories pair threatening information with fear cues, anxious respondents are significantly more likely to support protective foreign policy than are less anxious respondents, even when that policy is hawkish.

Threatening events such as a terrorist attack not only increase a collective sense of threat but also contract the political space and elite discussions of foreign policy options. Generally, in the domain of foreign policy, the views of the presidential administration are most prominent in news, and opposition voices are less likely to be heard (Entman 2004; Nacos 1990). Particularly after threatening events, one dominant foreign policy message tends to emerge as elite dissonance fades, leading, at least in the short term, to a political environment where one elite message leads news coverage and thus, public opinion. In the wake of the 9/11 terrorist attacks, George W. Bush's definition of the attacks as a commencement of a War on Terror dominated other potential news frames, and the president's hawkish foreign policy views became the prominent argument about how to effectively protect the country. Not only did the news media adopt the president's frame as the dominant one, but mainstream news coverage did not consistently feature opposition voices from the Democratic Party or from outside of the government, thus cementing the president's frame as the main one for the public to rely on in forming their own foreign policy attitudes (Bennett, Lawrence, and Livingston 2007; Boydstun and Glazier 2012; Entman 2003, 2004). We expect that the Republican Party's long-term issue ownership of national security and terrorism (Egan 2013; Goble and Holm 2009), paired with the dominance of the president's frame, advantaged hawkish policy over dovish or less interventionist policy because hawkish policy like the Iraq War and increased national security spending was framed as protecting the United States from future terrorism. Military action may not always have been viewed as a protective policy because it brings significant risks. Lupia and Menning (2009) contend that a government *not* acting also constitutes a risk and that citizens may be anxious not only about personal danger of anti-terrorism policies but also about what the consequences of a failure to act may be. To that end, pursuing an active foreign policy may be framed as the more protective option for anxious citizens. For citizens seeking solace and protection after 9/11, both the balance of elite discussion and media coverage offered hawkish policies almost to the exclusion of other policies. To the extent that citizens anxious about future terrorism seek protection, we expect that, during the Bush administration, they were more likely to support hawkish policies than were citizens unconcerned about terrorism.[8]

We also expect that, under the conditions of anxiety when one party's message dominates, anxiety may overcome the powerful effects of partisanship on attitudes. Threat and fear increase the potential for persuasion by increasing individuals' interest and information. Anxiety tends to lead people to pay closer attention to their environment and seek relevant information (Brader 2006; MacKuen et al. 2010), and more engaged citizens are likely to encounter political information that may help them to form attitudes (Zaller 1992). As anxious citizens sought terrorism information, their attention was likely drawn to the plethora of threatening information about the potential for future attacks (Nacos, Bloch-Elkon, and Shapiro 2011). Anxious Democrats, faced with the threat of future terrorism and one dominant set of counterterrorism policies, should be more likely to support hawkish policies than are Democrats less anxious and less in need of emotional regulation.

If military action is framed as providing a safer environment, then we expect that anxious people will be supportive of hawkish policies. To test our hypothesis, we used the Terrorism YG/P Study 2006, an experiment that manipulated emotion with a television news story. The study recruited a nationally representative online sample of 809 respondents

---

[8] There are scholars who argue that it is anger, not anxiety that increases the propensity to support hawkish policies. According to Lambert et al. (2010), the boost in support that a president benefits from following an attack ("rally 'round the flag") is driven by anger, rather than anxiety, and that effect is confined to the president as a military leader – his popularity in other domains, such as economic policy is not improved. In fact, their findings suggest that anger and anxiety can have opposing effects; anxiety decreases support for a pro-war candidate whereas anger increases support. Huddy et al. (2005a) find that, in the aftermath of the attacks of September 11, anxiety was negatively related to support for military action and approval of President Bush, whereas perceived threat had opposite effects. Both articles point to the importance of distinguishing among negative emotions. Also, both suggest that anxiety causes people to support more protective policies. Where we diverge from these authors is that we expect that hawkish policy can be perceived as protective when it is framed as such and not strongly countered by opposition voices.

recruited through YouGov/Polimetrix (see Chapter 2, Table 2.3 for sample characteristics). We utilized a news story as the means of evoking emotion because most Americans receive information about terrorism from the news media.

Respondents were randomly assigned to watch one of two real television stories about foreign policy: (1) a neutral control story or (2) an evocative terrorism story. The control story described India's economy and provided neither verbal information on threat nor a visual emotional cue to threat. Subjects in the treatment condition watched a story entitled "Wave of Terror" that outlined recent terrorist attacks and suggested that a terrorist attack was imminent. The experimental story suggested that the pattern of terrorist attacks in the past year, including the increase in smaller scale attacks like those in London and Madrid, might indicate a new wave of terrorism. In the story, terrorism experts warned the public to expect further attacks. In the terrorism treatment, the news story was edited to enhance the threatening nature of the visual imagery by adding video such as the burning World Trade Center and bloodied victims of the 2005 London transit bombings to further enhance the emotional experience.

We expect that respondents who watched a threatening story about terrorism paired with emotional imagery will support hawkish foreign policy. The news stories did increase respondents' emotions. After watching the news story, each subject received a set of questions designed to tap into particular negative emotions; respondents rated how anxious (worried, fearful, anxious), sad (sad, depressed, grief-stricken), and angry (angry, mad, and furious) they felt. Respondents rated their emotional reactions on a 9-point scale from "did not feel the emotion" at the low end to "felt the emotion very strongly" at the high end of the scale, which we rescaled to vary between 0 and 1. Figure 5.2 shows that exposure to evocative terrorism imagery and information increased respondents' anxiety. The anxiety measure combines the "worried," "fearful," and "anxious" scales. The terrorism news stories increased respondents' level of anxiety significantly by .11 (se = .03), or 37 percent over the control condition ($M_{anxiety}$ = .29 in control).

To establish that terrorism anxiety increases support for protective and hawkish policies like those advocated by the Bush administration, we measure respondents' foreign policy attitudes by experimental condition using a set of six dependent variables. The *militarism* measure asked respondents whether they thought that the best way to ensure peace was through military strength or diplomacy. The dichotomous measure is scored from 0 to 1, with 1 representing the "military" position.

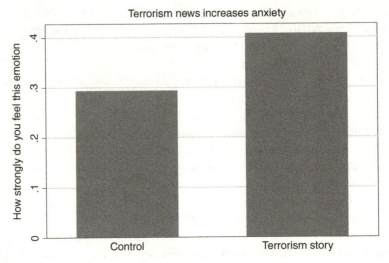

FIGURE 5.2: Terrorism news increases respondent anxiety
Source: Terrorism YG/P Study 2006.

Respondents also answered three questions about whether federal spending on the defense budget, homeland security, and border security to
prevent illegal immigration should be increased, decreased, or kept the
same. Each question was scaled from −1 (spend less) to 1 (spend more).
The *civil liberties* question measured how much respondents agreed with
the premise that it's necessary to give up civil liberties to curb terrorism on
a 5-point scale from "strongly disagree" at 0 to "strongly agree" at 1. The
Iraq measure asked respondents to evaluate retrospectively whether they
believed that the war in Iraq was worth the cost and is scored on a 5-point
scale from "strongly disagree" to "strongly agree," which we rescaled to
vary between 0 and 1.

We expect that terrorism stories significantly affect attitudes because
they evoke anxiety. Looking at respondents within the terrorism condition,
those respondents at high levels of anxiety are more supportive of all the
protective policies by large margins than even those people who watched
the terrorism news but felt less anxious. Highly anxious individuals (i.e.,
higher than the mean anxiety of .35) prefer military action over diplomacy
in foreign affairs ($M_{lowanx} = .41$, $M_{highanx} = .71$, $t = 4.85$, $p<.01$),[9] support

_____

[9] The t- and p-values come from an OLS model that predicts foreign policy attitudes based
on whether a respondent is above or below the mean in anxiety for respondents in the
terrorism news condition, weighted with post-stratification weights.

higher defense spending by *eight times* ($M_{lowanx} = .04$, $M_{highanx} = .39$, $t = 3.98$, $p<.01$), support higher homeland security spending by *three times* ($M_{lowanx} = .14$, $M_{highanx} = .59$, $t = 5.35$, $p<.01$), are more accepting of sacrificing civil liberties for security ($M_{lowanx} = .31$, $M_{highanx} = .44$, $t = 2.37$, $p<.01$), and even are more positive toward the Iraq war by 56 percent ($M_{lowanx} = .24$, $M_{highanx} = .38$, $t = 3.45$, $p<.01$). High anxiety did not translate into more support for border security spending, perhaps because border security to prevent immigration is not as clearly tied to terrorism as homeland security or defense. The effect of emotion is to substantively increase support for a range of more militaristic policies that respondents do not prefer in the absence of anxiety. We contend that anxiety motivates people to seek protection from the source of their anxiety, and here, terrorism anxiety led citizens to embrace a set of policies framed as protective by the Bush administration. Anxiety wasn't completely absent from respondents in the control condition, but their anxiety should not have been related to terrorism and thus terrorism policy. To demonstrate that the effect of anxiety is directed toward policies effective at mitigating the threats causing the anxiety in the first place, in Figure 5.3, we show the predicted values of the foreign policy measures at different levels of anxiety for both conditions. The gray line represents respondents in the terrorism news condition, and the black line represents those in the control condition. As the level of anxiety increases in the terrorism condition, so does support for foreign policy that relies on the military, increased spending on homeland security and defense, sacrificing civil liberties for safety, and even more positive retrospections about Iraq. For those in the control condition, rising levels of anxiety don't translate into higher support for protective policies, suggesting that respondents want policies that can effectively keep them safe from the harms that caused their anxiety. We also formally test whether anxiety mediates the effect of the terrorism condition in Table A5.5 in the Appendix, using the causal mediation approach we used previously.

During times of threat, we expect that anxiety can override the strong effects of partisanship in creating support for protective policies that citizens may not support in calmer times. Figure 5.4 displays the average level of support for the counterterrorism policies among Democrats in the terrorism condition, the partisan group least likely to support conservative policies associated with a Republican president. Although the absolute levels of support for hawkish policy are low among Democrats even after watching evocative terrorism news, Figure 5.5 shows that evoking anxiety can increase support for a range of policies framed as protective to the United States. For example, when asked to pick whether the United

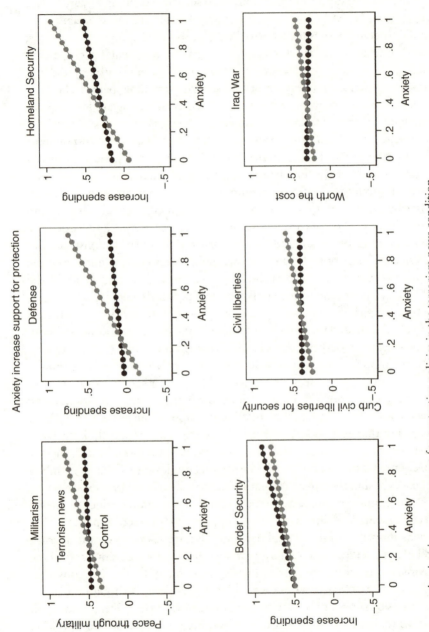

FIGURE 5.3: Anxiety increases support for protective policies in the terrorism news condition
Source: Terrorism YG/P Study 2006.

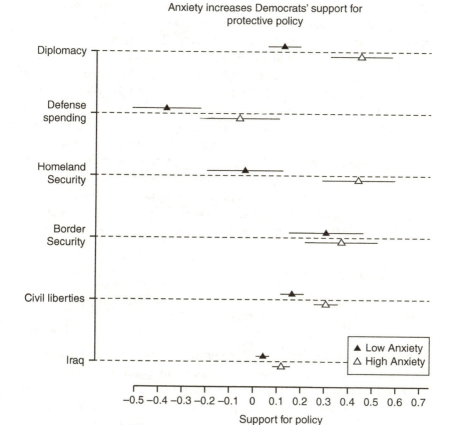

FIGURE 5.4: Terrorism anxiety increases Democrats' support for hawkish foreign policy
Source: Terrorism YG/P Study 2006.

States should pursue foreign policy through diplomatic means or through military strength, 12 percent of low-anxiety Democrats in the terrorism condition chose military strength, compared to 45 percent of high-anxiety Democrats, a threefold increase (t = 3.35, p<.01).[10] Although anxious Democrats do not reach the same level of support for military action as anxious Republicans (92 percent) or Independents (60 percent), the emotional experience pushed Democrats toward a foreign policy that

---

[10] The t-values and p-values come from an OLS model that predicts foreign policy attitudes based on whether a respondent is above or below the mean in anxiety for respondents in the terrorism news condition, weighted with post-stratification weights provided by YouGov/Polimetrix.

only 10 percent of them espoused prior to watching the terrorism news.[11] Looking across the other measures, feeling anxious increased Democrats' support for defense spending by .30, actually switching Democrats from wanting less defense spending to wanting to keep the budget the same (t = 2.25, p<.05), support for homeland security spending by .48 (t = 3.41, p<.01), support for the Iraq war by .08 (or double the support of less anxious Democrats [t = 2.51, p<.05]), and sacrificing civil liberties by .14 (again doubling the support of less anxious Democrats). Again, anxiety did not significantly influence attitudes about border security spending. Overall, though, we find that anxiety created by terrorism news increased support for a variety of assertive counterterrorism policies even among those respondents least predisposed to support them. Citizens seeking safety and a relief for their terrorism anxiety found policies effectively framed as protective by the presidential administration.

ANTI-IMMIGRATION APPEALS

We have terrorists coming into the country both through our northern and southern borders. I guarantee you that it's happening.

Tom Tancredo

Politicians use threatening appeals to promote more restrictive immigration policies and to curb immigrant access to government programs. Images of people dashing across the border, waiting menacingly at area stores, and crime are frequently deployed in immigration ads and discussions of the dangers of illegal immigration. We argue that these appeals are effective, at least in part, because they generate anxiety. The connection between immigration threats and anti-immigrant attitudes is well established. We expect that, for most Americans, anxiety about immigration increases support for restrictive immigration policies and for denying undocumented immigrants state services. In contemporary political rhetoric, elites and interest groups that advocate immigration restrictions, both in terms of the flow of immigration and access to services, tend to frame these arguments in terms of protecting America. These policies

---

[11] It is not the case that anxious Republicans have significantly different foreign policy attitudes than low-anxiety Republicans. We believe that this is, in part, because Republican respondents were already motivated to support the foreign policy from the Bush administration because they share partisanship and ideological predispositions and that anxiety had no room to move these attitudes further. For instance, 88 percent of low-anxiety Republicans in the terrorism condition preferred military action over diplomacy in world affairs, providing a ceiling on how much anxiety could affect these opinions.

are portrayed as protective of American jobs and way of life by interest groups and the political parties, most strongly by the Republican Party. In the 2012 Republican platform, the party called for the completion of a border fence with Mexico, employment verification, and linked illegal immigration to terrorism, drug trafficking, and gangs (The Republican Party 2012).

We also use immigration to demonstrate some constraints on the effectiveness of threatening appeals. Because the parties take different positions on immigration, we expect that partisanship shapes what immigration messages individuals accept.[12] When threatening appeals appear manipulative to recipients, those individuals with strong prior attitudes or values that are inconsistent with the message presented in the message may react by rejecting the emotional appeal itself or rejecting the policy implications of the message. In the case of immigration, we expect that partisanship conditions the acceptance of immigration messages. Republicans are more likely than Democrats to be persuaded by immigration ads that call for more restrictive immigration policy.

Worries that immigrants have detrimental effects on the economy and are costly to the state decrease support for immigration and immigrant access to the government (Brader, Valentino, and Suhay 2008; Citrin et al. 1997). Anxiety over national economic conditions is related to opposition to illegal immigration and support for policies such as delaying immigrants' access to government programs, including Medicaid and Food Stamps (Citrin et al. 1997). In their study of attitudes about Proposition 187, Lee and Ottati (2002) find that support for the anti-immigration bill was related to economic worries, among other concerns. In two experiments, Brader et al. (2008) show immigration cues that reference low-skilled Latinos induced anxiety about immigration, which led to support for decreased immigration levels, English-only policies, and an interest in anti-immigration information. The increase in immigration opposition was not due to changes in beliefs about immigration or different perceptions of threat, but rather, to anxiety provoked by out-group cues.

The evidence for partisan differences in immigration attitudes is mixed. Over time, the political coalitions formed around immigration reform have crossed partisan and ideological boundaries (Tichenor 2002), meaning that elite cues may not be an easy heuristic for forming attitudes.

---

[12] We also argue that racial differences affect people's reactions to threatening immigration appeals (Albertson and Gadarian 2012). Other research on racial differences in immigration attitudes includes Ha (2010) and Brader et al. (2010).

Citrin et al. (1997) find that partisanship is unrelated to preference for limiting immigration in the United States based on 1992 and 1994 American National Election Studies data. Neiman, Johnson, and Bowler (2006) find weak evidence of partisan differences in immigration attitudes in California. They conclude that partisan differences are often due to correlated factors, such as race, and that there are many Democrats and Independents whose views overlap with Republicans. Others have found stronger evidence of a partisan divide in immigration attitudes. Tolbert and Hero (1996) found that the percentage of Republicans in a county related to the level of support for California's Proposition 187. More recently, a survey about the 2010 Arizona legislation found that Republicans are more supportive of requiring people to produce documents verifying legal status than are Democrats, although majorities of both parties approve of this measure (Pew Research Center for the People and the Press 2010a). Given increasing partisan polarization (Levendusky 2009), we anticipate that partisanship shapes not only support for immigration policy framed as protective but also respondents' willingness to accept persuasive communication on immigration.

To demonstrate the effects of immigration worries on attitudes, we use Immigration KN Study 2007 and Immigration KN Study 2011. We start our discussion with Immigration KN Study 2007. This study uses a bottom-up anxiety manipulation, where respondents list what makes them worried about immigration. To evoke anxiety about immigration, respondents in the treatment condition read the prompt, *Now, we'd like you to take a moment to think about the debate over immigration in the United States. When you think about immigration what makes you worried? Please list everything that comes to mind.* In the control condition, respondents were asked to simply list everything that came to mind when they thought about immigration with the prompt *First, we'd like you to take a moment to think about the debate over immigration in the United States. When you think about immigration, what do you think of?* Importantly, because subjects generate their own anxiety in this study, we anticipate that anxiety will move respondents broadly toward protective policies and will not evoke significant reactance. We conceive of this bottom-up manipulation as a proxy for the ways individuals become anxious as a result of less mediated means like events, social experiences, and/or political talk.

Respondents had unlimited time to complete the thought listing and were provided a text box to type as much as they wished. After completing the thought-listing exercise and engaging in the information-seeking component of the study (see Chapter 3), respondents answered a series of questions about whether illegal immigrants should be eligible for the following government services: (1) Elementary education, (2) In-state tuition at state universities, (3) Emergency room care, (4) Food Stamps, and (5) Medicaid. Respondents answered on a 5-point scale that ranged from 1 (definitely not eligible) to 5 (definitely eligible). Respondents also answered a question about whether federal spending for border security should be increased (1), decreased (0), or kept at the same level (.5). To test our hypothesis that anxiety generates more restrictive attitudes toward services for undocumented immigrants, we reverse-coded the eligibility questions and scaled them from 0 to 1, so that higher values mean that immigrants should *not* be eligible for government programs. Based on factor analysis,[13] we combined the services into two indices: (1) A "humanitarian" index (emergency room [ER] access, elementary school access) and (2) An "entitlement" index (Food Stamps, drivers licenses, and in-state tuition). On average, the sample was much more supportive of providing basic humanitarian services to undocumented immigrants (M_{human} = .52) than allowing immigrants access to entitlements such as Food Stamps or Medicaid (M_{entit} = .81). Respondents were also strongly supportive of increasing border security spending; 68 percent of all respondents wanted to increase spending compared to only 8 percent who wished to decrease spending.

Our expectation is that immigration anxiety will increase support for restrictions on the access illegal immigrants have to state services and will increase support for increased border spending.[14] As we established in Chapter 3, the bottom-up manipulation successfully increased anxiety among treatment respondents, and treatment affects information seeking through making respondents anxious. In this section, we trace how the level of anxiety is related to immigration policy attitudes. Figure 5.5

[13] The principal component factor analysis revealed a two-factor structure after varimax rotation. All variables had a factor loading of greater than .50, and each scale was highly consistent. We determined the internal consistency for each of the scales using Cronbach's alpha (Humanitarianism α = .74, Entitlement α = .74).

[14] To measure immigration anxiety, we had two research assistants unaware of our hypotheses code the open-ended answers for the intensity of anger, anxiety, and excitement on a scale from 0 (no emotion), 1 (some), to 2 (extreme). Coders showed a great deal of agreement for both anxiety (70 percent agreement, Cohen's kappa = .53, z = 15.01, p<.01) and anger (78 percent agreement, kappa = .52, z =13.05, p<.01), so we averaged across the codes to create one anger score and one anxiety score for each respondent. The treatment conditions significantly increased respondents' anxiety by .55 (se = .07, p<.01) or by more than doubling the level of anxiety.

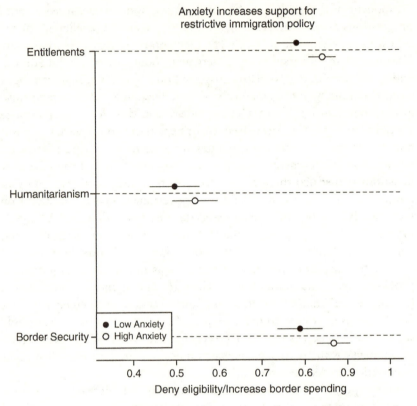

FIGURE 5.5: Immigration anxiety increases support for immigration protection
Source: Immigration KN Study 2007.

displays mean immigration attitudes divided by whether respondents are high in immigration anxiety (greater than the overall mean of .74) or low (lower than the mean).[15] The figure demonstrates that immigration anxiety does significantly shape immigration attitudes by increasing support for entitlement restrictions by .06 or 6 percent of the scale (se = .03, p<.05) and increasing support for border security spending by .16 or 16 percent of the scale (se = .06, p<.05). Yet, anxiety does not affect attitudes about services that help those in medical need or children, perhaps because these are less closely tied to protection.

[15] More formally, Table A5.6 in the Appendix shows how the treatment condition affects immigration attitudes through increasing respondents' level of anxiety (and not through affecting anger).

As expected, immigration anxiety increased support for policies framed as protective of the United States. One of the advantages of Immigration KN Study 2007's design, though, is that not only do we know the level of respondents' anxiety, but we also know the substance of that anxiety. If respondents worried about the toll that illegal immigration takes on the American economy, public safety, and the cultural make-up of the country (i.e., conservative immigration worries), what policies they prefer to "protect" the country should be different than if concerns about immigrant exploitation or deportation (i.e., liberal immigration worries) raised their anxiety. We had two research assistants unaware of our hypotheses code the number of liberal worries and conservative worries listed by each respondent. Worries about what immigration does to the country ("the strain on the taxpayer in terms of welfare programs," "violence, drugs, job loss") were coded as conservative worries, whereas worries about the treatment of immigrants themselves ("Lou Dobbs and his mistreatment of immigrants," "the rising sentiment against immigrants") were coded as liberal worries. If respondents mentioned different types of worries, then these different types of worries may translate into preferences for different types of policies.

Conservative worries were far more prominent in the thought-listing exercise; 28 percent of the sample listed a conservative worry, and 34 percent of the sample listed more than one conservative worry. Only 38 percent of the sample failed to mention any conservative worries, which is striking given that half of the sample was in the control condition. On the other hand, just 11 percent of the sample listed one liberal worry, and only 4 percent of the sample listed more than one liberal worry. These kinds of worries are not as widespread in the public. Not surprisingly, liberal and conservative worries are related to partisanship. The sample consists of 186 Democrats and 192 Republicans and Independents. Figure 5.6 shows the average number of worries listed for Democrats (including Democratic-leaning Independents) and Independents together with Republicans (including Republican-leaning Independents) in the treatment condition. On average, Democrats mentioned .31 liberal worries, whereas Republicans mentioned an average of just .08 liberal worries (t = 3.38, p<.01). On the other hand, Democrats mentioned an average of .96 conservative worries, and Republicans mentioned an average of 1.71 conservative worries (n = 355, t = 4.44, p<.01).

The substance of worries about immigration differs by partisanship. Furthermore, there are clear differences when subjects are asked to worry about immigration. The treatment condition does not significantly

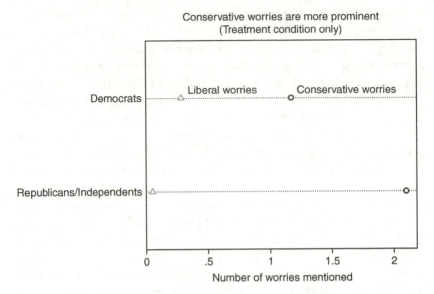

Number of worries mentioned

FIGURE 5.6: Conservative immigration worries are prominent in the treatment condition
Source: Immigration KN Study 2007.

increase the number of liberal immigration worries over the control condition, neither among Democrats ($M_{control}$ = .32 vs. $M_{treatment}$ = .28, t = .40, p = .69) nor among Republicans ($M_{control}$ = .11 vs. $M_{treatment}$ = .09, t = .33, p = .74). Asking a respondent to worry about immigration did not trigger liberal worries. On the other hand, both groups of partisans expressed more conservative worries when they were in the treatment condition (Democrats: $M_{control}$ = .68 vs. $M_{treatment}$ = 1.31, t = 3.41, p<.01; Republicans: $M_{control}$ = 1.22 vs. $M_{treatment}$ = 2.12, t = 4.01, p<.01).

Democrats clearly are able to summon anxieties about the detrimental effects of immigration on their own, but what effect do those anxieties have on their attitudes? Table 5.3 shows respondents' mean immigration policy attitudes separated by level of conservative worry and respondent partisanship. There are two major take-aways from this table: (1) Democrats who become anxious on their own about immigration's detrimental effects on the United States prefer more restrictions than do less anxious Democrats, and (2) anxious Democrats have similar immigration attitudes to anxious Republicans and Independents. Similarly to the terrorism case, anxiety moves Democrats toward policies advocated by the Republican Party to protect the country. Immigration anxiety can be

TABLE 5.3: *Conservative immigration anxiety increases protective attitudes among Democrats*

	Entitlement		Humanitarianism		Border Security	
	Dem	Rep/Ind	Dem	Rep/Ind	Dem	Rep/Ind
Low conservative Anxiety	0.70	0.83	0.40	0.57	0.43	0.67
	(0.04)	(0.04)	(0.05)	(0.05)	(0.09)	(0.09)
High conservative anxiety	0.82	0.89	0.55	0.59	0.71	0.77
	(0.03)	(0.01)	(0.04)	(0.03)	(0.06)	(0.04)
% increase	18.26	7.55	37.73	3.43	67.12	13.71
t	2.81	1.32	2.58	0.60	2.74	0.91
P	0.01	0.19	0.01	0.55	0.01	0.37

Source: Immigration KN Study 2007.
Means immigration attitudes. Dependent variable ranges from 0 to 1, with higher values indicating more support for restrictive policies and higher border security spending.

a boon for Republican leaders to increase support for their preferred immigration policies, but, in the next section, we show that there are limitations to immigration fear appeals.

A CAVEAT IN OUR MODEL: ARE THERE LIMITS ON THE EFFECTIVENESS OF THREATENING APPEALS?

I used to be a conservative and I watch these debates and I'm wondering, I don't think I've changed, but it's a little troubling sometimes when people are appealing to people's fears and emotion rather than trying to get them to look over the horizon for a broader perspective . . .

Jeb Bush

Using Immigration MT Study 2011, we show that when persuasive communications like ads try to raise conservative worries about immigration, Democrats are less easily persuaded to react by updating their attitudes than when they raise their own anxiety. In the study, we created a thirty-second ad that detailed arguments against illegal immigration (see Chapter 4 for study details). We chose to create an ad that outlined the costs of illegal immigration because this is a prominent part of political rhetoric about immigration (Simon and Alexander 1993), and immigration attitudes are significantly shaped by concerns over the costs of immigration (Alvarez and Butterfield 2000). The ad focuses on immigration from Mexico because Latinos are the focus of the vast majority of anti-immigrant appeals in the United States. Although Lapinski, Peltola, Shaw, and Yang (1997) note that Americans express negativity toward immigrants of most nationalities, work by Brader, Valentino, and Suhay (2008) and McAdams, Sochi, and Weisberg (2008) show that a focus on Latinos and undocumented status in political communication increases opposition to immigration. In a study of Iowa caucus-goers, Knoll, Redlawsk, and Sanborn (2011) show that immigration frames that explicitly mention immigrants' ethnicities can induce more conservative policy preferences among Republican voters concerned about immigration. Hopkins (2012) demonstrates that even mere exposure to Spanish-language ballots can decrease support for bilingual education among Republican respondents and in heavily Republican districts.

In this study, the advertisement highlighted the public's main areas of concern about illegal immigration – jobs, security, and social benefits. The only difference between the treatment condition and the control condition was the evocative imagery and threatening music. Across the control and treatment condition, the script was the same, while the images and presence of threatening music varied.[16] Because only the images and music varied across conditions, differences in opinions can be attributable to these emotional cues rather than to information.

As a reminder, the 174 subjects in this study were recruited through Amazon's Mechanical Turk to take a study on political advertising. Once respondents agreed to take the survey, they were directed to a website that randomly assigned them to watch either the control condition (threatening verbal information, neutral imagery, no music) or the treatment condition (threatening verbal information, imagery, and music) and then answer a series of questions on their level of trust in various political actors to handle immigration and attitudes about illegal immigrants' access to state services. As we established in Chapter 4, the threatening music successfully increased respondents' anxiety.

We expect that evoking anxiety over the costs of immigration will increase support for more restrictive immigration policies. Political elites and thinkers often tout restrictions on immigration as ways of protecting the United States from economic costs and cultural changes (Borjas 1999; Huntington 2004). The political ad that respondents watched both highlighted the costs of immigration and advocated restrictive immigration policies in order to protect the nation and therefore alleviate the anxiety caused by immigration.

---

[16] See the Appendix for the full script of the ad, which is based on one of the commercials run by California governor Pete Wilson in his 1994 campaign.

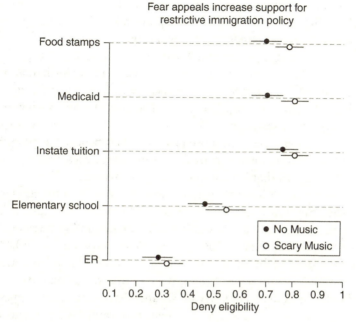

FIGURE 5.7: Threatening immigration ad increases support for restrictive immigration policies
Source: Immigration MT Study 2011.

Respondents answered a series of questions about whether illegal immigrants should have access to ER care, elementary school for children, Medicaid, Food Stamps, and in-state tuition on a 5-point scale from definitely not eligible to definitely eligible. We rescaled each variable to vary between 0 and 1, with higher values corresponding to more restrictive attitudes. We expect that increased anxiety will increase support for restrictive policies. Forty-two percent of respondents answered that illegal immigrants should definitely be eligible for ER care, and 24 percent said that the children of illegal immigrants should definitely be eligible for elementary school. In contrast, less than 10 percent of respondents thought that illegal immigrants should be eligible for Medicaid (7 percent), Food Stamps (8 percent), or in-state tuition (8 percent). Figure 5.7 shows respondents' mean attitudes for these five measures by experimental condition and 90 percent confidence intervals.[17] The white open circles

[17] We use 90 percent confidence intervals here because of the small number of respondents per condition.

represent the treatment condition, and the black circles represent the control condition. Consistent with Immigration KN Study 2007, immigration anxiety decreases support for access to Food Stamps ($M_{control}$ = .69, M_{treat} = .79, t = 2.09, p<.05) and Medicaid ($M_{control}$ = .70, M_{treat} = .82, t = 2.38, p<.05) but does not significantly affect support for humanitarian services (ER: $M_{control}$ = .28, M_{treat} = .31, t = .70, p<.49 and elementary education: $M_{control}$ = .46, M_{treat} = .55, t = 1.62, p<.11). Although immigration anxiety increases support for more restrictive policies, individuals seem to differentiate between those programs that benefit the offspring of undocumented immigrants or provide care in emergencies, in contrast with sustained programs that benefit immigrants themselves.

As with Immigration Study KN 2007, we use a factor analysis to divide the immigration policies into an "entitlement" index (Food Stamps, Medicaid, and in-state tuition at colleges and universities) and a humanitarianism index (ER access, elementary education).[18] We model the effect of being in the treatment condition on this attitude index using OLS (with no controls). We find that watching the immigration ad with the addition of scary music and visuals increases support for denying immigrants access to entitlement programs by 8 percent of the scale (although this misses significance at the conventional levels: b = .08, se = .05, p<.08), whereas exposure to the emotional ad does not significantly influence attitudes about humanitarian policies (b = .06, se = .05, p<.27). Support for state programs is partially a function of general beliefs about what the state should provide, so we also run a model controlling for respondents' ideology. When controlling for the effect of ideology on attitudes, the treatment condition significantly increases support for restricting immigrant access to entitlement programs by .10 (se = .04, p<.05) but did not significantly influence humanitarian policy preferences (b = .10, se = .08, p<.11). The ad that all respondents watched called for restricting illegal immigrants' access to the economy and state resources, but the addition of evocative imagery and music served to further decrease support for those services, suggesting that emotion can powerfully affect attitudes above the informational component of campaign ads.

---

[18] The principal component factor analysis revealed a two-factor structure after varimax rotation. All variables had a factor loading of greater than .50, and each scale was highly consistent. We determined the internal consistency for each of the scales using Cronbach's alpha (Humanitarianism α = .75, Entitlement α = .89).

Differences by Party

Unlike in the cases of terrorism or in Immigration KN Study 2007, immigration anxiety increases support for protective policies most forcefully among Republicans and Independents in this study (see Table A5.7 in the Appendix). Exposure to an evocative anti-immigration ad increased support for restrictions in access to entitlement programs by .11 (or 14 percent over the control condition) among Republicans and Independents over simply watching the same ad with no music or scary imagery (se = .05, p<.05). Support for these programs was already low among Republicans in the control condition. In the control condition, 86 percent of Republicans thought undocumented immigrants should not have access to in-state tuition, and 82 percent thought Medicaid and Food Stamps access should be restricted. In contrast, the treatment did not significantly influence Republicans' and Independents' attitudes toward humanitarian programs. Among Democrats in the sample, the anti-immigration ad did move respondents toward more protection (i.e., decreasing support for state services), but the effects did not reach statistical significance on any of the measures. The effect of the threatening ad was significantly larger on Republicans and Independents, compared to Democrats ($\chi^2 = 6.92$, p<.05).

Why does immigration anxiety fail to convince Democrats to support more protective/restrictive policy? We infer that the nature of the anxiety manipulation rather than the type of the anxiety itself matters in who will accept and be affected by fear-inspiring messages. Issue ads, like the one used in this study, are likely to be seen as more overtly persuasive than newspaper or television coverage of the immigration issue. When facing persuasive messages that are more in line with typical Republican messages (e.g., protect the border), Democrats may be more wary of accepting threatening information that would lead them to update their attitudes. When Democrats created or tapped into their own anxieties about immigration, they preferred immigration policies similar to their Republican counterparts. When faced with a persuasive message intended to manipulate their anxiety, though, Democrats were less likely to support restrictionist immigration policies not normally in line with their predispositions, a pattern we attribute to reactance (Brehm and Brehm 1981).

CONCLUSION

Political attitudes are one way that we express what is important to us. Opinions can help define who we are and what we prioritize. In times of threat, we can use our attitudes to help us feel safer. A strong leader might make us feel more secure in a highly uncertain world, a high (possibly electrified) fence could keep us safe from dangerous immigrant "others," and vaccinations might protect us from a public health threat. We show that the emotional experience of anxiety has broad implications for political attitudes. Whether the anxiety is generated by an outside threat such as smallpox or by a threat that is arguably created by government action, such as immigration, we find that anxious people are more supportive of protective policies. People anxious about climate change supported a wide variety of policies to reduce carbon emissions and protect the environment. In our immigration research, we found that anxiety generated by campaign ads can trigger attitude change for many respondents. Our findings were not confined to politically generated anxiety. In the smallpox study, we manipulated anxiety through varying newspaper content, and in the terrorism study we relied on television news reports. Strategic politicians might trigger political alarms, but there is plenty to be alarmed about when simply watching the news.

The effect of anxiety on political attitudes is complicated by the politics of who can scare us effectively. Partisanship conditions who feels anxious and what policies people support to cope with anxiety. For instance, Democrats are more likely to experience anxiety over climate change whereas Republicans are more likely to experience anxiety over immigration. Despite these associations, our studies show that anxiety can overwhelm partisanship, particularly when the anxiety is a function of events or mass media coverage. Anxious citizens are motivated to support protective policies regardless of partisanship, and the party that owns a policy area is advantaged on what policies are deemed effective. This might be a reason why threatening appeals are so commonplace in political discourse. They may not be successful at making all people feel anxious, but if they are, these appeals are particularly successful at persuading them to support a range of policies meant to protect them from harm.

We do not rule out the possibility that the public can be persuaded to be anxious about the wrong things nor that protective policies that strip others of rights are either the most effective or costless to the republic. For political thinkers (Edelman 1985) concerned that elites can simply use emotional rhetoric to manipulate citizens into adopting their preferred policy, this chapter should provide some relief. Anxiety increases the desire for protection, but when elites overtly appeal to fear, citizens can use their partisan identities to buffer against the anxiety and potentially reject the policy solutions offered. When events, elites, or issues can bypass the strong effects of partisanship and group identity to induce the public's fears, an anxious public is one that will support protective policies to bring themselves affective balance and to bring safety to the nation.

6

Anxiety and Democratic Citizenship

Neither a man nor a crowd nor a nation can be trusted to act humanely or to think sanely under the influence of a great fear.

Bertrand Russell

Contemporary American political life abounds with crises and worry. Terrorist attacks, a warming planet, and flu pandemics all trigger the public's anxieties. Meanwhile, politicians use fears of economic downturns and cultural changes to evoke the public's worries about immigration. Given that politics often involves anxiety, in this book, we ask how and when is anxiety successful at causing citizens to engage with politics? In addition, we ask what is the substance of that political engagement?

Political thinkers and democratic theorists express concern that anxiety may undercut citizens' abilities to make rational political choices, yet recent research from political science and psychology paints a more hopeful picture of anxiety, suggesting that political fears may lead to more knowledgeable and trusting citizens. Our theoretical contribution reconciles the normatively attractive portrait of anxiety in recent political science literature with the uses of fear in contemporary politics. We use four policy areas to test how anxiety shapes citizens' engagement with political information and political trust. Together, these components paint a fuller picture of the ways that anxiety shapes political life than accounts that either simply vilify or praise the role of emotion in politics. Anxiety does not preclude man or nation from acting or thinking sanely, but "under the influence of great fear" the public is likely to support protective policies that may undercut democracy.

Throughout the course of the book, we find that political anxiety systematically shapes citizen engagement by encouraging attention to politics and increasing acceptance of leaders and policies framed as able to protect the public. Political anxiety leads citizens to learn more about politics, but anxious citizens are systematically drawn to threatening news. Political anxiety increases trust in political actors, but trust is confined to those actors seen as useful for handling the source of the anxiety. Political anxiety makes people more likely to take protective policy positions, and the dominant protective policies are shaped both by partisanship of individuals and the partisan politics around the issues. An anxious politics both helps citizens to reach a democratic ideal of an informed, interested polity *and* leaves the public open to manipulation. In this chapter, we consider what this book contributes to the study of political psychology and emotion in public life. We also reflect on when anxiety strengthens democracy and when it may undermine democracy.

Not all politics is emotive. Citizens need to be paying a modicum of attention for an issue to be relevant and cause them to feel emotional. Political issues that are far below the attention radar are unlikely to make someone feel something. Yet, looking at the bulk of modern political behavior scholarship on how individuals form opinions, make voting decisions, process information, or evaluate political leaders in American politics, one may get the idea that citizens do these things sedately, with little emotional force. Elections spark enthusiastic cheers for favored candidates, government gridlock engenders angry phone calls, and hurricanes create anxiety for those in the path of possible destruction. Prominent theories of political behavior emphasize citizens' knowledge (Delli Carpini and Keeter 1996), self-interest (Erikson and Stoker 2011), resources (Verba, Schlozman, and Brady 1995), partisanship (Campbell et al. 1960), and feelings about social groups (Sniderman, Brody, and Tetlock 1993) with little emphasis placed on how emotion colors each of those elements or, ultimately, behaviors like voting.

Emotion is certainly not absent from discussions of political life. Political philosophers recognize that emotions, including anxiety, are a prominent, albeit not always constructive, political phenomenon. Both liberal and conservative thinkers recognize the power of anxiety to prompt citizens to stop, pay attention, and act (Robin 2006). In Hobbes's state of nature, people fear for their security and willingly cede autonomy to a sovereign willing to protect them (as in Hobbes's *Leviathan*; Hobbes 2008). Machiavelli's prince recognized that fear is persuasive and can create a compliant polity (Machiavelli 1997). John Locke pointed to fear as "an uneasiness of the mind" and pointed to this uneasiness as the most potent incentive to action (Locke 1950). Conservative writer Edmund Burke argued that a lack of emotion, particularly fear, leads to passivity, whereas fear can rouse an otherwise inactive public (Burke 2013). Writers like Alexis de Tocqueville in *Democracy in America* (1945) recognized that emotions had utility for political leaders and could lead to a strengthened democracy or an enfeebled society with citizens too terrorized to participate. This book squares well with de Tocqueville's view of emotion; anxiety can either bolster or damage democracy depending on how it is deployed by political leaders.

For us, taking emotion seriously means looking more broadly at the consequences of emotion in politics. We see emotion as central to understanding political life. At the same time, we argue that politics shapes the ways that anxious citizens cope. Our first main substantive contribution with this work is that we consider the effects of anxiety on civic life broadly. Citizens might vote once a year, but every day they make millions of other decisions that are relevant to politics. If they start their day with a morning paper or a glance at an online news source, which storylines catch their eyes? Do they choose to read stories or just skim headlines? Do they accept what they read, or do they argue against it? In deciding whether to vaccinate their newborns, whose medical advice do they trust? – a decision that affects not only their family but public health broadly. When terrorism seems likely, do they acquiesce to government surveillance to stay safe or rail against it for the sake of privacy? These decisions might all take place before a first cup of coffee.

Our second major substantive contribution in this work is that we situate anxiety in a messy, emotionally evocative, decidedly partisan context. Anxious people seek out information, and an emotionally charged media environment provides fertile ground for their bias toward threatening information. Anxious citizens put their trust in relevant, expert political elites and government agencies, and partisanship shapes who counts as a relevant expert. Finally, anxiety prompts people to support protective policies, and political parties fight over whose policies protect us best.

By putting the study of anxiety squarely within a partisan context, this book departs from other political psychology work on emotion. Affective intelligence theory (Marcus, Neuman, and MacKuen 2000; Brader 2005) sees anxiety supplanting or at least significantly attenuating the effect of partisanship on how citizens form opinions and decide who to vote for at election time. In this view, anxiety is a call to evaluate the political environment, stop relying on standing decisions, and make choices based on the contemporary political environment. We find that there are conditions under which anxiety influences partisans in similar ways, but these conditions are a subset of political life. That is, when threats are new and not communicated in an overtly persuasive way, anxiety affects Republicans and Democrats in broadly similar ways. Yet, anxiety more commonly exists in a partisan world. Most of the time, we are in the realm of framed threats rather than unframed threats, and partisan actors are involved in conveying threatening messages. When politicians communicate threat through ads, speeches, or other overtly persuasive ways, anxiety can bump up against partisanship. People from the "other political party" might resist the message and not experience anxiety. Even if they do feel anxious, they might not react in the manner prescribed by the communication. Partisanship and other identities can act as a filter on threatening information, lessening or heightening the emotional impact. As party polarization continues, these findings imply that anxiety's effect may be not be universal or may be short-lived. By considering how political anxiety exists as part of partisan conflict, we contribute to a broad understanding of how emotions significantly affect political behavior during times of both ordinary (i.e., partisan) politics and more extraordinary times.

We argue that anxious people seek protection. From this very general motivation, we trace out the impact of anxiety on three specific and politically relevant aspects of civic life: (1) citizens ought to pay attention to the news, (2) they need to figure out who to trust, and (3) they should hold attitudes on the important issues of the day. We find that anxiety affects all three.

LEARNING

Anxious minds want to know – what threats await them, who to trust and who to avoid, and how to resolve the threats. Citizens made anxious by observing events in the world or convinced to be anxious by elites seek out information to resolve the uncertainty that underlies anxiety. As one example, Nielsen ratings estimated that 79.5 million Americans watched television news coverage on the night of September 11, 2001, as they struggled to understand who attacked the United States and how they should react. In the week following the attacks, the television news audience doubled in comparison to the prior week

(Althaus 2002). In the face of public health crises like anthrax attacks or flu pandemics, Americans also want to learn more, and they search the Internet for symptoms and cures for illness and anxiety (Bar-Ilan and Echerman 2005; Ginsberg et al. 2008). This behavior is regular enough that public health officials can predict outbreaks from these searches and potentially deploy vaccines and other medical equipment (Ginsberg et al. 2008).

Although anxiety increases information-seeking and interest in politics, it also biases the type of information that individuals gather and how they process that information. After asking individuals to generate their own anxiety about immigration, we observed the type of news that they sought out and how they engaged with this news. Anxious individuals sought more relevant information than did those less concerned about immigration by choosing more stories about immigration. Yet, anxious individuals did not simply choose immigration stories at random. They were systematically drawn toward stories that portray immigration as threatening the safety and security of the United States through increasing crime and immigrants taking undeserved social benefits. Not only are anxious citizens drawn toward these types of stories, but they are also more likely to remember and agree with these stories compared with those people who are less anxious about immigration. We theorize that anxious citizens deem this threatening information as more informative or useful for decision making because negative information is more helpful in avoiding future harm.

Partisanship affects what anxious people learn. When asked to list their anxieties, Republicans and Democrats expressed similar levels of anxiety in both the treatment and control conditions. Anxious partisans were also equally likely to read threatening immigration stories. However, partisanship affects what information people ultimately take away from anxiety-driven learning. Anxious people all seek out threatening information, but only anxious Republicans were more likely to recall that information and agree with it. This might suggest that the effects of anxiety are short-lived – perhaps anxiety overrode other considerations at first, but the effect didn't last. It's also possible that recall and agreement are more complex than choosing materials to read. Either way, this presents a departure from Affective Intelligence (Marcus et al. 2000), where anxiety causes people to cast aside standing decisions like partisanship and rely on more contemporary information. Our work suggests that acceptance of contemporary information depends on a standing decision like partisanship.

TRUST

Without trust, governments are difficult to manage – policy making is more contentious (Bianco 1994), tax receipts harder to collect (Scholz and Lubell 1998), and even public health mandates are harder to enforce (Leavitt 2003), so anxiety may benefit the functioning of government. Trust may increase the speed and functioning of government, but it is not without potential downsides itself. Our results also point to some potentially troubling implications. Anxious citizens became more trusting of a variety of experts, but in the case that "experts" offer misleading or false information, trust may be a problem itself. Many parents anxious about autism trusted an expert, Dr. Andrew Wakefield, when he published a study linking a common childhood vaccine to autism, a study later debunked and potentially responsible for outbreaks of preventative diseases like measles (Robin 2006).

Our research shows that anxiety-driven trust differs by policy area. In the wake of anxiety, citizens not only want to know more about politics, but they also increase their trust in elites deemed expert in avoiding or thwarting threats. In policy areas with best practices and a clear demarcation of knowledge and expertise, such as public health, determining who to trust is more straightforward for citizens than in policy areas like immigration, where "experts" differ on their definition of what is threatening, as well as on their policy solutions. In both public health studies, when anxious, citizens were significantly more trusting of doctors and federal health agencies compared to when they were less concerned about pandemics such as the flu and smallpox. Across the two health studies, there was no instance in which health anxiety *decreased* trust in an actor, even in actors not directly related to health outcomes like the IRS and the Federal Reserve. These findings suggest that public health officials may be able to harness anxiety in communicating about pandemics but that messages about treatments or vaccines need to originate from the right sources.

In policy areas that could be blamed on government action or inaction, anxiety lowers trust in some actors while increasing trust in others. In policy areas like immigration that are more contested on partisan grounds, anxiety pushes citizens toward elites from parties that "own" the policy area, even when these anxious citizens may disagree with that party's policies. Anxiety also pushes people away from political elites of the non-owning party. The Republican Party consistently ranks as the party best able to "handle" immigration (Egan 2013), and we saw a boon in trust in our studies among those who watched threatening immigration ads. Across the immigration studies, anxious subjects, both Democrats and Republicans, put more trust in Republican actors than did citizens less anxious about immigration. Democratic actors, including President Obama, suffer a decline in trust when people are anxious about immigration. Anxious citizens want protection and may view the owning party as more able to implement their solutions, even if the policies offered are not their ideal policies. However, we also find that anxious citizens do not simply want elites who offer empty, threatening rhetoric, but rather they trust in actors who have expertise and, in the case of immigration, offer conservative policy solutions.

If an anxious public places its trust in leaders who betray the polity for the sake of their policies or re-election, then this may further erode trust when the crisis abates. In a *New York Times* column, philosopher Peter Ludlow argued that political elites use fear to manipulate the public:

Fear is a primal human state. From childhood on, we fear the monsters of our imaginations, lurking in dark closets, under beds, in deserted alleyways, but we also now fear monsters in the deserts of Yemen and the mountains of Pakistan. But perhaps it is possible to pause and subdue our fears by carefully observing reality – just as we might advise for trying to calm and comfort a fear-stricken child. We might find that, in reality, the more immediate danger to our democratic society comes from those who lurk in the halls of power in Washington and other national capitols and manipulate our fears to their own ends.

Even if elites do not purposely use fear to manipulate the public, when an anxious public advantages one party over another, that party has an incentive to focus elections and policy debates on those issues. If anxious citizens are willing to trust a party that they normally disagree with in times of crisis, this may facilitate policy making, but it also potentially shuts down debate and democratic deliberation. Owning parties may be effective in policy making, and anxious citizens may want to allow them more leeway in making policy (Egan 2013). However, this suggests that anxious citizens may not receive close representation of their views. This representative gap becomes normatively troubling if citizens simply turn toward leaders who will protect the public at any costs to democracy. Similarly, if elected leaders create crises in order to maintain power, cynically portray their policies, and provide false information about policies' consequences, or if no opposition voices create alternative policies for the public to adopt, the state of democracy is impoverished.

POLITICAL ATTITUDES

Political anxiety leads to an increasingly informed and trusting public but a public focused on threatening information and trusting of political "experts" in the pursuit of safety and security. In an attempt to remedy anxiety, citizens also support policies framed as effective protection against the threats that inspire their anxiety, even when these policies conflict with their political predispositions, such as partisanship. Across varied policies, citizens in a state of anxiety want to feel better, and they support policies that they believe will keep them safe from disease, war, and a changing climate.

Anxious citizens do not indiscriminately support the most conservative policies and politicians. Rather, the dynamics of the political environment shape which policies are most effectively framed as protective, even if a variety of policies may actually mitigate threats. When the political environment surrounding a particular issue is dominated by one party, citizens are likely to embrace that party's policies, sometimes despite their own partisan attachments. Sometimes the dominant policy is one that is agreed upon as the most effective. When made anxious about a smallpox outbreak, respondents were significantly more likely to support a set of practices designed by health agencies like the World Health Organization to thwart an epidemic against a disease for which few people have any protection. Sometimes policies are dominant because opposition voices are quiet or silenced by the potential (electoral and otherwise) consequences of advocating different policies. Citizens worried about terrorism supported hawkish counterterrorism policies like the ones advocated by President George W. Bush, policies not countered, at least initially, by strong voices in the press or the Democratic Party (Bennett, Lawrence, and Livingston 2007; Boydstun and Glazier 2012).

When the policy space is more contested, anxious people tend to be more supportive of policies offered by the party that "owns" the policy. Both Republicans and Democrats anxious about climate change were more supportive of Democratic-backed climate change policies, such as increasing fuel efficiency standards. In immigration policy, anxiety leads to a public less supportive of immigration flows and immigrant rights, both among Democrats and Republicans. Across both Climate Change Study PMR 2012 and Immigration KN Study 2007, respondents actively created their own anxiety, either outside the study (Climate Change Study PMR 2012) or through a bottom-up manipulation (Immigration KN Study 2007), meaning that some partisans feel anxiety on issues for which their own party does not "own" the issue. These findings suggest that owning parties not only have an incentive to focus election campaigns on the issues where they are favored (Simon 2002), but also may actively benefit from a public worried about the owning party's prominent issues.

Although some issues are evocative or threatening enough to create anxiety across the political spectrum, how anxious messages are communicated matters for whether citizens will accept these messages and adjust their policy attitudes. Democrats who generated their own anxiety about immigration in Immigration KN Study 2007 have immigration policy attitudes that are more similar to anxious Republicans than to their own partisan brethren not worried about immigration. However, when anxious messages come through persuasive communications like ads, Democratic constituents were more likely to reject the emotion and the policy recommendations linked to ads. Immigration MT Study 2011 and Immigration KN Study 2011 both used issue ads that portrayed immigration as harming the country economically and socially, complete with evocative images and scary music, ads reminiscent of those run by politicians like former California governor Pete Wilson. When faced with these persuasive messages, Democrats were unmoved in their support for restrictionist immigration policy. Threatening appeals do not automatically resonate with all citizens when they are clearly meant to persuade and can potentially lead to backlashes (Wright and Brehm 1982). Politicians looking to benefit from an anxious public face constraints when attempting to persuade those across the aisle to support their policies. Political persuasion can be a tricky game. Our research suggests that persuasion using anxiety is best done through less overtly persuasive means.

LOOKING OUTWARD: WHERE ELSE DOES ANXIETY PLAY OUT?

Anxiety influences how citizens think, behave, and act on the issues of immigration, public health, climate change, and terrorism – four very different types of policy areas. We expect that these dynamics play out across a variety of policy areas, not just the four that we explore in this book. Public health issues like infectious diseases easily frighten the public with little work on the behalf of elites because of their potentially deadly consequences. On unframed issues, partisanship is less likely to influence who becomes anxious and (at least at first) what types of policies anxious citizens support. Televised images of crime and riots stoke the public's anxieties about physical safety and increase support for more punitive crime policy (Iyengar 1991; Gilliam, Valentino, and Beckmann 2002), similar dynamics that we observe with terrorism attitudes. As citizens increasingly face anxiety-producing natural disasters like hurricanes, tornados, or floods, we expect that they will increasingly seek information and be biased toward useful but potentially threatening information. Our findings also suggest that in areas like crisis communication, some information sources are viewed as more trustworthy, and their policy recommendations will be more heeded. On unframed issues, those who can most effectively communicate about the nature of threats and policies to mitigate threats are likely to be nonpartisan experts.

Issues like immigration and climate change require more work by elites to point out dangers, and partisanship may either enhance or mitigate the effects of anxiety based on the political context. Anxiety can overcome the powerful effects of partisanship in framed policy areas under the conditions where anxiety is high and there are clear policy recommendations with little partisan opposition. These conditions are relatively rare though, and anxiety exists in a partisan world most of the time, where partisans are involved in conveying threatening messages and policy recommendations. In policy areas that are more clearly politicized – that is, where the parties differ on their evaluations of the threat as well as on potential solutions – the effect of anxiety may be more limited in scope or would need to be at extremely high levels to move the broad public. Policy areas like economic crises, gun control, and abortion create anxiety more on one side of the political aisle than the other, or at least create different types of anxieties for different groups, and are likely to function like immigration anxiety and climate change. For instance, although an anxiety ad about immigrants being exploited might resonate with Latino respondents, messages about immigrants exploiting the U.S. state and economy may generate more anxiety in whites. We expect that for an issue like abortion, messages about restrictions on abortion access will create more anxiety in some citizens, whereas messages about abortion's effect on women are more likely to cause anxiety in others. These different types of anxieties will lead to different sets of policies that can lessen these feelings. For some policy areas, like abortion, we think that the anxieties are relatively entrenched, and it would be difficult to make a pro-life respondent anxious about abortion access restrictions. However, for many policy areas, especially where knowledge is low, policy positions are not firm, or fundamental identities are not evoked, individuals can be made to feel anxious about a wide variety of issues. When outside events, social networks, or new information can break through partisan filters and create anxiety in those people who would not normally feel anxious, political leaders have the opportunity to persuade. Even if political leaders may not always successfully persuade members of the other party to become anxious or support their policies, political entrepreneurs can stoke anxieties in their own followers.

Our focus is on how political anxiety functions within a stable democratic state, but our theory has implications for understanding how anxiety influences politics in less stable regimes and how political elites utilize anxiety to win support. In explaining the origins of ethnic conflict, Lake and Rothchild (1996) argue that when states are weak, conflict is likely when political leaders build on fears of a group's future and place in society. When states cannot arbitrate between groups and provide credible protection, groups become more fearful about survival and violence becomes more likely. Even in strong states with strong legal systems and norms, political leaders can use anxieties about minority groups (e.g., immigrants) or potentially bad future events (e.g., terrorism) to increase support for policies that harm citizens by denying them rights and liberties (Brooks and Manza 2013). Particularly when opposition voices are quiescent or silent, leaders in power may stoke anxieties to increase support for electoral purposes or for their favored policies. In states with fragile rule of law, citizens may not simply support policies that they deem protective but may also more actively defend against perceived threats when they do not trust the state to protect them. When politics elicits anxiety, its effects may be significantly more dramatic in weaker states, but, on the whole, we expect that as citizens try to regulate their anxiety across a variety of policies and places, they will support leaders and policies that they believe will keep them safe.

HOW WE STUDY EMOTION

The bulk of our research relies on experiments, and the appropriateness of experiments for studying causal mechanisms is well established. However, the ability of an experiment to isolate the effect of emotion has received less attention, and we argue that our work makes a methodological contribution on this front. Some experimental manipulations are straightforward. If this were a study of attack advertising, we could randomly assign study participants to view an attack ad and measure the effects. We might struggle with establishing a control condition (should we show a positive ad, a neutral ad, or perhaps no political advertisement?), and we might waver over how to present the advertise-ment (we might embed it in a television program, so that the goals of our study are less obvious and the viewing experience is more natural). We would have a number of judgment calls to make, but claiming that we manipulated our independent variable – exposure to an attack ad – would be relatively straightforward. Manipulating an emotion like anxiety is much less obvious. There are no magic "political anxiety pill" and placebo that can be randomly assigned to participants.

There are three main steps we take in our experimental approach, and we advocate these for any experimental studies of subjective experiences. First, we manipulate anxiety in multiple ways. Our bottom-up manipula-tion is perhaps the method that gets us closest to the magic pill metaphor. We ask subjects in the treatment condition to list their worries about a particular subject (immigration or a public health threat) and then com-pare those subjects to others who simply listed their thoughts about the same subject. The advantage of this approach is that everyone is asked to take a version of the pill – perhaps different things are anxiety-inducing to different people, but because the worries are self-generated, we expect that the treatment group is generally anxious. This approach is not perfect – surely some in the treatment group were unable or unwilling to generate worries. Also, some in the control group might experience anxiety in the course of listing their thoughts.

We might also wonder if self-generated anxiety is anything like the anxiety that comes about because of news or political campaigns. This concern inspires our other two methods of manipulation. We rely on (1) news manipulations (print and television) and (2) campaign advertise-ments because anxiety in response to these stimuli is relevant to our concern: what happens when events trigger anxiety? A frightening news report or a threatening campaign advertisement are common triggers of political anxiety. These are more complex manipulations, which make them more relevant to real-world experiences but also more complicated analytically. An anti-immigration advertisement might trigger anxiety, anger, and/or indifference in varying combinations for different groups in the population. Similarly, a public health scare announced through a news report might encounter some skeptics. The messiness in these stimuli makes our experiments more relevant to real-world politics but also weaker in terms of internal validity.

Across our experiments, anxiety manipulations are attached to policy (i.e., anxiety about immigration or terrorism), which reflects our theory that citizens seek effective protection from threats. That is, we expect that citizens anxious over climate change turn to leaders and policies that protect them on climate change, not the flu. Other studies of emotion utilize stimuli such as movie clips (Renshon, Lee, and Tingley 2014) or pictures of angry faces (Banks 2014) that are removed from the policy context. The advantage of those stimuli is the ability to make a strong causal claim that is the experience of anger or anxiety free of politics that influences policy attitudes. The policy-specific anxiety that we utilize gets closer to the type of messages utilized by news outlets and political elites. Campaign ads include not only emotive music and faces but also messages about how to resolve the feeling, usually by supporting the candidate or policy advocated in the ad.

Acknowledging that there is no perfect manipulation of political anxiety, we advocate varied approaches. Bottom-up manipulations might achieve greater internal validity because they allow the participant to tell us what makes them anxious. In contrast, external stimuli like news stories or campaign advertisements cannot generate the same emotional experience in all participants, but they allow us to test our hypotheses in relation to real-world stimuli. These manipulations allowed us to better situate the emotional experience of anxiety in a political environment that is often partisan.

Our second methodological suggestion is extensive pretesting of experimental manipulations. This is vital to establish that our manipulations trigger anxiety and also to measure whether they have effects on other emotions (most notably anger) and on cognition. For many of our studies, we pretested a variety of manipulations to choose the best materials. When it comes to public health threats, would a smallpox outbreak or the bubonic plague generate more anxiety? (In our pretesting, smallpox "won.") In our anti-immigrant advertisements, we borrowed materials from both Pete Wilson and Ron Paul, and found that Pete Wilson's advertisement was more anxiety producing. Pretesting allowed us to pick the appropriate materials for our studies with less expensive convenience samples. Pretesting also allowed us to measure a variety of emotions right after the stimulus was received.

There is some debate over the appropriate place of emotion measures in experiments – they might fit after the manipulation but before the dependent variable, but we would question whether asking participants to answer a survey question about emotion changes their emotional experience. Emotion questions could be positioned after the dependent variable, but then we would question whether the emotional experience is expected to last. This is especially a concern if the dependent variable of interest is expected to alleviate an uncomfortable emotional experience. Both of these approaches have their critics, and this book relies on studies that take up different approaches on the placement of emotion measures.

The third methodological approach we take to establish the connection between anxiety and our dependent variables is mediation models. Extensive pretesting allowed us to pick materials that were best suited to triggering anxiety and not other emotions, but, of course, picking good materials is not the same as picking perfect materials. Anti-immigrant advertisements trigger anxiety, but they also trigger some anger. On the other hand, news about a smallpox outbreak causes anxiety, but it also generates sadness. Given that our stimuli triggered a variety of emotions, we need to show that anxiety mediates the relationship between the stimuli and the dependent variables. An experimental approach allows us to test a causal hypothesis, and our mediation models grant us more precision in saying that anxiety is doing the causal work. Although the magic political anxiety pill is still elusive, we advocate using multiple manipulations, extensive pretesting, and mediation models. These approaches have allowed us to situate a discrete emotional experience in a complex political environment.

LOOKING FORWARD: WHAT DOES THIS LINE OF RESEARCH LOOK LIKE IN THE FUTURE?

The seven studies in this book can illuminate a great deal about how political anxiety influences citizen attitudes and behaviors, but even with multiple studies across four policy areas, we are left with a number of open questions about anxiety's impact on politics. These questions provide opportunities for future political psychology research, and we outline some future paths for scholars interested in uncovering the ways that emotional politics functions.

One set of open questions from our research is about the duration of anxiety effects. How long do the effects of immigration anxiety or worries over a public health crisis last? What if threatening stimuli are ever-present? If citizens face daily reminders of economic crisis, increasing crime, or the threat of terrorism when they flip on the television or talk to a neighbor, do people remain vigilant and trusting, or do they tune out? Anxiety could continue to affect political life even after the original threat is less salient or even forgotten through shaping memories or through information seeking (Lodge and Taber 2005). If anxiety is to have a long-term impact on political behavior, we need first to be able to demonstrate that it has a short-term impact.

Our experiments are well-suited to establishing the connection between short-term anxiety and attitudes because we both manipulate anxiety and measure outcomes in a relatively constrained period of time. We do not employ a panel design and revisit our subjects later to measure if (and how much) anxiety continues to influence decision making and opinion formation, but this is a relatively straightforward extension of our work. Another avenue for studying the duration of anxiety and its downstream effects is through exploiting the variation in threat across places and time. Utilizing a "lab in the field" type of design, researchers could manipulate anxiety in sites that are similar on most dimensions but vary on how common a particular threat is. As an example, in a study of how anger influences intragroup relations, Zeitzoff (2014) leverages variation in underlying violence by running a study in two Israeli communities that experienced different levels of rocket fire. For scholars interested in how constant exposure to threat impacts the ability of any event or elite to utilize anxiety for political purposes, this type of lab in the field design would provide a sense of how generalizable our findings are for societies in times of crisis.

Anxious people cope with anxiety in three specific ways that we track: they seek information, they trust in experts, and they support policies that they believe will protect them. Another set of open questions that this research raises is how these coping mechanisms interact and are shaped by social context. It is plausible and likely that political anxiety leads people toward social networks and trusted others, not just impersonal sources of information and political leaders. Like other survey-based experiments, we observe how anxious people react individually. We do not observe how social institutions like the family, friendship networks, or religious organizations may blunt or strengthen the effects of anxiety or offer individuals alternative coping mechanisms such as interpersonal trust or avoidance. Our findings also lend themselves to studying how the coping strategies are related to each other. Does employing one coping mechanism (i.e., information seeking) minimize the need for others (i.e., trust), or do they enhance one another (i.e., trust increases the likelihood of supporting an expert's protective policy). Are some strategies more effective at alleviating anxiety than others? Are there individual differences in personality that make some coping mechanisms more attractive? A follow-up to our research could be a study that would induce anxiety and then allow people to choose among a set of strategies and allow a test of which ones ultimately decreased respondents' anxiety and which ones generated effective political decisions and behaviors.

ANXIETY AND DEMOCRATIC CITIZENSHIP

Are anxious citizens victims of emotional politics and elite manipulation, or are they good citizens closer to our democratic ideals? They might be both – anxiety motivates an often apathetic public to engage in democratic life, but it also gives us more than a few things to worry about. American citizens tend to fall far short of the ideal of a knowledgeable public, but an anxious citizenry is a more informed public. When a hurricane is barreling toward New Orleans or a terrorism suspect is on the loose in Cambridge, an anxious public is an attentive public and maybe a safer public. Emotions are motivating, and when anxiety motivates Americans to seek protection and trust in their government, this may enable speedier and (potentially) better policy making. Yet, anxiety also reveals the "dark side" of American politics (Brooks and Manza 2013), one in which citizens more readily sacrifice the rights and liberties of groups that are perceived to be physical or existential threats to the American public. When citizens do not pay close attention and verify the reliability of the emotional claims being made, they are likely to be moved toward policies and elites they would not otherwise agree with under more sedate circumstances. Citizens can rely on their predispositions, such as partisanship, ideology, and group membership, as a screen on anxious information, but they must be careful to not uncritically accept information from their own partisan leaders as well.

When politicians can define what the public is supposed to fear (Robin 2006), they may also be particularly successful in offering policies to alleviate that anxiety and benefit electorally from this anxiety. Republican elites are more able to convince Republican and Democratic voters alike to support restrictionist types of immigration policies when immigration creates anxiety for these individuals. The challenge for the Republican Party is that, although immigration is a frequent policy issue, it is often pushed off the agenda by other pressing issues like the economy. Nascent issues are unlikely to raise and maintain anxiety. Our findings reveal another complicating factor for party leaders who wish to benefit from anxiety. For party leaders who want to persuade partisans of the other party to be anxious, explicitly appealing to anxiety may be less effective than relying on other means, such as social networks or the news media. Self-generated anxiety is more likely to affect respondents of both political parties than anxiety that is used overtly persuasively because individuals are not motivated to resist it. The policies offered by an "owning" party may or may not be in the best interests of individual citizens or the nation as a whole. For instance, restricting immigration or strengthening domestic surveillance may potentially head off a future terrorist attack, but these policies risk damaging privacy, freedom of association, and a diverse polity, all important to the health of a democracy.

Political candidates have incentives to focus citizen anxiety on issues that are most electorally beneficial for their party, and they often choose to focus campaign communications on those issues. Our research shows why anxiety-inducing communication may influence the electorate. Negative advertisements are memorable (Wattenberg and Brians 1999), and our research suggests that they are particularly effective because anxious citizens are motivated to seek out additional threatening information. A campaign ad might leave us anxious about immigration for several reasons, and, in an anxious state, we are attracted to and remember threatening information. If an attack advertisement gives us one or two reasons to fear immigration, our attention to the media when we are anxious might give us a few more. Even if the effect of the original anxiety-producing ad fades quickly (D. P. Green and Gerber 2002), it may have larger downstream effects through shaping how people process information. Beyond information gathering, an anxious citizen needs someone to trust, and a strategic candidate from the issue-owning party can reassure us and presumably lead us toward policies favored by his party.

There are several worrisome elements in anxious politics. First, are threats real, and are they relevant to politics? Knowing how anxiety affects citizens' attitudes makes it clear that politicians have something to gain by stoking fears. Sometimes we ought to be anxious because of a legitimate threat to our livelihood, but the solution to the threat might not be political. Achen and Bartels (2002) raise the political consequences of irrelevant threats, such as shark attacks; our concerns go a step further – beyond politically irrelevant threats, we worry about politically relevant, politically constructed threats. Although some threats are real and imminent, others are politically constructed. Journalists and political elites have incentives to hype threats, and whether the sky is falling or not can be difficult for an ordinary citizen to figure out. Throughout our writing, we have been agnostic on the veracity and importance of different threats. Immigration triggers anxiety for many Americans, but should they feel that way? While people on the left find the immigrant threat overhyped, people on the right doubt the role of people in climate change. In the immediate aftermath of a terrorist attack on U.S. soil, we expect that all Americans feel some level of anxiety, and likely the same is true in the event of a widespread public health crisis. Empirically, these factors matter in our research because a threat has to generate anxiety in order to trigger the effects we have studied. But the contested nature of some of threats illustrates that one person's anxious politics can be another person's hoax. Not every threat is real, and our research on the persuasive potential of anxious politics makes us particularly concerned about politically manufactured threats.

We worry that people might pay attention to the wrong threats, but it is also concerning if people aren't paying attention to the right threats. Americans were late to recognize the economic threat facing the country prior to the 2008 crisis. Threats that are not immediate are difficult to sell to the public. Climate change is an area where the threats that cause anxiety may be less immediate than other policy areas (e.g., disease outbreak, riots, mass shootings), and, thus, it is harder to convince people to worry, harder to make them care about the problem, perhaps even when they should.

Another factor that makes anxious politics troubling is if threats are not countered by other messages. Politicians want to be responsive to threats that could do real damage and that are immediate. No one wants to be on the wrong side of history – let the dictator rise, or the pandemic get out of control, or the flood drown a city. Alternative voices like the media and whistleblowers may fill a void when the opposition party is quiet or focusing on its own scary issues, yet the media also faces an incentive to scare the public to increase ratings and attention (Zaller 1999). In the face of anxiety, opposition voices, particularly from the party not in power, are necessary so that threats do not get overhyped. Without multiple voices helping the public to distinguish what issues to worry about and what policies to support to alleviate that anxiety, the party in power has monopoly on scaring the public.

FINAL THOUGHTS

When politics is emotive, when citizens are anxious because of melting icecaps, bombings in Boston or Mumbai, or measles outbreaks harming children, this anxiety systematically affects political beliefs and behavior. Emotion is not simply a residual in our models of political behavior, an error to be corrected for or lamented in how we conceive of citizenship. Our theories of democracy conceive of good citizens as those who are informed, participatory, and with enough trust in government to comply with prescribed policy. In many ways, anxiety helps citizens meet those standards. Anxious citizens cope with this uncomfortable emotion by searching out news to help them understand, back trustworthy leaders, and throw their support behind policies framed as protective. However, anxiety is not an unalloyed good. Anxiety leads citizens to support policies that deny others rights in times of crisis and to support leaders who may continually provoke anxiety to maintain power and support for favored policies. Anxiety's role in democracy is complex, but what this book shows is that the components of democratic life – learning, trust, opinion formation – often run through emotional experiences.

APPENDIX

Anxious Politics: 7 Main Studies

Name of Study	Immigration KN Study 2007	Immigration MT Study 2011	Immigration KN Study 2011
Date	Spring 2007	Winter 2011	Summer 2011
Sample	384 Adults, representative. Knowledge Networks (KN)	174 Adults, online opt-in. Mechanical Turk (MT)	1,053 Adults, representative. KN
DVs	Info seeking, Attitudes	Trust, Attitudes	Trust, Attitudes
Anxiety manipulation	Thought listing	Campaign ad (video)	Campaign ad (video)

Name of Study	Public Health H1N1 2010	Public Health Smallpox YG/P Study 2011	Terrorism YG/P Study 2006	Climate Change PMR Study 2012
Date	Spring 2010	Spring 2011	Fall 2006	Summer 2012
Sample	156 UT students	600 Adults, representative. YouGov/ Politmetrix (YG/P)	809 Adults, representative. YG/P	250 Adults, online panel. PMR
DVs	Trust	Trust, Attitudes	Attitudes	Attitudes
Anxiety manipulation	Thought listing	Newspaper	TV News	Cross-sectional

IMMIGRATION KN STUDY 2007

DATE: Spring 2007

SAMPLE: 384 adults, nationally representative online sample recruited from GfK/Knowledge Networks panel.

MANIPULATION: Bottom-up anxiety manipulation

First, we'd like you to take a moment to think about the debate over immigration in the United States. *When you think about immigration, what makes you worried?* [*When you think about immigration, what do you think of?*] Please list everything that comes to mind.

DEPENDENT VARIABLES:

1. Information seeking
   a. Time spent per story
   b. Number of stories read
   c. Total time spent on reading stories
2. Here is a list of services that the government could provide for illegal immigrants. Do you think that illegal immigrants should be eligible for these services? (In random order)
   a. Do you think that illegal immigrants should be eligible for elementary education (grades K–6)?
   b. Do you think that illegal immigrants should be eligible for in-state tuition at state universities?
   c. Do you think that illegal immigrants should be eligible for drivers' licenses?
   d. Do you think that illegal immigrants should be eligible for Food Stamps?
   e. Do you think that illegal immigrants should be eligible for emergency room treatment?
   f. Should federal spending on tightening border security to prevent illegal immigration be increased, decreased, or kept about the same?

FULL TRANSCRIPT OF SEARCH STORIES: News stories used in the information search. Respondents only saw the headlines and could choose any story. The headlines appeared in random order on the computer screen.

Category	Headlines
Immigration stories: Threatening	Gangs in the U.S.: How Illegal Immigrants Complicate Law Enforcement; Why Unskilled Immigrants Hurt America
Immigration stories: Nonthreatening	Immigrants to Be Proud of; A Story of Two Immigrants
Non-immigration stories	One in Five Children Will Become Obese; Mysterious Stone Slab Bears Ancient Writing

STORY 1

Gangs in the U.S.: How Illegal Immigrants Complicate Law Enforcement

Police commanders may not want to discuss, much less respond to, the illegal alien crisis, but its magnitude for law enforcement is startling. Some examples:

- In Los Angeles, 95 percent of all outstanding warrants for homicide (which total 1,200 to 1,500) target illegal aliens. Up to two-thirds of all fugitive felony warrants (17,000) are for illegal aliens.
- A confidential California Department of Justice study reported in 1995 that 60 percent of the bloody 18th Street Gang in California is illegal (estimated membership: 20,000); police officers say the proportion is undoubtedly much greater. The gang collaborates with the Mexican Mafia, the dominant force in California prisons, on complicated drug distribution schemes, extortion, and drive-by assassinations, and is responsible for an assault or robbery every day in Los Angeles County. The gang has dramatically expanded its numbers over the last two decades by recruiting recently arrived youngsters, a vast proportion illegal, from Central America and Mexico.
- The leadership of the Columbia Li'l Cycos gang, which uses murder and racketeering to control the drug market around L.A.'s MacArthur Park, was about 60 percent illegal in 2002, says former Assistant U.S. Attorney Luis Li. Frank "Pancho Villa" Martinez, a Mexican Mafia member and illegal alien, controlled the gang from prison, while serving time for felonious reentry following deportation.

Good luck finding any reference to such facts in official crime analysis. The LAPD and the Los Angeles City Attorney recently requested a judicial injunction against drug trafficking in Hollywood. The injunction targets the 18th Street Gang and, as the press release puts it, the "non-gang members" who sell drugs in Hollywood on behalf of the gang. Those "non-gang members" are virtually all illegal Mexicans, smuggled into the country by a trafficking ring organized by 18th Street bigs. The illegal Mexicans pay off their transportation debt to the gang by selling drugs; many soon realize how lucrative that line of work is and stay in the business.

The immigration status of these non-gang "Hollywood dealers," as the City Attorney calls them, is universally known among officers and gang prosecutors. But the gang injunction is silent on the matter. And if a Hollywood officer were to arrest an illegal dealer (known on the street as a "border brother") for his immigration status, or even notify Immigration and Customs Enforcement (ICE), he would be severely disciplined for violation of Special Order 40, the city's sanctuary policy.

STORY 2

Why Unskilled Immigrants Hurt America

The day after Librado Velasquez arrived on Staten Island after a long journey from his home in Mexico, he waited on a street corner with other illegal immigrants looking for work. Velasquez, had been a farmer until he heard about work in the U.S. from his cousin, who is also here illegally. He eventually got work loading trucks at a small New Jersey factory, which hired illegals for jobs that required few special skills. The arrangement suited both, until a work injury sent Velasquez to the local emergency room. After five operations, he is now permanently disabled and has remained in the United States to pursue compensation claims.

Velasquez's story illustrates some of the fault lines in the nation's highly charged debate on immigration. Since the mid-1960s, America has welcomed nearly 30 million legal immigrants and received perhaps another 15 million illegal immigrants. These immigrants have picked our fruit, cleaned our homes, cut our grass, worked in our factories and washed our cars. But they have also crowded into our hospital emergency rooms, schools and government-subsidized aid programs, sparking a fierce debate about their contributions and costs.

Advocates of open immigration argue that welcoming the Velasquezes of the world is essential for our American economy: our businesses need workers like him. Like tax cuts, supporters argue, immigration pays for itself.

But the tale of Velasquez helps show why supporters are wrong about today's immigration. America does not have a vast labor shortage that requires waves of low-wage immigrants; in fact, unemployment among unskilled workers is high – about 30 percent. Like Velasquez, many of the unskilled, uneducated workers now journeying here labor in shrinking industries, where they force out native workers.

These workers come at great cost. Increasing numbers of them arrive with little education and few skills necessary to succeed in a modern economy. Many may wind up stuck on our lowest economic rungs, where they will rely on a vast U.S. welfare and social-services apparatus. Even as welfare reform and other policies are helping to shrink America's underclass by weaning people off such social programs, we are importing a new, foreign-born underclass.

Immigration can only pay off again for America if we reshape our policy, organizing it around what's good for the economy by welcoming workers we truly need and excluding those who, because they have so little to offer, are likely to cost us more than they contribute, and who will struggle for years to find their place here.

STORY 3

A Story of Two Immigrants

AMID THE DIN over illegal immigration, I have been thinking about two immigrants I happen to know rather well.

One is a 3-year-old boy from southern Guatemala. He was brought to the United States in March 2004, one of 11,170 adopted orphans to immigrate that year. The other, who will turn 81 in August, comes from a small village in what is now Slovakia. He entered the United States in the spring of 1948, a few months before his 23d birthday.

Born an ocean and 78 years apart, these two immigrants might seem on the surface to have little in common. But as naturalized U.S. citizens, they in fact have a great deal in common. English, to mention the most obvious example, is the primary language for both. Neither retains the customs of his native land.

The little boy from Guatemala is my younger son. The older man from Slovakia is my father.

America is a richer place because my father and son are here, and no doubt most Americans even those now clamoring for a crackdown on illegal immigration would agree. To countless Americans, the difference between legal and illegal immigration is self-evident and meaningful. But is that really what distinguishes the immigrants we want from those we don't that the former enter the country lawfully, while the latter break the rules to get here? Are immigrants like my father and son inherently desirable merely because a lot of exasperating bureaucratic requirements were met before they came? Are the 11 million illegal immigrants living within our borders unwelcome and problematic only because they got in the wrong way?

A foreigner who enters the United States without first running the immigration-law gantlet is not congenitally unfit to be a good American any more than someone who operates an automobile without a license is congenitally unfit to drive. Our immigration laws are maddening and Byzantine. They are heavily skewed in favor of people related to U.S. citizens nearly two-thirds of all legal immigrants qualify to enter the United States because they are the relatives of someone already here.

In so many other contexts, Americans admire self-starters and risk-takers who find ways to get around roadblocks that would defeat less inventive, determined, or gutsy individuals. Of course it is vital, especially after 9/11, to properly control the nation's borders. But there is still something to be said for the self-starters and risk-takers who look at the formidable roadblocks we place in the path of most would-be immigrants, especially those not related to a U.S. citizen and make up their minds to find a way around them.

STORY 4

Immigrants to Be Proud Of

The exclusionists are wrong when they say the current wave of immigration is tearing our social fabric. The facts show that the recent rise in immigration hasn't been accompanied by social breakdown, but by social repair. As immigration has surged, violent crime has fallen by 57 percent. Teen pregnancies and abortion rates have declined by a third. Teenagers are having fewer sexual partners and losing their virginity later. Teen suicide rates have dropped. The divorce rate for young people is on the way down.

Over the past decade we've seen the beginnings of a moral revival, and some of the most important work has been done by Catholic and evangelical immigrant churches, by faith-based organizations like the Rev. Luis Cortés's Nueva Esperanza, by Hispanic mothers and fathers monitoring their kids. The anti-immigration crowd says this country is under assault. But if that's so, we're under assault by people who love their children.

Immigrants themselves are like a booster shot of traditional morality injected into the body politic. Immigrants work hard. They build community groups. They have traditional ideas about family structure, and they work heroically to make them a reality. This is evident in everything from divorce rates (which are low, given immigrants' socioeconomic status) to their fertility rates (which are high) and even the way they shop.

Hispanics and Hispanic immigrants have less money than average Americans, but they spend what they have on their families, usually in wholesome ways. According to Simmons Research, Hispanics are 57 percent more likely than average Americans to have purchased children's furniture in the past year. Mexican-Americans spend 93 percent more on children's music.

According to the government's Consumer Expenditure Survey, Hispanics spend more on gifts, on average, than other Americans. They're more likely to support their parents financially. They're more likely to have big family dinners at home.

This isn't alien behavior. It's admirable behavior, the antidote to the excessive individualism that social conservatives decry.

Good values lead to success, and that immigrants' long-term contributions more than compensate for the short-term strains they cause. There's no use denying the strains immigration imposes on schools, hospitals and wage levels in some markets (but economists are sharply divided on this). So over the long haul, today's immigrants succeed. By the second generation, most immigrant families are middle class and paying taxes that more than make up for the costs of the first generation.

STORY 5

Report: One in Five Children Will Become Obese

One in five children is predicted to be obese by the end of the decade.

But efforts to turn that tide are scattershot and underfunded, and the government killed one of the few programs proven to work, say specialists at the Institute for Medicine.

No one knows which programs really help kids slim down, said the institute said in calling for research to identify best methods.

More troubling, the country lacks the national leadership needed to speed change, lamented an expert panel convened by the scientific group.

Dr. Jeffrey Koplan of Emory University, who led the IOM's panel, said, "This is a major health problem. It's of a different nature than acute infectious threats, but it needs to be taken just as seriously."

To reinforce that point, Wednesday's report spotlighted the government's VERB campaign, a program once touted as spurring a 30 percent increase in exercise among the preteens it reached. It ended this year with Bush administration budget cuts.

Koplan was blunt, calling it a waste of taxpayer money to develop a program that works and then dismantle it.

The report cites other examples of promising federal programs that have yet to reach their potential. Kids gobbled fruits and vegetables in an Agriculture Department school snack program, but it only reaches 14 states. And CDC's main anti-obesity initiative had enough money this year to fund just 28 states starting childhood nutrition and exercise programs.

The report also lauded some creative state and local efforts, including:

- A California program, started in Marin County, to build new sidewalks and bike paths to get children to walk or bike to school.
- An effort by Arkansas schools notify parents when students are over-weight. The initiative recently reported a leveling off of the state's child obesity rate.

In 2004 the IOM called for a joint attack on childhood obesity by parents, schools, communities, the food industry and government. Wednesday's report was the first checkup.

"We still are not doing enough to prevent childhood obesity, and the problem is getting worse," concluded Koplan, a former CDC director. "The current level of public and private sector investments does not match the extent of the problem."

Some 17 percent of U.S. youngsters already are obese, and millions more are overweight. Obesity can lead to diabetes, high blood pressure and cholesterol, sleep problems and other disorders.

STORY 6

Mysterious Stone Slab Bears Ancient Writing

An ancient slab of green stone inscribed with insects, ears of corn, fish and other symbols is indecipherable so far, but one message is clear: It is the earliest known writing in the Western Hemisphere.

The ancient Olmec civilization probably produced the faintly etched symbols around 900 B.C., or roughly three centuries before what previously had been proposed as the earliest examples of writing in the Americas.

"We are dealing with the first, clear evidence of writing in the New World," said Stephen Houston, a Brown University anthropologist. Houston and his U.S. and Mexican colleagues detail the tablet's discovery and analysis in a study appearing this week in the journal Science.

The text contains 28 distinct glyphs or symbols, some of which are repeated three and four times. The writing system does not appear to be linked to any known later scripts and may represent a dead end, according to the study.

Other experts not involved in the study agreed with Houston and his colleagues that the horizontally arranged inscription shows patterns that are the hallmarks of true writing, including syntax and language-specific word order.

"That's full-blown, legitimate text – written symbols taking the place of spoken words," said William Saturno, a University of New Hampshire anthropologist and expert in Mesoamerican writing.

Villagers in the Mexican state of Veracruz discovered the tablet sometime before 1999, while quarrying an ancient Olmec mound for road-building material. News of the discovery slowly trickled out, and the study's authors traveled to the site this year to examine and photograph the block.

"This is centuries before anything we've had. People have debated whether the Olmecs had any writing. This clears it up. This nails it for me," David Stuart, a University of Texas at Austin expert in Mesoamerican writing, said of the new find.

The find bolsters the early importance of the Olmecs, who flourished between about 1200 B.C. and 400 B.C., before other great Central American civilizations such as the Maya and Aztec. They are best known for the massive heads they carved from stone. The village where the block was found is close to a site called San Lorenzo, believed to be the center of the Olmec world.

"To me, this find really does bring us back to this idea that at least writing and a lot of the things we associate with Mesoamerican culture really did have their origin in this region," Stuart said.

IMMIGRATION MT STUDY 2011

DATE: Winter 2011

SAMPLE: 174 adults, opt-in online sample recruited from Amazon's Mechanical Turk workplace.

MANIPULATION: Campaign Ad focused on the costs of immigration (see transcript below)

1. Control condition – no music
2. Treatment condition – threatening music

DEPENDENT VARIABLES:
1. Trust in political actors
   a. How much do you trust the <u>President Obama</u> to address immigration? (Not at all, not very much, somewhat, a great deal)
   b. How much do you trust the <u>Governor Brewer</u> to address immigration?
   c. How much do you trust <u>the Democratic Party</u> to address immigration?
   d. How much do you trust <u>the Republican Party</u> to address immigration?
   e. How much do you trust <u>U.S. Customs & Border Control</u> to address immigration?
   f. How much do you trust <u>the Minuteman Project</u> to address immigration?
   g. How much do you trust <u>Citizens Concerned about Immigration</u> to address immigration?
2. Immigration attitudes

Here is a list of services that the government could provide for illegal immigrants. Do you think that illegal immigrants should be eligible for these services? (Definitely not eligible, probably not eligible, Unsure, probably eligible, definitely eligible) (In random order)

a. Do you think that illegal immigrants should be eligible for <u>elementary education (grades K–6)</u>?
b. Do you think that illegal immigrants should be eligible for <u>in-state tuition at state universities</u>?
c. Do you think that illegal immigrants should be eligible for <u>Medicaid</u>?
d. Do you think that illegal immigrants should be eligible for <u>Food Stamps</u>?
e. Do you think that illegal immigrants should be eligible for <u>emergency room treatment</u>?

TRANSCRIPT OF AD:

It's how most of us got here. It's how this country was built. American citizenship is a treasure.

But now the rules are being broken. Today more than 11 million illegal immigrants overwhelm our borders, our economy, and our hospitals.

Illegal immigrants take American jobs.

On-screen text: Immigrant labor depresses American wages by $200 billion a year.

Open borders bring crime and a threat to national security.

On-screen text: More than 10% of federal prisoners are serving time for immigration crimes.

Illegal immigrants take welfare, health care, and education dollars that should go to hard working Americans.

There is a right way to do things and a wrong way. Enough is enough. Say NO to illegal immigration.

On-screen text: Enough is enough

IMMIGRATION KN STUDY 2011

DATE: Spring 2011

SAMPLE: 1053 adults, nationally representative online sample recruited from GfK/Knowledge Networks panel.

MANIPULATIONS:

A. Campaign ad focused on the costs of immigration (See transcript below)
   a. Control condition – no music
   b. Treatment condition – threatening music

B. Trust evaluations. When asked to rate how much a political figure was trusted, respondents saw either (see transcript of statements below):
   a. Statement by the figure about immigration that was threatening
   b. Statement by the figure about immigration that was solution focused
C. Citizens Concerned about Immigration. This group was randomized to offer either a (see transcript of policy positions below):
   a. Liberal policy solution for immigration
   b. Conservative policy solution for immigration

Ad with no music and neutral visuals followed by liberal solution for CCAI	Ad with no music and neutral visuals followed by conservative solution for CCAI	Ad with threatening music and images followed by liberal solution for CCAI	Ad with threatening music and images followed by conservative solution for CCAI
Control video Group 1	Control video Group 2	Treatment video Group 1	Treatment video Group 2

GROUP 1: (RANDOMIZE ORDER SHOWN, LIBERAL SOLUTION FOR CCAI)
1. Obama – threat
2. Department of Homeland Security/BorderPatrol- threat
3. Republican Party – threat
4. Citizens Concerned about Immigration (CCAI) – [citizen group – liberal solution]
5. Jan Brewer – solution
6. Minutemen – solution
7. Democratic Party – solution

GROUP 2: (RANDOMIZE ORDER SHOWN; CONSERVATIVE SOLUTION FOR CCAI)
1. Obama – solution
2. Department of Homeland Security/Border Patrol – solution
3. Republican Party – solution
4. Citizens Concerned about Immigration – Solution [citizen group – conservative solution]
5. Brewer – threat
6. Minutemen – threat
7. Democratic Party – threat

DEPENDENT VARIABLES:

1. Trust in political actors
    a. How much do you trust the <u>President Obama</u> to address immigration? (Not at all, not very much, somewhat, a great deal)
    b. How much do you trust the <u>Governor Brewer</u> to address immigration?
    c. How much do you trust <u>the Democratic Party</u> to address immigration?
    d. How much do you trust <u>the Republican Party</u> to address immigration?
    e. How much do you trust <u>U.S. Customs & Border Control</u> to address immigration?
    f. How much do you trust <u>the Minuteman Project</u> to address immigration?
    g. How much do you trust <u>Citizens Concerned about Immigration</u> to address immigration?
2. Immigration attitudes

Here is a list of services that the government could provide for illegal immigrants. Do you think that illegal immigrants should be eligible for these services? (Definitely not eligible, probably not eligible, Unsure, probably eligible, definitely eligible) (In random order)

a. Do you think that illegal immigrants should be eligible for <u>elementary education (grades K–6)</u>?
b. Do you think that illegal immigrants should be eligible for <u>drivers' licenses</u>?
c. Do you think that illegal immigrants should be eligible for <u>Medicaid</u>?
d. Do you think that illegal immigrants should be eligible for <u>Food Stamps</u>?
e. Do you think that illegal immigrants should be eligible for <u>emergency room treatment</u>?

TRANSCRIPT OF AD: (Half of respondents see this ad accompanied by scary music. The other half see the ad without music.)

It's how most of us got here. It's how this country was built. American citizenship is a treasure.

But now the rules are being broken. Today more than 11 million illegal immigrants overwhelm our borders, our economy, and our hospitals.

Illegal immigrants take American jobs.

On-screen text: Immigrant labor depresses American wages by $200 billion a year.

Open borders bring crime and a threat to national security.

On-screen text: More than 10% of federal prisoners are serving time for immigration crimes.

Illegal immigrants take welfare, health care, and education dollars that should go to hard working Americans.

There is a right way to do things and a wrong way. Enough is enough. Say NO to illegal immigration.

On-screen text: Enough is enough

THREAT AND SOLUTION STATEMENTS:

President Barack Obama

Solution Statement [This line was not visible to respondents]

"There are an estimated 11 million undocumented immigrants in the United States. Because they live in the shadows, crimes go unreported as victims and witnesses fear coming forward. We need to create a pathway for legal status that is fair, reflective of our values, and works."

Threat Statement [This line was not visible to respondents]

"There are an estimated 11 million undocumented immigrants in the United States. Because they live in the shadows, crimes go unreported as victims and witnesses fear coming forward. This makes it harder for the police to catch violent criminals and keep neighborhoods safe."

Governor of Arizona (R), Jan Brewer

Solution Statement [This line was not visible to respondents]

"Border-related violence and crime due to illegal immigration are critically important issues to the people of our state and to the country. We cannot sacrifice our safety to the murderous greed of drug cartels. I support a law that requires that the police determine a person's immigration status if there is reasonable suspicion that the person is an illegal alien."

Threat Statement [This line was not visible to respondents]

"Border-related violence and crime due to illegal immigration are critically important issues to the people of our state and to the country. We cannot sacrifice our safety to the murderous greed of drug cartels. Kidnappings and violence are compromising our quality of life."

Democratic Party

Solution Statement [This line was not visible to respondents]

"We cannot ignore the nearly 12 million immigrants currently living in the United States illegally. The exploitation of undocumented immigrant workers threatens to drive down wages for Americans. We support comprehensive reform grounded in the principles of responsibility.

Employers who exploit undocumented workers undermine American workers, and they have to be held accountable."

Threat Statement [This line was not visible to respondents]

"We cannot ignore the nearly 12 million immigrants currently living in the United States illegally. The exploitation of undocumented immigrant workers threatens to drive down wages, benefits and working conditions for middle-class workers and low-income Americans striving to earn a middle-class standard of living."

Republican Party

Solution Statement [This line was not visible to respondents]

"We cannot ignore the nearly 12 million immigrants living in the United States illegally. Illegal immigration undercuts the American middle class, places unsustainable burdens on social service programs, and poses a significant risk to national security. Our determination to uphold the rule of law begins with more effective enforcement, completing the border fence quickly and securing the borders."

Threat Statement [This line was not visible to respondents]

"We cannot ignore the nearly 12 million immigrants currently living in the United States illegally. Illegal immigration undercuts the American middle class, places unsustainable burdens on our social service programs, and poses a significant risk to our national security."

The Department of Homeland Security/Border Patrol

Solution Statement [This line was not visible to respondents]

"Most illicit drugs available in the United States and thousands of illegal immigrants are smuggled into the United States across the nearly 2,000-mile Southwest Border. We propose more agents to patrol our borders, secure our ports of entry and enforce immigration laws and expanded removal capabilities to eliminate 'catch and release.'"

Threat Statement [This line was not visible to respondents]

"Most illicit drugs available in the United States and thousands of illegal immigrants are smuggled into the United States across the nearly 2,000-mile Southwest Border. Intercartel warfare has resulted in unprecedented violence in northern Mexico and the potential for increasing violence in the United States."

The Minuteman Project

Solution Statement [This line was not visible to respondents]

"The failure of elected and appointed officials to enforce immigration laws poses a threat to the security, sovereignty, and prosperity of our nation, particularly to our middle class and labor union work forces, and to the safety of our families.

The Minuteman project will recruit Americans to observe, report, and deter illegal border crossings in Arizona."

Threat Statement [This line was not visible to respondents]

"The failure of elected officials to enforce immigration laws poses a threat to the security, sovereignty, and prosperity of our nation, particularly to our middle class and labor union work forces, and to the safety of our families."

Citizens Concerned about Immigration

Conservative solution [This line was not visible to respondents]

"We believe that security of our borders is an urgent national interest. We oppose illegal immigration and all forms of amnesty, or legal status for illegal immigrants. We support suspending automatic U.S. citizenship to children born to illegal immigrant parents and eliminating government funding to illegal immigrants for education, housing, and business loans. We also support eliminating all laws that require hospitals to give non-emergency medical care to illegal immigrants."

Liberal solution [This line was not visible to respondents]

"We believe that today's immigration laws do not reflect our values or serve our security. Undocumented immigrants within our borders who clear a background check, work hard, and pay taxes should have a path to earn full participation in America. We support hastening family reunification for parents and children, husbands and wives, and offering more English- language and civic education classes so immigrants can assume all the rights and responsibilities of citizenship."

PUBLIC HEALTH H1N1 STUDY 2010

DATE: Spring 2010

SAMPLE: 156 undergraduates in a political science lab at the University of Texas at Austin

MANIPULATION: Bottom-up anxiety manipulation

First, we'd like you to take a moment to reflect on the H1N1 virus (swine flu). What makes you feel worried about the H1N1 virus (swine flu)? Please describe how you feel as vividly and in as much detail as possible. [What comes to mind when you think about the H1N1 virus (swine flu)? Please list everything that comes to mind.]

DEPENDENT VARIABLES:

1. Information seeking
   a. Time spent per story
   b. Number of stories read
   c. Total time spent on reading stories
2. Do you think the following behavior is important for staying healthy during flu season (Very important, somewhat important, not at all important)
   a. Washing your hands
   b. Using hand sanitizer
   c. Getting a seasonal flu vaccine
   d. Getting an H1N1 vaccine
   e. Exercising
   f. Taking vitamins
   g. Getting enough sleep
3. How confident are you that the federal government will be able to handle an outbreak of the H1N1 virus (swine flu) in this country – very confident, somewhat confident, not too confident, or not confident at all?
4. How confident are you that the president will be able to handle an outbreak of the H1N1 virus (swine flu) in this country?
5. A number of groups provide information about H1N1. We'll show you a series of people and groups, and we'd like to know if you trust each of the following sources for information about the H1N1 flu. (A great deal, somewhat not very much, not at all)
   a. Your personal doctor
   b. The Centers for Disease Control and Prevention (a government funded source of research about health)
   c. The Food and Drug Administration (FDA, a federal government agency with the mission of assuring the drugs, vaccines, and the food supply)
   d. Websites from health organizations like WebMD
   e. President Obama

FULL TRANSCRIPT OF SEARCH STORIES: News stories used in the information search. Respondents only saw the headlines and could choose any story. The headlines appeared in random order on the computer screen.

Category	Headlines
H1N1 stories: Threatening	Texas Should Take H1N1 Seriously
	Deaths Still High as Low-Level Flu Spread Continues
H1N1: Nonthreatening	Was the Swine Flu Fuss Necessary?
	Swine Flu Outbreak Appears to Be Headed toward a Close
Non-H1N1 stories	One in Five Children Will Become Obese
	Mysterious Stone Slab Bears Ancient Writing

STORY I

Texas Should Take H1N1 Seriously

This year's flu season is the worst in many years, and young adults have been hit especially hard by the H1N1 flu. Who is in the age group most likely to get H1N1? People under 25. Who gets so sick they need to be hospitalized? Half of them are under 25. And who is least likely to get a flu shot? People under 25.

But H1N1 mainly hits the young. And even though most cases are mild, some can be quite severe. The Centers for Disease Control and Prevention estimates that about 540 children and teenagers have died from H1N1 flu since April, and we are only at the beginning of the official flu season. Some of those who died were perfectly healthy when they caught the flu.

So what can you do to protect yourself and people around you from flu?

Get vaccinated. It's the most effective way to prevent the flu. The H1N1 flu vaccine is made the same way as the seasonal flu vaccine, which has a decades-long safety track record. And it's undergone more testing than other flu vaccines.

If you're someone with a health condition like diabetes or asthma, the CDC says you should get vaccinated as soon as your community has vaccine available. Other groups at high risk for serious complications include young children and pregnant women. Also, people who care for babies younger than six months, health care workers and emergency medical personnel should go to the head of the vaccination line.

In addition, many people do not realize that simply being younger than 25 also puts you in a priority group to receive the vaccine. So look into getting vaccinated at school. Check out the flu.gov flu vaccination locator to find the best place for you to go to get vaccinated quickly.

Stay home when you're sick. If you do get the flu, there are things you should do to protect yourself and those around you. College campuses – dormitories, classes, wherever a lot of people are indoors together – are places the flu can spread. If you get sick, don't go out, and don't invite visitors in.

Make it part of your daily routine to keep the flu from spreading. The HıNı vaccine may not have arrived in your area yet, so keep doing the simple things everyone does to keep germs in check: Wash your hands, cough and sneeze into your sleeve and disinfect surfaces like computer keyboards and counter tops.

No one knows whether this wave of HıNı will get worse, taper off or be followed by another wave later in the season.

But we do know that preventing the flu depends on all of us, and everyone will be safer if each one of us is serious about preventing and reducing the HıNı flu.

I am writing today to urge you to take HıNı flu seriously, not just as the secretary of the Department of Health and Human Services, who has read lots of scientific studies saying this is a young person's pandemic, but also as a mother of two sons who not long ago were sitting exactly where you are today.

I know it's easy to believe that the flu is something that only the very old or the very young need to worry about, that catching the flu is no big deal. But no flu should ever be dismissed as "just the flu." The regular, seasonal flu is responsible for 36,000 deaths every year – mainly in people over 65.

STORY 2

Deaths Still High as Low-Level Flu Spread Continues

HıNı swine flu is no longer widespread in any state, but new infections continue and the death rate remains high, the CDC reported today.

Across the country so far there have been some 16 million more cases than in the average seasonal flu season and 13,000 more hospitalizations, said Mike Osterholm, an infectious disease expert at the University of Minnesota. There have been nearly 10,000 deaths, and the vast majority of deaths were in people younger than 65, he said.

A Harvard poll shows that about half of Americans believe the HıNı swine flu outbreak is over, and only a third remain concerned. That may explain why three in four U.S. residents still haven't been vaccinated against the pandemic virus, despite now-plentiful vaccine supplies.

CDC figures clearly show that the fall/winter wave of H1N1 swine flu has passed its peak. The number of people seeing a doctor about flu symptoms has for three weeks hovered just below epidemic levels.

Yet for the same three weeks, deaths from pneumonia and influenza have been above what CDC calculates to be the seasonal "epidemic threshold."

While flu isn't the cause of all these deaths, this figure – and reports of nine new pediatric swine flu deaths in the last week of January – are troubling reminders that H1N1 swine flu continues to infect, sicken, and even kill susceptible people.

"This virus is still around," CDC respiratory disease chief Anne Schuchat, MD, said at a news conference. "People are being hospitalized and are dying. . . . The virus is still spreading and those not who have not been vaccinated still are vulnerable."

Schuchat admits that there may not be another huge wave of H1N1 swine flu infections. But she noted that ongoing spread means cases "really can add up over time."

A CDC survey conducted in the last week of January found that about 70 million U.S. residents – 23.4% of the population – have been vaccinated with the 2009 H1N1 vaccine. Extensive data on the first 61 million doses administered indicate that the vaccine is safe.

The Harvard poll, conducted Jan. 20–24, shows that over half of parents either got their children vaccinated or plan to do so by the end of February.

However, the CDC survey shows that only 37% of children who got a first dose of the vaccine got their second dose. Without a second dose, a child remains unprotected.

"I urge parents to take their kids back for their second dose," Schuchat said. "It would be tragic for you to go so far to do the right thing and then have your child get sick."

Since vaccine distribution began, 124 million doses of the vaccine have been shipped around the U.S. At least 155 million doses will be made available in the U.S., which has enough bulk vaccine to make 229 million doses.

STORY 3

Was the Swine Flu Fuss Necessary?

More than a month has passed since swine flu was considered widespread anywhere in Texas. The H1N1 vaccine is widely available, but demand has fallen off along with the threat from the virus.

Although they warn that H1N1 is still circulating and flu season is far from over, officials are starting to step back and reflect on the most extensive public health campaign in years.

From the school closings in the early days of the outbreak to the frustrating vaccine shortages at its peak, no one will soon forget the swine flu virus that sickened tens of millions nationally but proved less dangerous than feared.

"It wasn't severe to where we were seeing hundreds of thousands of deaths," said Sharlene Edwards, public health preparedness manager for the Pinellas County Health Department. Nor, she noted, was it mild. "It was making people sick, so we had to respond."

In planning for pandemic influenza in the past, however, experts often anticipated many more people becoming critically sick and dying than they saw with the swine flu virus.

"We always prepared for the worst," Edwards said. "A lot of us are now going to go back and take a different approach to future pandemic planning."

Now vaccine is sitting on pharmacy shelves, and it's hard to know how much will get used during the remaining weeks of the flu season. Some may be donated to other countries, Skinner said. Leftovers will be thrown away, as scientists prepare an updated flu vaccine to administer next flu season.

But in the United States, public health officials say their response to the outbreak had some positive results, including expanded surveillance to monitor the spread of flu.

And the H1N1 outbreak may have finally gotten people to follow health officials' long-standing advice to take the seasonal flu seriously. Walgreens, for example, saw unprecedented demand for seasonal vaccine.

With children among the most vulnerable to swine flu, health officials took immunization clinics directly to local schools once the H1N1 vaccine became available. Austin health officials administered more than 50,000 doses of the H1N1 vaccine in schools, reaching about 25 percent of the target audience, a figure that officials say they are pleased with. Houston provided about 35,000 vaccine doses in schools.

But even as he promotes it, Austin's Pedigo understands why people aren't lining up to receive the vaccine. "As the incidence of the disease dropped, he said, the community lost interest."

STORY 4

Swine Flu Outbreak Appears to Be Headed toward a Close

If the U.S. swine flu epidemic isn't over, it certainly looks as if it's on its last legs.

While federal health officials are not ready to declare the threat has passed and the outbreak has run its course, they did report Friday that for the fourth week in a row, no states had widespread flu activity. U.S. cases have been declining since late October.

One U.S. expert said the epidemic has "one foot in the grave," and there are many reasons to believe there won't be another wave later in the year.

For one thing, the virus has shown no signs of mutating. The vaccine against it is effective. And roughly half the people in the U.S. probably have some immunity because they were infected with it or got vaccinated.

The World Health Organization is witnessing an international decline as well, and is discussing criteria for declaring the pandemic over. Britain this week shut down its swine flu hot line, which was set up to diagnose cases and give out Tamiflu.

"Clearly, the last four weeks have been one of the quietest January flu seasons I can remember in my career," said Michael Osterholm, a prominent expert on global flu outbreaks with the University of Minnesota.

Since its emergence last April, swine flu has caused an estimated 15,200 deaths worldwide, mostly in the U.S. – a much lower number than initially feared. The positive outcome is primarily because the virus didn't mutate into a deadlier form.

Even so, experts have praised the actions of the U.S. and Mexican governments and scientists who quickly developed an effective vaccine.

Criticizing the government for its intense response would be like chastising officials for building dikes in New Orleans to withstand a Category 5 hurricane and then seeing only a Category 3 come ashore, Osterholm said.

"The government did not overreact," said University of Michigan flu expert Dr. Arnold Monto, echoing Osterholm's point.

Whether it will stay quiet for the rest of the winter is hard to say, but some experts are beginning to lean that way.

"If it's not dead, it's weakening fast. It's got one foot in the grave," said Dr. William Schaffner, a flu authority at Vanderbilt University.

STORY 5

Report: One in Five Children Will Become Obese

[Please see the full text of this story on page 163.]

STORY 6

Mysterious Stone Slab Bears Ancient Writing

[Please see the full text of this story on page 165.]

PUBLIC HEALTH SMALLPOX YG/P STUDY 2011

DATE: Spring 2011

SAMPLE: 600 adults, nationally representative online sample recruited from YouGov/Polimetrix panel.

MANIPULATION: Newspaper story that varied evocative language

a. Control condition – Ancient language
b. Treatment – past outbreak
c. Treatment – present outbreak

DEPENDENT VARIABLES:

1. Civil liberties

A number of emergency powers have been proposed that state officials could use in the event of a smallpox outbreak. Please tell me if you would favor or oppose giving state officials the authority to take the following steps: (5 points: Strongly oppose to Strongly favor) [Presented in random order)

a. Requiring hospitals and health clinics to provide services to people who think they may have smallpox, even if a hospital or clinic does not want to provide them.
b. Requiring a person to be vaccinated against smallpox. Exceptions for special medical cases would be made. People who do not have exceptions and refuse vaccination could be arrested
c. Requiring a person to have a medical exam or test to diagnose whether the person has smallpox. People who refuse could be arrested.

   d. Quarantining people suspected of having been exposed to small-
      pox. People who refuse could be arrested.
   e. Requiring people who actually have smallpox to be isolated in a
      special health facility with other people who have the disease.
      People who refuse could be arrested.
   f. Destroying personal effects that might be contaminated by
      smallpox.
2. If state officials were given emergency powers like the ones that we
   have been discussing, how much do you agree that they would
   administer properly and not abuse these powers? (Strongly agree,
   Agree, Neither agree nor disagree, Disagree, Strongly disagree)
3. If state officials were given emergency powers like the ones that we
   have been discussing, how much do you agree that that it would
   threaten your personal rights and freedoms? (Strongly agree, Agree,
   Neither agree nor disagree, Disagree, Strongly disagree)
4. Trust

   How much do you trust the following person/group as a source for
   information about smallpox: (A great deal, somewhat, not very
   much, not at all)
a. Surgeon General Regina Benjamin

Manipulation (randomly assign within each condition):

   1. Surgeon General Regina Benjamin
   2. Expertise (this line not visible to respondent):

   Surgeon General Regina Benjamin, Benjamin holds an MD from
   the University of Alabama-Birmingham. She attended Morehouse
   School of Medicine and completed her family medicine residency
   in Macon, Ga.

   3. Relevance (this line not visible to respondent):

   Surgeon General Regina Benjamin, Benjamin is Founder and
   Former CEO of the Bayou La Batre Rural Health Clinic in
   Alabama, a health care facility with expertise in infectious disease.

   4. Politicization (this line not visible to respondent):

   Surgeon General Regina Benjamin. Benjamin was appointed as the
   18th Surgeon General of the United States Public Health Service by
   President Barack Obama.

b. the head of the Federal Reserve, Ben Bernanke
c. Department of Homeland Security
d. Internal Revenue Service
e. Personal doctor
f. Center for Disease Control
g. Food and Drug Administration
h. American Medical Association
i. Oprah Winfrey
j. Department of Health and Human Services
k. Friends and family in the medical field
l. Websites from health organizations like WebMD
m. President Obama

5. How confident are you in the federal government's ability to handle a smallpox outbreak? (Not too confident, Somewhat confident, Very confident)

6. How confident are you in President Obama's ability to handle a smallpox outbreak? (Not too confident, Somewhat confident, Very confident)

FULL TRANSCRIPT OF NEWSPAPER STORIES:

CONTROL

Mysterious Stone Slab Bears Ancient Writing

[Please see the full text of this story on page 165.]

TREATMENT – PRESENT OUTBREAK

The New York Times

(In the font and layout of *The New York Times*)

Smallpox Outbreak the First in 30 Years

Published: January 10, 2011

Smallpox, a disease that scientists once thought eliminated from nature, has reemerged in Cleveland, Ohio and is threatening to kill thousands and sicken hundreds of thousands of residents. Seven people have been hospitalized, including a 10 year old girl, with high fevers, red rashes, and severe headaches. Officials from the state department of health and the Centers for Disease Control have verified the diagnosis of smallpox.

Public health experts are seriously concerned about the spread of smallpox and point out that this strain of the disease is particularly virulent. Because smallpox is highly communicable through face to face contact and has a death rate of 30 percent, the CDC has placed the patients under quarantine in Cleveland Memorial Hospital. Two cases with similar symptoms were just confirmed in Pennsylvania and one in Florida, and officials are urgently trying to stop the spread of the disease.

Symptoms of smallpox usually begin within 12–14 days of exposure and consist of high fever, malaise, headache, and backache. Skin lesions on the face, forearms, hands, and feet, then appear. Victims are contagious with the onset of the fever, often before they realize they are ill. There is no treatment for smallpox.

It is unclear where the outbreak originated, but experts do not believe that smallpox is not being used as a weapon. However, the weaponization of smallpox and other viruses remains a concern among public health officials.

Now that several new cases of smallpox have been diagnosed, health officials and the state government are on alert to contain the threat. The patients, their immediate family, as well as health workers in direct contact will be vaccinated against smallpox with vaccines specifically shipped from the CDC headquarters in Atlanta.

Officials at the Food and Drug Administration are working hard to increase the production and supply of smallpox vaccines. Individuals born before 1972 and members of the military are currently the only Americans with immunity against smallpox. Under the provisions of a 2003 law named Project BioShield, the FDA is able to rapidly deploy medical defenses in a crisis.

Smallpox, which emerged more than 3,000 years ago, was one of the most devastating diseases known to humanity. In the 20th century alone, smallpox killed 300 million people, and left many others forever scarred, blind and wounded. The fight against smallpox began in 1959, with the WHO officially making the eradication of smallpox its goal. It was in May 1980 that the World Health Assembly certified the world free of naturally occurring smallpox and the war against smallpox was won.

Now, it appears that they were wrong.

Given the lethal nature of the disease, CDC officials urge individuals to stay cautious for smallpox symptoms and contact their doctors or local hospitals if they develop.

TREATMENT — PAST OUTBREAK

The New York Times

(In the font and layout of *The New York Times*)

Anniversary of Smallpox Outbreak

Published: January 10, 2011

This weekend marked the 25th anniversary of smallpox's reemergence in Cleveland, Ohio. Scientists thought the disease had been eliminated from nature. It threatened to kill thousands and sicken hundreds of thousands of residents. Seven people were hospitalized, including a 10 year old girl, with high fevers, red rashes, and severe headaches. Officials from the state department of health and the Centers for Disease Control verified the diagnosis of smallpox.

Public health experts were seriously concerned about the spread of smallpox and pointed out that this strain of the disease was particularly virulent. Because smallpox is highly communicable through face to face contact and has a death rate of 30 percent, the CDC placed the patients under quarantine in Cleveland. Two cases with similar symptoms were confirmed in Pennsylvania and one in Michigan, and officials worked urgently to stop the spread of the disease.

Symptoms of smallpox usually begin within 12–14 days of exposure and consist of high fever, malaise, headache, and backache. Skin lesions on the face, forearms, hands, and feet, then appear. Victims are contagious with the onset of the fever, often before they realize they are ill. There is no treatment for smallpox.

It is unclear where the outbreak originated, but experts did not believe that smallpox is being used as a weapon. However, the weaponization of smallpox and other viruses remains a concern among public health officials.

Once several new cases of smallpox were diagnosed, health officials and the state government were on alert to contain the threat. The patients, their immediate family, as well as health workers in direct contact were vaccinated against smallpox with vaccines specifically shipped from the CDC.

Officials at the CDC worked hard to increase the production and supply of smallpox vaccines. Individuals born before 1972 and members of the military were the only citizens with immunity against smallpox.

Smallpox, which emerged more than 3,000 years ago, was one of the most devastating diseases known to humanity. In the 20th century alone, smallpox killed 300 million people, and left many others forever scarred, blind and wounded. The fight against smallpox began in 1959, with the WHO officially making the eradication of smallpox its goal. It was in May 1980 that the World Health Assembly certified the world free of naturally occurring smallpox and the war against smallpox was won.

The 1986 outbreak in Ohio demonstrated that they were wrong.

Given the lethal nature of the disease, CDC officials urge individuals to stay cautious for smallpox symptoms and contact their doctors or local hospitals if they develop.

CLIMATE CHANGE PMR STUDY 2012

DATE: Summer 2012
   SAMPLE: 250 Adults, Pacific Market Research

ANXIETY MEASURE (no manipulation):

Are you at all worried about climate change? (No, not at all; Yes, a little; Yes, somewhat; Yes, a great deal).

CONTROL VARIABLES:

1. Partisanship:

Generally speaking, do you think of yourself as a Republican, a Democrat, an Independent, or what? (Democrat; Republican; Independent; Other)

(For Partisans): Would you consider yourself to be a strong (Democrat/ Republican) or a not strong (Democrat/Republican)?

(For Independents): If you identify as an independent, would you consider yourself to be closer to the Republican Party or closer to the Democratic Party? (Closer to the Republican Party; Closer to the Democratic Party; Closer to neither)

2. Trust in Scientists:

How much do you trust the things that scientists say about the environment? (Not at all; A moderate amount; A lot; Completely)

3. Felt Knowledge:

How much do you feel you know about climate change? (Nothing; A little; A moderate amount; A lot)

4. Knowledge Scale Questions:

For the following statements, just choose the option that comes closest to your opinion of how true it is . . .

a. Every time we use coal or oil or gas, we contribute to the greenhouse effect. How true is this? (Definitely true; Probably true; Probably not true; Definitely not true). (84% Correct)
b. The greenhouse effect is caused by a hole in the earth's atmosphere. How true is this? (Definitely true; Probably true; Probably not true; Definitely not true). (56% Correct)
c. To the best of your knowledge, what was the previous Bush administration's position on the Kyoto Protocol? (Supported it; Opposed it; Neither supported nor opposed it; Don't know) (18% Correct)

DEPENDENT VARIABLES:

1. How much do you support or oppose building more nuclear power plants? (strongly support, somewhat support, somewhat oppose, strongly oppose)
2. How much do you support eliminating all federal subsidies from all forms of energy production – including oil, gas, coal, nuclear, corn ethanol, solar, and wind.
3. How much do you support or oppose expanding offshore drilling for oil and natural gas off the U.S. coast?
4. How much do you support or oppose signing an international treaty that requires the United States to cut its emissions of carbon dioxide 90% by the year 2050?
5. How much do you support or oppose requiring electric utilities to produce at least 20% of their electricity from wind, solar, or other renewable energy sources, even if it cost the average household an extra $100 a year?
6. How much do you support or oppose regulating carbon dioxide (the primary greenhouse gas) as a pollutant?
7. How much do you support or oppose providing tax rebates for people who purchase energy efficient vehicles or solar panels?
8. How much do you support or oppose funding more research into renewable energy sources, such as solar and wind power?

TERRORISM YG/P STUDY 2006

DATE: Spring 2006

SAMPLE: 809 adults, Nationally representative sample from YouGov/Polimetrix

MANIPULATION: TV news story that varied in evocative imagery

a. Control condition – "India Inc.": Neutral story about Indian economy, neutral imagery
b. Treatment "Wave of Terror": Evocative terrorism news story, evocative imagery

DEPENDENT VARIABLES:

1. Civil liberties: In order to curb terrorism in this country, it is necessary for the average American to give up some civil liberties. (Strongly Agree, Agree, Neither agree nor disagree, Disagree, Strongly disagree)
2. Iraq: Taking everything into account, do you agree or disagree that the U.S. war in Iraq has been worth the cost. (Strongly Agree, Agree, Neither agree nor disagree, Disagree, Strongly disagree)

3. Militarism: Which of the following statements comes closer to your view: a. The best way to ensure peace is through military strength or b. Good diplomacy is the best way to ensure peace.

4. Spending preferences: Foreign aid, border security, homeland security, war on terrorism, and defense: "Should federal spending on foreign aid [homeland security, etc] be increased, decreased, or kept about the same?" (Increase, Keep the same, Decrease)

MODERATING VARIABLES:

1. Threat of terrorism (measured prior to the experimental treatment)– "How likely to you think it is that the U.S. will suffer an attack as serious as the one in New York and Washington some time in the next 12 months? Would you say very likely, somewhat likely, somewhat unlikely, or very unlikely?"

FULL TRANSCRIPT OF NEWS STORIES:
March 1, 2006 Wednesday
LENGTH: 537 words
HEADLINE: INDIA INC.;
ECONOMIC EXPLOSION
DIANE SAWYER (ABC NEWS)
(Off-camera) And one of the reasons, one of the goals, of course, is to cement the growing economic partnership between the U.S. and India. To make sure American companies get a piece of the action from India's stunning economic surge. India, now the world's second-fastest growing economy, after China. One billion people live in India, 300 million of them middle class. Tonight, we begin a special series on this seismic rumble half a world away. ABC's Jim Sciutto is in India.
JIM SCIUTTO (ABC NEWS)
(Voice-over) This is India booming. Western culture and technology coming East. Indian know-how going West, by high-speed connection. And it's not just call centers feeding the surge, but accountants in New Delhi preparing U.S. tax returns. Radiologists in Bangalore reading MRIs for doctors in Texas.
DOCTOR ARJUN KALYANPUR (RADIOLOGIST)
One occasion, he asked me, he said, "Just where are you, anyway?" And I said "I'm in Bangalore." And he said, "Bangor, Maine?" I said, "No, Bangalore, India." He said, "Get out of here."
JIM SCIUTTO (ABC NEWS)
(Voice-over) Today, more than half of Fortune 500 companies outsource some work to India, to an educated, English-speaking workforce, at a fraction of U.S. salaries.

SUHEL SETH (MARKETING EXECUTIVE)

I think what America and India have found in each other are enduring partners who can trust each other.

JIM SCIUTTO (ABC NEWS)

(Voice-over) U.S. exports to India have doubled in the last two years. And U.S. firms have become market leaders by adapting, such as McDonald's, which now sells vegetarian hamburgers here. Today, there are more middle-class Indians with buying power than the entire U.S. population.

JIM SCIUTTO (ABC NEWS)

(Off-camera) The challenge for India is spreading the new wealth from the cities to rural areas like this one, where nearly 80% of the population lives. It's coming, but slowly.

JIM SCIUTTO (ABC NEWS)

(Voice-over) In a village in northwest India, we found a new cleaners, a new private doctor. An old saying goes here, India seems to live in several centuries at once. But it's educating itself for the 21st. Vesting small town students with big-city career plans.

STUDENT (FEMALE)

Accountant.

STUDENT (MALE)

Doctor.

STUDENT (FEMALE)

I want to be a broadcast journalist.

JIM SCIUTTO (ABC NEWS)

(Voice-over) Like many Indians, Elangovan left a high-tech job in America for high-tech in India, and now lives in one of the many new gated communities that bring a touch of California to Calcutta.

ELANGOVAN KULANDAIVELU (IGATE CORPORATION SOFTWARE EXECUTIVE)

I think the same kind of opportunities that you would find in the U.S., you know, you could find very similar or even better opportunities out here in India.

JIM SCIUTTO (ABC NEWS)

(Voice-over) For some Americans, as well. India's rapidly-expanding airlines are now hiring out-of-work American pilots, outsourcing in reverse. The next step for an India on the move. Jim Sciutto, ABC News, Jakhauli, India.

THREATENING STORY — VARIATION IN VISUALS

WAVE OF TERROR (ABC News, July 25, 2005)

ELIZABETH VARGAS: (Off-camera) The investigations of London and Sharm el-Sheikh attacks are massive, involving intelligence agencies on four continents. As we said at the beginning of the broadcast, there is a real urgency. Intelligence officials are deeply worried that global terrorism has entered a dangerous, new phase. Here's ABC's Pierre Thomas.

PIERRE THOMAS, ABC NEWS : (Voice-over) U.S. officials say al Qaeda is evolving. Now relying on largely independent, regional groups to launch smaller-scale attacks designed to produce huge international aftershocks.

ROGER CRESSEY, TERRORISM EXPERT: The intelligence community believes there was a terrorist summit in 2004 in Pakistan, where targets were approved by the al-Qaeda leadership or people representing them.

JACK CLOONAN, ABC NEWS CONSULTANT: If you looked at this as bin Laden, as the chief executive, he has franchised a lot of this stuff out. And now, you have his acolytes around the world carrying out his mission statement.

PIERRE THOMAS: (Voice-over) Al Qaeda's mission statement has consistently called for attacks against the U.S. and its allies. April 8th, 2003, a month after the U.S. invaded Iraq, Osama bin Laden called on extremists to "get up and raise your weapons against America and Britain." Five months later, bin Laden warns, "we reserve to ourselves the right to respond against all the countries participating in this war, especially Britain, Spain." Six months later, Madrid was bombed. In February, al Qaeda number two in command, Ayman al Zawahiri, criticized Egyptian president Hosni Mubarak "and his gang" for pursuing a "policy of normalization with Israel." Five months later, an Egyptian resort was bombed,

Experts linking the recent bombings, are worried about the frequency of the attacks, one after another, and that the attacks appear to exploit specific political events. The 2004 Madrid train bombing came on the eve of the Spanish national elections. The July 7th London bombing coincided with the G-8 summit of western leaders. The Egyptian bombing came the same weekend as their independence day.

PIERRE THOMAS: (Off-camera) Tonight, intelligence officials around the world are sharing information, trying to figure out if this is only the beginning of a wave of attacks. Elizabeth?

CHAPTER 2

TABLE A2.1: *Anxious politics: Six pretests*

Name of Study	UW Immigration Article Pretest	Princeton Immigration Pretest	UT Immigration Pretest	Disease Pretest	Smallpox Article Pretest	Terrorism
Date	2006/2007	2007	2008	2011	2011	2005
Sample	20 University of Washington students	30 Princeton University students	60 University of Texas students	100 Mechanical Turk, Adults	210 Mechanical Turk, Adults	40 Princeton University students
DVs	Ratings of articles in TESS study in terms of valence and interest	Effect of bottom-up manipulation on beliefs about immigrants – cognition vs. emotion	Effect of bottom-up manipulation on anxiety, anger	Ratings of emotions after reading articles about plague, smallpox, E. coli	Ratings of emotions after reading articles about smallpox	Ratings of images to make sure that increased anxiety

TABLE A2.2: *Immigration MT Study 2011 manipulation check*

	Anxiety	Anger	Enthusiasm
Scary music	0.44	−0.36	−0.60
	(0.26)	(0.29)	(0.27)
Anger	0.51		−0.06
	(0.06)		(0.08)
Enthusiasm	0.26	−0.07	
	(0.07)	(0.08)	
Anxiety		0.61	0.29
		(0.07)	(0.08)
Constant	−0.20	2.99	1.51
	(0.33)	(0.28)	(0.33)
N	165	165	165
R^2	0.37	0.32	0.11

Source: Immigration MT Study 2011.
Model specification: OLS, coefficients in bold are significant at p<.10.
Scary music is an indicator for the treatment condition (0 = control condition, 1 = treatment condition). Anger, Anxiety, Enthusiasm range from 0 (do not feel emotion) to 8 (feel emotion very strongly).

CHAPTER 3

TABLE A3.1: *Bottom-up immigration manipulation – UT student sample pretest*

	Anxiety	Anger	Enthusiasm
Treatment	0.39	0.30	−0.33
	(0.23)	(0.28)	(0.25)
Constant	1.42	1.55	2.73
	(0.37)	(0.44)	(0.39)
Observations	60	60	60
R^2	0.05	0.02	0.03

Source: UT immigration pretest 2007.
Model specification: OLS, coefficients in bold are significant at p<.10, based on a two-tailed test. Treatment condition is an indicator that respondents were asked to list their worries about immigration (0 = control condition, 1 = worried condition). This is the same manipulation used in Immigration KN Study 2007.

TABLE A3.2: *Treatment condition does not affect beliefs about immigrants*

	Burden the U.S. Economy	Do Not Pay Fair Share of Taxes	Threaten Traditional Values and Customs	Take Jobs Americans Don't Want	Try to Learn English	Strengthen the U.S. Because of Talents
	Coef. (se)	Coef. (se)	Coef. (se)	Coef. (se).	Coef. (se)	Coef. (se).
Treatment	0.05 (0.43)	0.22 (0.35)	0.24 (0.45)	−0.63 (0.39)	0.39 (0.37)	−0.10 (0.30)
Constant	3.00 (0.33)	3.57 (0.27)	2.28 (0.34)	4.00 (0.30)	3.32 (0.28)	3.78 (0.23)
N	33	33	33	33	33	33

Source: UT immigration pretest 2007.
Model specification: OLS. Coefficients in bold are significant at $p<.05$, based on a two-tailed test. Treatment condition is an indicator that respondents were asked to list their worries about immigration (0 = control condition, 1 = worried condition).

TABLE A3.3: *Treatment condition increases number of worries and anxiety*

	Number of Worries	Anxiety	Anger
Treatment condition	**0.80** (0.16)	**0.54** (0.07)	0.11 (0.06)
PID	0.35 (0.28)	−0.01 (0.13)	0.14 (0.11)
Ideology	0.19 (0.43)	**0.40** (0.18)	0.12 (0.16)
Female	−0.12 (0.16)	−0.17 (0.07)	0.02 (0.07)
High school degree	−0.06 (0.28)	0.11 (0.13)	0.12 (0.16)
Some college	0.31 (0.29)	**0.25** (0.12)	−0.25 (0.16)
College graduate	0.20 (0.26)	**0.26** (0.12)	**−0.34** (0.16)
White	0.18 (0.43)	−0.02 (0.09)	0.05 (0.08)
Constant	0.63 (0.32)	0.16 (0.15)	0.38 (0.15)
N	384	384	384
R^2	0.11	0.22	0.09

Source: Immigration KN Study 2007.
Model specification: OLS. Coefficients in bold indicate $p<.05$, based on a two-tailed test. The treatment variable is 0 for respondents in the control condition and 1 for respondents in the treatment condition. Number of worries is a count of the number of unique worries mentioned by respondent in the open-ended manipulation (range 0–8). Anxiety and anger are the levels of emotion coded from open-ended responses (0 = none, 1 = some, 2 = extreme).

TABLE A3.4: *Summary of ANOVA results*

	n	F	p-value
Selective exposure			
Immigration stories proportion	327	4.58	0.03
Nonthreatening immigration stories proportion	327	0.79	0.38
Selective attention			
Proportion recalling an immigration story (among those who read an immigration story)	266	5.90	0.02
Proportion recalling a threatening story (among those who read a threatening story)	232	5.78	0.02
Proportion recalling a nonthreatening story, (among those who read a nonthreatening story)	200	0.43	0.51

Source: Immigration KN Study 2007.
Model specification: ANOVA. The dependent variables are proportions and vary from 0 to 1. The treatment variable is 0 for respondents in the control condition and 1 for respondents in the treatment condition.

TABLE A3.5: *Proportion of stories read: Mediation models (Baron and Kenney method)*

	All Immigration Stories		Threatening Immigration Stories		Nonthreatening Immigration Stories	
Treatment	−0.02	−0.04	0.02	−0.01	−0.03	−0.03
	(0.04)	(0.04)	(0.03)	(0.03)	(0.03)	(0.03)
Number of worries	0.05		0.04		0.01	
	(0.01)		(0.01)		(0.01)	
Anxiety		0.10		0.10		0.01
		(0.03)		(0.03)		(0.02)
Constant	0.50	0.52	0.26	0.25	0.25	0.26
	(0.03)	(0.03)	(0.03)	(0.02)	(.02)	(0.02)
N	384	384	384	384	384	384
R^2	0.04	0.04	0.04	0.05	0.01	0.01
Sobel test – Z-value	3.25	3.45	3.14	3.64	0.93	0.37
p-value	0.01	0.01	0.01	0.01	0.35	.71

Source: Immigration KN Study 2007.
Model specification: OLS. Coefficients in bold indicate $p<.05$, based on a two-tailed test. The dependent variables are proportions and vary from 0 to 1. The treatment variable is 0 for respondents in the control condition and 1 for respondents in the treatment condition. Number of worries is a count of the number of unique worries mentioned by respondent in the open-ended manipulation (range 0–8). Anxiety is the level of anxiety coded from open-ended responses (0 = none, 1 = some, 2 = extreme). Sobel tests for mediation calculated with sgmediation command in Stata.

TABLE A3.6: *Proportion of stories remembered: Mediation models (Baron and Kenney method)*

	All Immigration Stories		Threatening Immigration Stories		Nonthreatening Immigration Stories	
Treatment	0.04	0.04	0.08	0.06	−0.03	−0.03
	(0.04)	(0.04)	(0.04)	(0.04)	(0.04)	(0.04)
Number of immigration stories read	0.13	0.13	0.06	0.06	0.07	0.07
	(0.01)	(0.01)	(0.01)	(0.01)	(0.01)	(0.01)
Number of worries	0.05		0.03		0.01	
	(0.01)		(0.01)		(0.01)	
Anxiety		0.08		0.07		0.01
		(0.03)		(0.03)		(0.03)
Constant	0.22	0.23	0.14	0.14	0.08	0.09
	(0.04)	(0.04)	(0.04)	(0.04)	(0.03)	(0.03)
N	384	384	384	384	384	384
R^2	0.25	0.23	0.09	0.08	0.11	0.10
Sobel test – Z-value	2.73	2.23	2.15	2.01	0.92	0.26
p-value	0.01	0.03	0.03	0.04	0.36	0.79

Source: Immigration KN Study 2007.

Model specification: OLS. Coefficients in bold indicate p<.05, based on a two-tailed test. The dependent variables are proportions and vary from 0 to 1. The treatment variable is 0 for respondents in the control condition and 1 for respondents in the treatment condition. Number of worries is a count of the number of unique worries mentioned by respondent in the open-ended manipulation (range 0–8). Anxiety is the level of anxiety coded from open-ended responses (0 = none, 1 = some, 2 = extreme). Sobel tests for mediation calculated with sgmediation command in Stata.

TABLE A3.7: *Immigration anxiety increases exposure to threatening immigration news*
Proportion of Stories Read

	All Immigration Stories	Threatening Immigration Stories	Nonthreatening Immigration Stories	All Immigration Stories	Threatening Immigration Stories	Nonthreatening Immigration Stories
Treatment condition	−0.01 (0.04)	0.03 (0.04)	−0.04 (0.04)	−0.04 (0.05)	0.01 (0.03)	−0.04 (0.04)
Number of worries	0.06 (0.01)	0.04 (0.01)	0.01 (0.06)			
Anxiety				0.11 (0.03)	0.09 (0.03)	0.02 (0.02)
Anger				0.10 (0.03)	0.10 (0.04)	0.00 (0.03)
PID	−0.12 (0.08)	−0.11 (0.07)	−0.01 (0.06)	−0.11 (0.08)	−0.10 (0.07)	−0.01 (0.06)
Ideology	0.06 (0.12)	0.08 (0.10)	−0.02 (0.10)	0.02 (0.13)	0.04 (0.11)	−0.02 (0.10)
White	0.01 (0.06)	0.03 (0.05)	−0.02 (0.05)	0.02 (0.06)	0.04 (0.05)	−0.02 (0.05)
Female	−0.05 (0.04)	−0.02 (0.04)	−0.03 (0.04)	−0.04 (0.04)	−0.02 (0.04)	−0.03 (0.04)
High school degree	−0.17 (0.09)	−0.11 (0.08)	−0.06 (0.09)	−0.15 (0.09)	−0.10 (0.09)	−0.06 (0.09)
Some college	−0.04 (0.09)	0.00 (0.09)	−0.039 (0.10)	−0.03 (0.09)	0.01 (0.09)	−0.04 (0.10)
College graduate	−0.10 (0.09)	−0.12 (0.08)	0.02 (0.09)	−0.08 (0.09)	−0.10 (0.08)	0.02 (0.09)

(continued)

TABLE A3.7: (continued)

	All			All		
	Immigration Stories	Threatening Immigration Stories	Nonthreatening Immigration Stories	Immigration Stories	Threatening Immigration Stories	Nonthreatening Immigration Stories
Constant	0.63	0.31	0.32	0.61	0.28	0.32
	(0.10)	(0.09)	(0.10)	(0.10)	(0.09)	(0.10)
N	384	384	384	384	384	384
R²	0.08	0.09	0.02	0.07	0.08	0.01
	Mediation by Anxiety				**Mediation by Anxiety**	
Mediation effect	0.04	0.03	0.01	0.06	0.05	0.01
95% CI	[0.02, 0.08]	[0.01, 0.07]	[−0.01, 0.03]	[0.02, 0.10]	[0.02, 0.09]	[−0.02, 0.04]
Direct effect	−0.01	0.04	−0.04	−0.03	0.01	−0.04
	[−0.10, 0.08]	[−0.05, 0.12]	[−0.12, 0.04]	[−0.13, 0.06]	[−0.08, 0.09]	[−0.12, 0.05]
Total effect	0.04	0.07	−0.03	0.03	0.06	−0.03
	[−0.08, 0.15]	[−0.03, 0.17]	[−0.11, 0.05]	[−0.10, 0.14]	[−0.04, 0.16]	[−0.12, 0.05]
				Mediation by Anger		
Mediation effect				0.01	0.01	0.00
95% CI				[−0.00, 0.03]	[−0.01, 0.03]	[−0.01, 0.01]
Direct effect				−0.03	0.01	−0.04
				[−0.14, 0.07]	[−0.08, 0.09]	[−0.12, 0.04]
Total effect				−0.03	0.02	−0.04
				[−0.15, 0.09]	[−0.09, 0.11]	[−0.12, 0.03]

Source: Immigration KN Study 2007.
Model specification: OLS with mediation effect calculated using algorithm in Imai, Keele, and Tingley (2010). Coefficients in bold indicate p<.05, based on a two-tailed test. The dependent variables are the proportion of all stories read that were about immigration, the proportion of all stories read that were threatening about immigration, and the proportion of all stories read that were nonthreatening about immigration. If a respondent did not read any stories, they are set to 0. The mediating coefficients for anger and anxiety come from separate models.

TABLE A3.8: *Anxiety increases agreement with threatening news*

	Argue Threatening vs. No Engagement	Agree Threatening vs. No Engagement	Argue Nonthreatening vs. No Engagement	Agree Nonthreatening vs. No Engagement
Treatment condition	0.42 (0.47)	0.57 (0.26)	−0.42 (0.46)	−0.53 (0.35)
Number of (non) threatening stories read	1.34 (0.35)	1.10 (0.17)	1.95 (0.40)	1.66 (0.26)
PID	0.79 (0.92)	0.39 (0.49)	2.83 (1.01)	0.87 (0.72)
Ideology	−0.79 (1.22)	0.95 (0.72)	−1.50 (1.34)	−1.81 (0.98)
White	−0.65 (0.56)	0.03 (0.37)	−0.57 (0.60)	−0.73 (0.43)
Female	−0.66 (0.50)	0.09 (0.26)	0.03 (0.47)	0.84 (0.36)
High school	12.36 (447.06)	0.02 (0.51)	0.12 (1.34)	1.04 (0.91)
Some college	12.50 (447.06)	−0.02 (0.49)	1.55 (1.19)	1.01 (0.89)
College graduate	12.98 (447.06)	−0.61 (0.48)	1.31 (1.16)	0.56 (0.87)
Constant	−15.56 (447.06)	−2.98 (0.67)	−5.95 (1.56)	−3.26 (1.03)
N	383	383	378	378
R^2	0.16	0.16	0.26	0.26

Source: Immigration KN Study 2007.

Model specification: Multinomial logit. Coefficients in bold indicate $p<.05$, based on a two-tailed test. Dependent variables indicate respondents' engagement with the stories: 0 (did not mention, neither agree nor disagree), 1 (agree with threatening [nonthreatening] story, no disagreement), 2 (argue with threatening [nonthreatening] story, no agreement). Respondents who both agreed and disagreed with stories were excluded (N = 7). The treatment variable is 0 for respondents in the control condition and 1 for respondents in the treatment condition. Number of relevant stories read is a count of how many threatening or nonthreatening stories respondent read during the information search.

TABLE A3.9: *Engagement with immigration stories – Alternative model*

	Argue Threatening	Agree Threatening	Argue Nonthreatening	Agree Nonthreatening
	Coef. (s.e.)	Coef. (s.e.)	Coef. (s.e.)	Coef. (s.e.)
Treatment	0.22 (0.52)	**0.75** (0.31)	−0.46 (0.43)	0.14 (0.36)
Number of relevant stories read	0.00 (0.57)	**−0.63** (0.31)	0.84 (0.48)	0.57 (0.38)
Constant	−4.09 (1.03)	0.41 (0.55)	−2.94 (0.80)	−2.06 (0.69)
N	232	232	200	200
Pseudo-R^2	0.03	0.04	0.03	0.01

Source: Immigration KN Study 2007.
Model specification: Logit. Coefficients in bold indicate $p<.05$, based on a two-tailed test.
Dependent variables indicate respondents' engagement with the stories: 0 (did not agree/
disagree), 1 (agree with (non)threatening story). The treatment variable is 0 for respondents
in the control condition and 1 for respondents in the treatment condition. Number of
relevant stories read is a count of how many threatening or nonthreatening stories
respondent read during the information search. Only respondents who read at least one
threatening story are included in the threatening model (N = 232) and only respondents who
read at least one nonthreatening story are included in the nonthreatening model (N = 200).

TABLE A3.10: *Immigration anxiety increases memory for threatening stories*
Proportion of Stories Remembered

	All Immigration Stories	Threatening Immigration Stories	Nonthreatening Immigration Stories	All Immigration Stories	Threatening Immigration Stories	Nonthreatening Immigration Stories
Treatment condition	0.07 (0.05)	0.08 (0.05)	0.00 (0.04)	0.07 (0.05)	0.05 (0.05)	0.01 (0.04)
Number of worries	**0.04** (0.02)	**0.04** (0.02)	0.00 (0.01)			
Anxiety				0.04 (0.04)	0.08 (0.04)	-0.03 (0.03)
Anger				0.09 (0.05)	0.08 (0.05)	0.00 (0.04)
PID	**-0.19** (0.08)	-0.11 (0.08)	-0.08 (0.07)	-0.19 (0.08)	-0.11 (0.08)	-0.08 (0.08)
Ideology	0.22 (0.13)	0.11 (0.12)	0.11 (0.11)	0.20 (0.13)	0.08 (0.12)	0.13 (0.11)
White	-0.03 (0.07)	0.06 (0.06)	-0.09 (0.06)	-0.03 (0.07)	0.06 (0.07)	-0.09 (0.06)
Female	-0.01 (0.05)	-0.02 (0.05)	0.01 (0.04)	-0.01 (0.05)	-0.01 (0.05)	0.00 (0.04)
High school degree	0.10 (0.09)	0.12 (0.09)	-0.03 (0.06)	0.12 (0.10)	0.14 (0.09)	-0.02 (0.07)
Some college	**0.21** (0.09)	0.14 (0.08)	0.06 (0.07)	**0.23** (0.10)	0.16 (0.09)	0.07 (0.07)
College graduate	0.13 (0.09)	-0.02 (0.07)	0.14 (0.07)	0.15 (0.09)	0.00 (0.08)	**0.15** (0.08)
Number of immigration stories read	**0.13** (0.01)	0.05 (0.02)	0.07 (0.01)	0.13 (0.01)	0.05 (0.02)	0.07 (0.01)

(continued)

TABLE A3.10: (continued)

	All Immigration Stories	Threatening Immigration Stories	Nonthreatening Immigration Stories	All Immigration Stories	Threatening Immigration Stories	Nonthreatening Immigration Stories
Constant	0.90 (0.10)	0.03 (0.09)	0.06 (0.09)	0.08 (0.11)	0.14 (0.05)	0.06 (0.08)
N	384	384	384	384	384	384
R^2	0.26	0.12	0.15	0.26	0.13	0.15
Mediation by Anxiety						
Mediation effect	0.03	0.03	0.00	0.03	0.04	-0.02
95% CI	[0.00, 0.07]	[0.00, 0.07]	[-0.03, 0.02]	[-0.01, 0.07]	[0.00, 0.09]	[-0.06, 0.02]
Direct effect	0.08	0.08	-0.01	0.06	0.06	0.02
	[-0.03, 0.18]	[-0.03, 0.18]	[-0.09, 0.08]	[-0.06, 0.16]	[-0.06, 0.16]	[-0.09, 0.09]
Total effect	0.11	0.11	0.00	0.09	0.10	0.00
	[-0.01, 0.23]	[-0.01, 0.24]	[-0.09, 0.09]	[-0.04, 0.21]	[-0.03, 0.23]	[-0.10, 0.09]
Mediation by Anger						
Mediation effect				0.01	0.01	0.00
95% CI				[-0.01, 0.04]	[-0.01, 0.04]	[-0.01, 0.01]
Direct effect				0.08	0.06	0.02
				[-0.03, 0.18]	[-0.05, 0.17]	[-0.07, 0.10]
Total effect				0.09	0.08	0.02
				[-0.03, 0.20]	[-0.05, 0.19]	[-0.07, 0.10]

Source: Immigration KN Study 2007.
Model specification: OLS with mediation effect calculated using algorithm in Imai, Keele, and Tingley (2010). Coefficients in bold indicate $p<.05$, based on a two-tailed test. The dependent variables are the proportion of all stories recalled that are about immigration, the proportion of all stories that are threatening, and the proportion of all stories that are nonthreatening. If a respondent did not read any stories or did not remember any stories, they are set to 0. The mediating coefficients for anger and anxiety come from separate models.

TABLE A3.11: *Immigration anxiety treatment affects Democrats and Republicans identically*

	Anxiety		Anxiety
Treatment	0.50	Treatment	0.58
	(0.10)		(0.11)
Democrat	0.11	Republican	−0.11
	(0.10)		(0.10)
Treatment * Democrat	0.07	Treatment * Republican	−0.07
	(0.14)		(0.01)
Constant	0.57	Constant	0.68
	(0.06)		(0.08)
N	359	N	359
R^2	0.15	R^2	0.15

Source: Immigration KN Study 2007.
Model specification: OLS. Coefficients in bold are significant at p<.05 based on a two-tailed test. Dependent variable is respondents' level of anxiety measured from 0 (not at all anxious) to 1 (very anxious). Models are weighted with post-stratification weights provided by KN.

CHAPTER 4

TABLE A4.1: *Smallpox anxiety increases trust in public health experts*

	IRS	Fed Reserve Chair	Oprah	DHS	Obama	Websites	Surgeon General (Political Framing)
Smallpox–present	-0.04 (0.03)	-0.03 (0.03)	-0.08 (0.04)	-0.06 (0.04)	0.00 (0.04)	-0.04 (0.04)	0.11 (0.09)
Smallpox–past	-0.08 (0.03)	-0.08 (0.03)	-0.09 (0.04)	-0.10 (0.04)	-0.03 (0.04)	-0.05 (0.03)	0.01 (0.08)
Anxious	0.16 (0.05)	0.10 (0.05)	0.21 (0.06)	0.30 (0.05)	0.13 (0.05)	0.19 (0.06)	-0.01 (0.12)
Angry	-0.02 (0.05)	0.07 (0.06)	-0.06 (0.06)	-0.07 (0.06)	-0.14 (0.05)	-0.02 (0.05)	-0.09 (0.12)
White	0.02 (0.03)	0.03 (0.04)	-0.01 (0.06)	0.13 (0.05)	0.06 (0.04)	0.01 (0.05)	-0.17 (0.15)
Black	0.22 (0.05)	0.16 (0.05)	0.16 (0.08)	0.22 (0.06)	0.32 (0.05)	-0.03 (0.06)	-0.11 (0.18)
Latino	0.05 (0.05)	0.04 (0.05)	0.01 (0.08)	0.20 (0.06)	0.14 (0.06)	0.09 (0.06)	-0.23 (0.16)
Female	0.02 (0.02)	0.09 (0.02)	0.09 (0.03)	0.06 (0.03)	0.04 (0.03)	0.04 (0.03)	-0.05 (0.07)
PID	0.02 (0.05)	0.02 (0.05)	-0.23 (0.06)	-0.06 (0.06)	-0.45 (0.06)	-0.05 (0.05)	-0.32 (0.13)
Ideology	-0.06 (0.06)	-0.07 (0.07)	-0.09 (0.08)	-0.07 (0.07)	-0.37 (0.07)	-0.02 (0.07)	-0.17 (0.16)
Health status	-0.05 (0.04)	-0.05 (0.05)	-0.02 (0.06)	0.08 (0.05)	0.12 (0.05)	0.05 (0.05)	0.18 (0.11)

(continued)

Age	-0.00	-0.00	0.00	-0.00	0.00	-0.00	0.00
	(0.00)	(0.00)	(0.00)	(0.00)	(0.00)	(0.00)	(0.00)
News interest	-0.06	-0.09	-0.13	-0.04	0.08	0.07	0.07
	(0.05)	(0.05)	(0.06)	(0.06)	(0.06)	(0.05)	(0.13)
Education	-0.01	-0.00	0.00	-0.00	0.01	0.01	0.04
	(0.01)	(0.01)	(0.01)	(0.01)	(0.01)	(0.01)	(0.02)
Constant	0.27	0.29	0.41	0.31	0.53	0.52	0.34
	(0.07)	(0.07)	(0.10)	(0.09)	(0.09)	(0.08)	(0.21)
Observations	554	551	555	551	553	552	183
R²	0.17	0.17	0.22	0.18	0.52	0.08	0.19
Anxiety mediation effect	**0.06**	0.03	**0.07**	**0.11**	**0.05**	**0.07**	-0.01
95% CI	[0.02, 0.09]	[-0.01, 0.07]	[0.03, 0.11]	[0.06, .014]	[0.01, 0.08]	[0.03, 0.10]	[-0.11, 0.09]
Direct effect	-0.04	-0.03	-0.08	-0.06	0.00	-0.04	0.12
	[-0.10, 0.03]	[-0.10, 0.04]	[-0.18, 0.01]	[-0.15, 0.03]	[-0.08, 0.09]	[-0.13, 0.05]	[-0.08, 0.32]
Total effect	0.02	0.00	-0.01	0.05	0.05	0.03	0.12
	[-0.06, 0.09]	[-0.08, 0.08]	[-0.11, 0.10]	[-0.06, 0.15]	[-0.04, 0.14]	[-0.07, 0.13]	[-0.08, 0.36]

Source: Public Health Smallpox YG/P Study 2011.

Model specification: OLS with mediation effect calculated using algorithm in Imai, Keele, and Tingley (2010).Coefficients in bold indicate p<.05, based on a two-tailed test. Dependent variables indicate how much respondents trust each actor from "not at all" (0) to "very much" (1). Models are weighted with post-stratification weights provided by YG/P.

	HHS	FDA	AMA	CDC	Friends and Family in the Medical Field	Personal Doctor	Surgeon General (Expert Framing)
Smallpox–present	-0.02	-0.00	-0.01	0.01	0.02	-0.00	-0.02
	(0.04)	(0.04)	(0.04)	(0.04)	(0.03)	(0.03)	(0.07)
Smallpox–past	-0.03	-0.04	-0.03	0.00	-0.02	-0.03	-0.00
	(0.03)	(0.04)	(0.03)	(0.03)	(0.03)	(0.03)	(0.06)
Anxious	**0.26**	**0.15**	**0.14**	**0.16**	0.07	0.06	**0.19**
	(0.05)	(0.06)	(0.04)	(0.05)	(0.04)	(0.04)	(0.09)
Angry	-0.19	-0.09	-0.18	-0.13	-0.06	-0.03	-0.20
	(0.05)	(0.06)	(0.05)	(0.05)	(0.05)	(0.04)	(0.09)
White	0.03	0.08	0.08	0.04	-0.02	-0.05	0.13
	(0.05)	(0.05)	(0.05)	(0.04)	(0.04)	(0.03)	(0.08)
Black	0.05	**0.15**	0.05	0.03	-0.07	-0.07	**0.23**
	(0.06)	(0.06)	(0.06)	(0.05)	(0.05)	(0.04)	(0.11)
Latino	0.05	0.10	**0.14**	0.03	-0.05	-0.00	0.16
	(0.06)	(0.06)	(0.05)	(0.05)	(0.05)	(0.04)	(0.11)
Female	**0.06**	**0.06**	**0.11**	**0.08**	0.05	0.04	**0.11**
	(0.03)	(0.03)	(0.03)	(0.03)	(0.02)	(0.02)	(0.05)
PID	-0.11	-0.12	-0.11	-0.15	-0.03	0.01	**-0.42**
	(0.05)	(0.06)	(0.05)	(0.05)	(0.04)	(0.04)	(0.08)
Ideology	-0.26	-0.12	-0.06	-0.13	0.02	-0.02	-0.14
	(0.07)	(0.07)	(0.07)	(0.07)	(0.06)	(0.05)	(0.11)
Health status	0.13	0.04	0.09	0.05	0.04	0.07	0.04
	(0.05)	(0.05)	(0.05)	(0.05)	(0.04)	(0.05)	(0.09)
Age	-0.00	0.00	0.00	0.00	0.00	0.00	0.00
	(0.00)	(0.00)	(0.00)	(0.00)	(0.00)	(0.00)	(0.00)
News interest	-0.10	-0.02	0.01	0.03	**0.10**	**0.15**	**0.19**
	(0.05)	(0.06)	(0.05)	(0.05)	(0.05)	(0.05)	(0.09)

(continued)

Education	0.01	0.01	0.01	0.02	-0.00	-0.00	0.02
	(0.01)	(0.01)	(0.01)	(0.01)	(0.01)	(0.01)	(0.02)
Constant	0.73	0.44	0.55	0.66	0.69	0.64	0.08
	(0.09)	(0.09)	(0.09)	(0.08)	(0.07)	(0.07)	(0.16)
N	554	553	554	551	553	553	370
R²	0.24	0.11	0.13	0.18	0.04	0.09	0.23
Anxiety mediation effect	0.09	0.05	0.05	0.06	0.02	0.02	0.07
95% CI	[0.06, 0.13]	[0.01, 0.09]	[0.02, 0.08]	[0.02, 0.08]	[-0.01, 0.05]	[0.02, 0.05]	[-0.01, 0.14]
Direct effect	-0.02	-0.01	0.04	0.01	0.03	0.00	-0.01
	[-0.10, 0.06]	[-0.09, 0.07]	[-0.06, 0.15]	[-0.07, 0.09]	[-0.04, 0.09]	[-0.05, 0.05]	[-0.16, 0.13]
Total effect	0.08	0.04	0.07	0.07	0.05	0.02	0.06
	[-0.02, 0.17]	[-0.04, 0.12]	[-0.04, 0.19]	[-0.02, 0.15]	[-0.02, 0.12]	[-0.04, 0.08]	[-0.11, 0.24]

Source: Public Health Smallpox YG/P Study 2011.

Model specification: OLS with mediation effect calculated using algorithm in Imai, Keele, and Tingley (2010). Coefficients in bold indicate p<.05, based on a two-tailed test. Dependent variables indicate how much respondents trust each actor from "not at all" (0) to "very much" (1). Models are weighted with post-stratification weights provided by YG/P.

CHAPTER 5

TABLE A5.1: *Smallpox anxiety decreases support for civil liberties (full controls)*

	Offer Services	Require Vaccine	Require Exam	Isolation	Quarantine	Destroy Property
Smallpox–present	0.03	0.32	0.30	0.31	0.36	0.10
	(0.12)	(0.14)	(0.14)	(0.13)	(0.12)	(0.13)
Smallpox–past	0.06	−0.03	−0.06	0.25	0.34	−0.10
	(0.12)	(0.14)	(0.14)	(0.13)	(0.13)	(0.13)
PID	−0.64	−0.55	−0.42	−0.42	−0.38	−0.56
	(0.17)	(0.20)	(0.21)	(0.20)	(0.18)	(0.19)
Ideology	−0.51	0.14	−0.11	0.04	0.01	−0.14
	(0.22)	(0.28)	(0.29)	(0.27)	(0.24)	(0.25)
Female	0.14	0.02	0.04	0.22	0.04	0.06
	(0.10)	(0.13)	(0.13)	(0.12)	(0.11)	(0.12)
Age	−0.00	0.01	0.01	0.01	0.00	0.01
	(0.00)	(0.01)	(0.01)	(0.00)	(0.00)	(0.00)
Student	−0.03	0.25	0.40	0.33	0.13	−0.14
	(0.14)	(0.17)	(0.18)	(0.16)	(0.15)	(0.17)
College graduate	0.08	0.25	0.21	0.31	0.13	0.13
	(0.10)	(0.14)	(0.14)	(0.13)	(0.12)	(0.13)
Voter registration	0.10	0.06	−0.35	0.20	0.12	0.07
	(0.17)	(0.20)	(0.22)	(0.20)	(0.19)	(0.21)
Employed	0.05	−0.03	−0.04	−0.12	−0.15	−0.17
	(0.10)	(0.13)	(0.13)	(0.12)	(0.11)	(0.11)
Black	−0.11	−0.20	0.00	−0.25	0.15	0.25
	(0.16)	(0.18)	(0.20)	(0.21)	(0.18)	(0.17)

(continued)

	(1)	(2)	(3)	(4)	(5)	(6)
Latino	-0.08	0.19	0.09	0.34	0.14	0.26
	(0.15)	(0.19)	(0.19)	(0.18)	(0.18)	(0.18)
Asian	-0.08	-0.16	-0.26	-0.31	**-0.65**	-0.07
	(0.29)	(0.41)	(0.26)	(0.35)	(0.29)	(0.35)
Other race	-0.13	-0.45	0.18	-0.19	**-0.48**	-0.44
	(0.26)	(0.29)	(0.30)	(0.26)	(0.24)	(0.26)
Christian	-0.05	-0.09	-0.14	-0.13	-0.29	0.02
	(0.20)	(0.24)	(0.23)	(0.20)	(0.20)	(0.22)
Jewish	0.31	0.20	-0.03	-0.15	-0.32	0.05
	(0.25)	(0.46)	(0.50)	(0.46)	(0.42)	(0.40)
Muslim	**-1.78**	-0.61	-1.35	-0.26	0.85	-0.98
	(0.89)	(0.99)	(0.72)	(1.06)	(0.36)	(1.13)
No religion	-0.08	-0.21	-0.40	-0.37	**-0.47**	-0.13
	(0.21)	(0.24)	(0.23)	(0.21)	(0.21)	(0.23)
Born-again Christian	-0.06	-0.17	-0.11	**-0.27**	-0.18	-0.18
	(0.13)	(0.15)	(0.15)	(0.14)	(0.14)	(0.15)
Religion is important	-0.16	-0.14	0.08	0.08	-0.34	0.14
	(0.19)	(0.23)	(0.22)	(0.22)	(0.22)	(0.22)
Frequency of prayer	-0.07	-0.20	-0.31	-0.35	-0.21	0.06
	(0.19)	(0.23)	(0.21)	(0.21)	(0.21)	(0.22)
News interest	**-0.36**	**-0.36**	-0.15	0.10	-0.17	0.06
	(0.18)	(0.24)	(0.24)	(0.23)	(0.21)	(0.23)
Health status	-0.33	0.01	0.10	0.18	0.30	-0.16
	(0.21)	(0.24)	(0.26)	(0.24)	(0.23)	(0.23)
Constant	5.03	3.11	3.30	2.40	3.73	3.28
	(0.39)	(0.46)	(0.48)	(0.43)	(0.40)	(0.46)
Observations	592	590	591	595	594	592
R^2	0.15	0.08	0.07	0.09	0.11	0.09

Source: Public Health Smallpox YG/P Study 2011.

Model specification: OLS. Coefficients in bold are significant at $p<.05$, based on a two-tailed test. Constant represents the average support for policies in the control condition. Treatment conditions are dichotomous variables for the assigned treatment condition. Dependent variables vary from 1 (strongly oppose) to 5 (strongly support). Models are weighted with post-stratification weights provided by YG/P. All variables are rescaled to vary between 0 and 1.

TABLE A5.2: *Present smallpox condition increases anxiety*

	Anxiety
Smallpox–present treatment	**0.35**
	(0.03)
Smallpox–past treatment	**0.18**
	(0.03)
N	551
R^2	0.30

Source: Public Health Smallpox YG/P Study 2011.
Model specification: OLS. Coefficients in bold are significant at $p<.05$, based on a two-tailed test. Dependent variable is respondents' level of anxiety measured from 0 (not at all anxious) to 1 (very anxious).

TABLE A5.3: *Present outbreak condition increases support for civil liberties restrictions through increasing anxiety*

	Offer Services	Require Vaccine	Require Exam	Isolation	Quarantine	Destroy Property
Smallpox–present	-0.10	-0.06	-0.09	-0.02	0.15	-0.27
	(0.13)	(0.16)	(0.17)	(0.16)	(0.15)	(0.15)
Smallpox–past	-0.16	**-0.31**	**-0.29**	0.03	0.15	**-0.38**
	(0.13)	(0.15)	(0.14)	(0.15)	(0.14)	(0.14)
Anxious	**0.67**	**0.79**	**1.10**	**0.88**	**0.80**	**0.84**
	(0.19)	(0.23)	(0.22)	(0.21)	(0.20)	(0.21)
Angry	-0.21	0.28	0.26	-0.03	-0.13	0.19
	(0.19)	(0.23)	(0.23)	(0.15)	(0.20)	(0.21)
Constant	3.89	2.84	2.63	2.87	3.15	3.15
	(0.09)	(0.11)	(0.10)	(0.10)	(0.10)	(0.10)
N	551	551	551	553	553	550
R^2	0.03	0.06	0.09	0.05	0.05	0.06
Anxiety mediation effect	**0.24**	**0.28**	**0.39**	**0.32**	**0.29**	**0.30**
95% CI	[0.09, 0.39]	[0.11, 0.45]	[0.22, 0.57]	[0.15, 0.47]	[0.13, 0.44]	[0.14, 0.46]
Direct effect	-0.10	-0.05	-0.09	-0.01	0.16	-0.26
	[-0.38, 0.18]	[-0.41, 0.30]	[-0.45, 0.26]	[-0.35, 0.31]	[-0.17, 0.48]	[-0.59, 0.05]
Total effect	0.14	0.23	0.30	0.30	**0.45**	0.04
	[-0.24, 0.49]	[-0.24, 0.65]	[-0.19, 0.75]	[-0.14, 0.70]	[0.01, 0.84]	[-0.40, 0.43]

Source: Public Health Smallpox YG/P Study 2011.
Model specification: OLS with mediation effect calculated using algorithm in Imai, Keele, and Tingley (2010). Dependent variables vary from 1 (strongly oppose) to 5 (strongly support). Coefficients in bold are significant at p<.05, based on a two-tailed test. All models are weighted with post-stratification weights provide by YG/P.

TABLE A5.4: *Anxiety increases support for civil liberties restrictions*

	Offer Services	Require Vaccine	Require Exam	Isolation	Quarantine	Destroy Property
Low anxiety (N = 293)	3.91	2.81	2.65	2.96	3.29	3.04
High anxiety (N = 306)	4.01	3.26	3.21	3.36	3.69	3.51
% increase	2.56	16.15	21.13	13.47	12.12	15.48
t	1.00	3.93	4.83	3.55	3.73	4.32
p	0.32	0.01	0.01	0.01	0.01	0.01

Source: Public Health Smallpox YG/P 2001.
Cells are the mean preference by category. Anxiety scores split on mean. Dependent variables vary from 1 (strongly oppose) to 5 (strongly support). Models weighted with post-stratification weights provided by YG/P.

TABLE A5.5: *Terrorism news increases support for protective policies through anxiety*

	Militarism	Homeland Security Spending	Defense Spending	Border Security Spending	Necessary to Sacrifice Civil Liberties	Iraq War Worth the Cost
Terrorism news	0.14	0.04	0.07	-0.06	-0.04	0.01
	(0.15)	(0.06)	(0.06)	(0.05)	(0.03)	(0.02)
Anxiety	**0.61**	**0.47**	**0.28**	**0.19**	**0.08**	0.05
	(0.26)	(0.10)	(0.10)	(0.09)	(0.04)	(0.04)
Threat perception (pre-test)	**1.52**	**0.59**	**0.78**	**0.25**	**0.30**	**0.22**
	(0.26)	(0.12)	(0.11)	(0.08)	(0.05)	(0.04)
PID	**0.24**	**0.07**	**0.14**	**0.03**	**0.03**	**0.08**
	(0.05)	(0.02)	(0.02)	(0.01)	(0.01)	(0.01)
Ideology	**2.12**	0.24	**0.50**	**0.85**	**0.30**	**0.24**
	(0.34)	(0.16)	(0.14)	(0.10)	(0.06)	(0.060)
Constant	-3.00	-0.57	-1.18	-0.11	-0.05	-0.28
	(0.26)	(0.09)	(0.07)	(0.06)	(0.03)	(0.03)
N	672	795	791	800	802	802
R²	0.37	0.19	0.36	0.21	0.28	0.42
Anxiety Mediation effect	0.01	0.05	0.03	0.02	0.01	0.01
95% CI	[0.00, 0.03]	[0.02, 0.09]	[0.01, 0.06]	[0.00, 0.05]	[-0.00, 0.02]	[-0.00, 0.02]
Direct effect	0.04	0.04	0.07	-0.06	-0.04	0.01
	[-0.04, 0.03]	[-0.09, 0.17]	[-0.05, 0.19]	[-0.16, 0.05]	[-0.09, 0.02]	[-0.04, 0.06]
Total effect	0.05	0.10	0.11	-0.03	-0.03	0.01
	[-.004, 0.14]	[-0.06, 0.27]	[-0.03, 0.25]	[-0.16, 0.09]	[-0.09, 0.03]	[-0.04, 0.07]
	Probit	OLS	OLS	OLS	OLS	OLS

Source: Terrorism YG/P Study 2006.

Model specification: OLS with mediation effect calculated using algorithm in Imai, Keele, and Tingley (2010). Coefficients in bold indicate p<.05, based on a two-tailed test. Dependent variables of militarism, civil liberties, and Iraq vary from 0 to 1 with higher values indicating support for more hawkish/protective policy. Dependent variables of spending on homeland security, defense, and border security vary from -1 (spend less) to 1 (spend more). All models are weighted with post-stratification weights provided by KN.

TABLE A5.6: *Immigration anxiety increase support for restrictions*

	Entitlements	Humanitarianism	Border Security
Treatment condition	**−0.11**	**−0.08**	**−0.10**
	(0.03)	(0.04)	(0.04)
Anxiety	**0.06**	**0.05**	**0.06**
	(0.02)	(0.03)	(0.02)
Anger	**0.07**	**0.15**	**0.04**
	(0.02)	(0.03)	(0.02)
PID	0.03	0.07	0.02
	(0.05)	(0.08)	(0.06)
Ideology	**0.25**	**0.15**	**0.18**
	(0.08)	(0.11)	(0.10)
White	**0.10**	**0.09**	**0.12**
	(0.04)	(0.05)	(0.05)
Female	−0.01	−0.02	0.01
	(0.03)	(0.04)	(0.04)
High school degree	0.03	0.02	−0.11
	(0.05)	(0.06)	(0.06)
Some college	−0.00	−0.02	**−0.12**
	(0.05)	(0.07)	(0.05)
College graduate	**−0.08**	**−0.17**	**−0.21**
	(0.05)	(0.06)	(0.05)
Constant	**0.59**	**0.36**	**0.76**
	(0.06)	(0.08)	(0.07)
N	377	377	373
R²	0.24	0.21	0.14
Mediation by Anxiety			
Mediation effect	**0.03**	**0.03**	**0.03**
95% CI	[0.01, 0.06]	[−0.00, 0.06]	[0.01, 0.06]
Direct effect	−0.11	−0.08	−0.10
	[−0.18, 0.04]	[−0.17, 0.01]	[−0.18, −0.02]
Total effect	−0.07	−0.05	−0.07
	[−0.15, 0.01]	[−0.15, 0.06]	[−0.16, 0.02]
Mediation by Anger			
Mediation effect	0.01	0.02	0.00
95% CI	[−0.00, 0.02]	[−0.00, 0.04]	[−0.00, 0.02]
Direct effect	−0.11	−0.08	−0.10
	[−0.18, 0.04]	[−0.17, 0.01]	[−0.18, −0.02]
Total effect	−0.10	−0.06	−0.10
	[−0.18, −0.02]	[−0.17, 0.04]	[−0.18, −0.02]

Source: Immigration KN Study 2007.
Model specification: OLS with mediation effect calculated using algorithm in Imai, Keele, and Tingley (2010).Coefficients in bold indicate p<.05, based on a two-tailed test. Dependent variables vary from 0 to 1 with higher values indicating that immigrants should not be eligible for services and increase border security spending. All models are weighted with post-stratification weights provided by KN.

TABLE A5.7: *Threatening music lowers support for immigration policy among Republicans/Independents*

	Entitlements		Humanitarianism	
	Republicans/Inds	Democrats	Republicans/Inds	Democrats
Scary music	0.11	0.08	0.11	0.05
	(0.05)	(0.11)	(0.07)	(0.07)
Constant	0.81	0.64	0.48	0.27
	(0.04)	(0.49)	(0.04)	(0.05)
N	76	89	76	89
R^2	0.05	0.02	0.03	0.01
Wald test of difference in coefficient				
χ^2	6.92		3.18	
P	0.03		0.20	

Source: Immigration Study MT 2011.
Model specification: OLS. Coefficients in bold are significant at p<.05, based on a two-tailed test. Dependent variable ranges from 0 to 1 with higher values indicating that immigrants should not be eligible for services. Wald tests are calculated after estimating a simultaneous equations model of the effect of the scary music condition on Republicans/Independents and Democrats separately.

References

Abelson, Robert. 1963. "Computer Simulation of 'Hot Cognition.'" In *Computer Simulation of Personality*, edited by S. Tomkins and D. Messick. New York: Wiley, 277–298.

Abelson, Robert, Donald Kinder, Mark D. Peters, and Susan Fiske. 1982. "Affective and Semantic Components in Political Person Perception." *Journal of Personality and Social Psychology* 42 (4): 619–630.

Achen, Christopher, and Larry Bartels. 2002. *Blind Retrospection: Electoral Responses to Droughts, Flu, and Shark Attacks*. Paper presented at the annual meeting of the American Political Science Association, Boston Marriott Copley Place, Sheraton Boston & Hynes Convention Center, Boston, Massachusetts.

Achen, Christopher, and Larry Bartels. 2005. "Partisan Hearts and Gallbladders: Retrospection and Realignment in the Wake of the Great Depression." Paper presented at the Midwest Political Science Association Annual Meeting, April 9, Chicago, Illinois.

Ackerman, Bruce A., and James S. Fishkin. 2004. *Deliberation Day*. New Haven, CT: Yale University Press.

Adorno, T. W., E. Frenkel-Brunswik, D. J. Levinson, and R. N. Sanford. 1950. *The Authoritarian Personality*. New York: Harper & Row.

Albertson, Bethany, and Shana Kushner Gadarian. 2012. *Who's Afraid of Immigration? The Effects of Pro- and Anti-Immigrant Threatening Ads among Latinos, African Americans and Whites, in Immigration and Public Opinion in the Liberal Democracies*. Gary Freeman, Randall Hansen, and David Leal, editors. New York: Routledge.

Allan, Nicole. 2010. "Immigration Politics a Boon for Jan Brewer and John McCain." *The Atlantic*, August 23. www.theatlantic.com/politics/archive/2010/08/immigration-politics-a-boon-for-jan-brewer-and-john-mccain/61904/.

Althaus, Scott L. 2002. "American News Consumption during Times of National Crisis." *PS: Political Science and Politics* 35 (3): 517–521.

Alvarez, Michael R., and Tara L. Butterfield. 2000. "The Resurgence of Nativism in California? The Case of Proposition 187 and Illegal Immigration." *Social Science Quarterly* 81: 167–179.

Arceneaux, Kevin, and Martin Johnson. 2013. *Changing Minds or Changing Channels? Media Effects in the Era of Expanded Choice.* Chicago: University of Chicago Press.

Archibold, Randal C. 2010. "Arizona Enacts Stringent Law on Immigration." *The New York Times*, April 23, sec. U.S./Politics. www.nytimes.com/2010/04/24/us/politics/24immig.html.

Arnold, Magda. 1960. *Emotion and Personality: Vol 1. Psychological Aspects.* New York: Columbia University Press.

Associated Press/GfK Poll. 2010. *Associated Press/GfK Poll.* iPOLL Databank, The Roper Center for Public Opinion Research. Gfk Roper Public Affairs & Corporate Communications. Storrs, CT: Roper Center for Public Opinion Research.

Banks, Antoine J. 2014. *Anger and Racial Politics: The Emotional Foundation of Racial Attitudes in America.* New York: Cambridge University Press.

Bar-Ilan, Judit, and Ana Echerman. 2005. "The Anthrax Scare and the Web: A Content Analysis of Web Pages Linking to Resources on Anthrax." *Scientometrics* 63 (3): 443–462.

Bar-Tal, Daniel, Eran Halperin, and Joseph De Rivera. 2007. "Collective Emotions in Conflict Situations: Societal Implications." *Journal of Social Issues* 63 (2): 441–460.

Barber, Benjamin. 1983. *The Logic and Limits of Trust.* New Brunswick, NJ: Rutgers University Press.

Bargh, John A., Shelly Chaiken, Paula Raymond, and Charles Hymes. 1996. "The Automatic Evaluation Effect: Unconditional Automatic Attitude Activation with a Pronunciation Task." *Journal of Experimental Social Psychology* 32 (1): 104–128.

Baron, R, and David Kenny. 1986. "The Moderator-Mediator Variable Distinction in Social Psychological Research: Conceptual, Strategic, and Statistical Considerations." *Journal of Personality and Social Psychology* 51: 1173–1182.

Bartels, Larry. 2002. "Beyond the Running Tally: Partisan Bias in Political Perceptions." *Political Behavior* 24 (2): 117–150.

Baum, Matthew, and Tim Groeling. 2010. *War Stories: The Causes and Consequences of Public Views of War.* Princeton, NJ: Princeton University Press.

Bennett, W. Lance. 2012. *News: The Politics of Illusion.* Vol. 9. Upper Saddle River, NJ: Longman.

Bennett, W. Lance, Regina G. Lawrence, and Steven Livingston. 2007. *When the Press Fails: Political Power and the News Media from Iraq to Katrina.* Studies in Communication, Media, and Public Opinion. Chicago: University of Chicago Press.

Berelson, Bernard, Paul Lazarsfeld, and William McPhee. 1954. *Voting: A Study of Opinion Formation in a Presidential Campaign.* Chicago: University of Chicago Press.

Berinsky, Adam. 2009. *In Time of War: Understanding American Public Opinion from World War II to Iraq*. Chicago: University of Chicago Press.

Berrebi, Claude, and Esteban F. Klor. 2007. "The Impact of Terrorism on Voters' Preferences." Working Paper. Santa Monica: RAND. http://ideas.repec.org/p/ran/wpaper/477-1.html.

Bianco, William. 1994. *Trust: Representatives and Constituents*. Ann Arbor: University of Michigan Press.

Blendon, Robert, John M. Benson, Caroline DesRoches, C. Pollard, W. Parvanta, and Melissa Hermann. 2002. "The Impact of Anthrax Attacks on the American Public." *Medscape General Medicine* 4(2): 1.

Blendon, Robert, Catherine M. DesRoches, John M. Benson, Melissa J. Herrmann, Kalahn Taylor-Clark, and Kathleen J. Weldon. 2003. "The Public and the Smallpox Threat." *New England Journal of Medicine* 348 (5): 426–432.

Blendon, Robert, Gillian K. SteelFisher, John M. Benson, Kathleen Weldon, and Melissa Herrmann. 2009. "Survey Finds That Just 40% Absolutely Certain They Will Get H1N1 Vaccine." Harvard School of Public Health. www.hsph.harvard.edu/news/press-releases/survey-40-adults-absolutely-certain-h1n1-vaccine/.

Bloch-Elkon, Yaeli. 2011. "The Polls – Trends: Public Perceptions and the Threat of International Terrorism After 9/11." *Public Opinion Quarterly* 75 (2) (June 20): 366–392.

Bonanno, George A., and John T. Jost. 2006. "Conservative Shift among High-Exposure Survivors of the September 11th Terrorist Attacks." *Basic and Applied Social Psychology* 28 (4): 311–323.

Borjas, George J. 1999. *Heaven's Door: Immigration Policy and the American Economy*. Princeton, NJ: Princeton University Press.

Boydstun, Amber, and Rebecca Glazier. 2012. "The President, the Press, and the War: A Tale of Two Framing Agendas." *Political Communication* 29 (4): 428–446.

Boyle, Michael, Mike Schmierbach, Cory Armstrong, Douglas McLeod, Dhavan Shah, and Zhongdang Pan. 2004. "Information Seeking and Emotional Reactions to the September 11 Terrorist Attacks." *Journalism and Mass Communication Quarterly* 81 (1): 155–167.

Brader, Ted. 2002. "Citizen Responses to Threat and Fear: New Developments and Future Directions." *The Political Psychologist* 7 (2): 3–8.

Brader, Ted. 2005. "Striking a Responsive Chord: How Political Ads Motivate and Persuade Voters by Appealing to Emotions." *American Journal of Political Science* 49 (2): 388–405.

Brader, Ted. 2006. *Campaigning for Hearts and Minds: How Emotional Appeals in Political Ads Work*. Studies in Communication, Media, and Public Opinion. Chicago: University of Chicago Press.

Brader, Ted. 2011. "Emotional Foundations of Democratic Citizenship." In *New Directions in American Politics*, edited by Adam Berinsky. New York: Routledge, 193–216.

Brader, Ted, Nicholas Valentino, Ashley Jardina, and Timothy Ryan. 2010. "The Racial Divide on Immigration Opinion. Why Blacks Are Less Threatened by Immigrants?" Paper presented at the Annual Meeting of the American Political Science Association. Washington, D.C.

Brader, Ted, Nicholas A. Valentino, and Elizabeth Suhay. 2008. "What Triggers Public Opposition to Immigration? Anxiety, Group Cues, and Immigration Threat." *American Journal of Political Science* 52 (4): 959–978.

Bradley, Margaret M., and Peter J. Lang. 2000. "Affective Reactions to Acoustic Stimuli." *Psychophysiology* 37 (2): 204–215.

Brehm, Jack Williams. 1966. *A Theory of Psychological Reactance*. New York: Academic Press.

Brehm, Sharon, and Jack Williams Brehm. 1981. *Psychological Reactance: A Theory of Freedom and Control*. New York: Academic Press.

Broad, William. 2002. "U.S. to Vaccinate 500,000 Workers against Smallpox." *New York Times*. July 7. www.nytimes.com/2002/07/07/us/us-to-vaccinate-500000-workers-against-smallpox.html?pagewanted=all&src=pm.

Brody, Richard A. 1991. *Assessing the President: The Media, Elite Opinion, and Public Support*. Stanford, CA: Stanford University Press.

Brooks, Clem, and Jeff Manza. 2013. *Whose Rights? Counterterrorism and the Dark Side of American Public Opinion*. New York: Russell Sage Foundation.

Budge, I., and D. J. Farlie. 1983. *Explaining and Predicting Elections: Issue Effects and Party Strategies in Twenty-three Democracies*. Boston: G. Allen and Unwin.

Burke, Edmund. 2013. *A Philosophical Inquiry into the Origin of Our Ideas of the Sublime and Beautiful*. (Oxford World's Classics). New York: Oxford University Press.

Busby, Joshua W. 2008. "Who Cares about the Weather?: Climate Change and US National Security." *Security Studies* 17 (3): 468–504.

Bushman, Brad. 1998. "Effects of Warning and Information Labels on Consumption of Full-fat, Reduced-fat and No-fat Products." *Journal of Applied Psychology* 83: 97–101.

Cacioppo, John T., and Gary G. Berntson. 1994. "Relationship between Attitudes and Evaluative Space: A Critical Review, with Emphasis on the Separability of Positive and Negative Substrates." *Psychological Bulletin* 115 (3): 401–423.

Campbell, Angus, Philip Converse, Warren E. Miller, and Donald Stokes. 1960. *The American Voter*. Midway Reprints. Chicago: University of Chicago Press.

Cassino, Dan, and Milton Lodge. 2007. "The Primacy of Affect in Political Evaluations." In *The Affect Effect*, edited by W. Russell Neuman, George Marcus, Ann Crigler, and Michael MacKuen. Chicago: University of Chicago Press, 101–123.

Centers for Disease Control and Prevention. 2003. *Executive Summary: Smallpox Response Plan*. Vol. 2012. April 27. http://emergency.cdc.gov/agent/smallpox/response-plan/files/exec-sections-i-vi.pdf.

Centers for Disease Control and Prevention, and Harvard School of Public Health. 2009. "Travelers Taking Significantly More Precautions against H1N1 and Seasonal Flu on Trips This Year, Citing Public Health Advice on Sneezing and Hand Sanitizing." www.hsph.harvard.edu/news/press-releases/h1n1-travel-1209/.

Centers for Disease Control and Prevention. 2014. "CDC Media Statement on Newly Discovered Smallpox Specimens." www.cdc.gov/media/releases/2014/s0708-nih.html.

Chanley, Virginia. 2002. "Trust in Government in the Aftermath of 9/11: Determinants and Consequences." *Political Psychology* 23 (3): 469–483.

Chanley, Virginia, Thomas J. Rudolph, and Wendy M. Rahn. 2000. "The Origins and Consequences of Public Trust in Government: A Time Series Analysis." *The Public Opinion Quarterly* 64 (3): 239–256.

Citrin, Jack. 1974. "Comment: The Political Relevance of Trust in Government." *American Political Science Review* 68 (3): 973–988.

Citrin, Jack, Donald Green, Christopher Muste, and Cara Wong. 1997. "Public Opinion toward Immigration Reform: The Role of Economic Motivations." *Journal of Politics* 59 (3): 858–881.

Citrin, Jack, and Christopher Muste. 1999. "Trust in Government." In *Measure of Political Attitudes*, edited by John Robinson, Phillip Shaver, and Lawrence Wrightsman. New York: Academic Press, 465–532.

Civettini, Andrew J. W., and David P. Redlawsk. 2009. "Voters, Emotions, and Memory." *Political Psychology* 30 (1): 125–151.

Cleary, Matthew, and Susan Stokes. 2006. *Democracy and the Culture of Skepticism: Political Trust in Argentina and Mexico*. New York: Cambridge University Press.

Clinton, William Jefferson. 1995. "State of the Union Address (as Prepared)," January 24. http://clinton6.nara.gov/1995/01/1995-01-24-president-state-of-the-union-address-as-prepared.html.

Clore, Gerald L., and Linda Isbell. 2001. "Emotion as Virtue and Vice." In *Citizens and Politics: Perspectives from Political Psychology*, edited by James Kuklinski. New York: Cambridge University Press, 103–126.

Clore, Gerald L., Norbert Schwarz, and Michael Conway. 1994. "Affective Causes and Consequences of Social Information Processing." In *Handbook of Social Cognition*, 2nd edition, edited by Wyer, Robert S., Jr., and Thomas Srull. Hillsdale, NJ: Erlbaum, 323–417.

CNN. 2011. "CNN/Opinion Research Corporation Poll – March 18–20 – Nuclear Power." March 22. http://politicalticker.blogs.cnn.com/2011/03/22/cnnopinion-research-corporation-poll-march-18-20-nuclear-power/.

Cohen, Florette, Daniel M. Ogilvie, Sheldon Solomon, Jeff Greenberg, and Tom Pyszczynski. 2005. "American Roulette: The Effect of Reminders of Death on Support for George W. Bush in the 2004 Presidential Election." *Analyses of Social Issues and Public Policy* 5 (1): 177–187.

Cohen, Micah. 2013. "Polls Show Growing Resolve to Live with Terror Threat." *FiveThirtyEight*. 23. http://fivethirtyeight.blogs.nytimes.com/2013/04/23/polls-show-growing-resolve-to-live-with-terror-threat/.

Conover, P. J., and Feldman, S. (1986). "Emotional Reactions to the Economy: I'm Mad as Hell and I'm Not Going to Take It Anymore." *American Journal of Political Science*, 50–78.

Converse, Philip. 1964. "Nature of Belief Systems in Mass Publics." In *Ideology and Discontent*, edited by David Apter. London: Free Press of Glencoe, 75–169.

Damasio, Antonio R. 1994. *Descartes' Error: Emotion, Reason, and the Human Brain*. New York: Putnam.

Davis, Darren W. 2007. *Negative Liberty: Public Opinion and the Terrorist Attacks on America*. New York: Russell Sage Foundation.

Dawood, Fatima, Danielle Iuliano, Carrie Reed, Martin Meltzer, David Shay, Po-Yung Cheng, and Don Bandaranayake. 2012. "Estimated Global Mortality Associated with the First 12 Months of 2009 Pandemic Influenza A H1N1 Virus Circulation: A Modelling Study." *The Lancet* 12 (9): 687–695.

Delli Carpini, Michael X., and Scott Keeter. 1996. *What Americans Know about Politics and Why It Matters*. New Haven, CT: Yale University Press.

Democratic National Committee. 2012. "Issues: Environment." www.demo crats.org/democratic-national-platform.

Dentzer, Susan. 2005. "Story of Polio Fight Wins Pulitzer Prize | PBS NewsHour." April 12. www.pbs.org/newshour/bb/health/jan-june06/polio_4–24.html.

De Tocqueville, Alexis. 1945. *Democracy in America*. 2 vols. *New York: Vintage*.

Dillard, James Price, Courtney Plotnick, Linda Godbold, Vicki Freimuth, and Timothy Edgar. 1996. "The Multiple Affective Outcomes of AIDS PSAs: Fear Appeals Do More Than Scare People." *Communication Research* 23 (1): 44–72.

Dillard, James Price, and Lijiang Shen. 2005. "On the Nature of Reactance and Its Role in Persuasive Health Communication." *Communication Monographs* 72: 144–168.

Downs, Anthony. 1957. *An Economic Theory of Democracy*. New York: Harper.

Druckman, James, and Rose McDermott. 2008. "Emotion and the Framing of Risky Choice." *Political Behavior* 30 (3): 297–321.

Dunlap, Riley E. 2008. "Climate-Change Views: Republican-Democratic Gaps Expand." Gallup. www.gallup.com/poll/107569/climatechange-views-republi candemocratic-gaps-expand.aspx.

Dunn, J. R., and M. E. Schweitzer. 2005. "Feeling and Believing: The Influence of Emotion on Trust." *Journal of Personality and Social Psychology* 88 (5): 736.

Edelman, Murray J. 1985. *The Symbolic Uses of Politics*. Champaign: University of Illinois Press.

Egan, Patrick. 2013. *Partisan Priorities: How Issue Ownership Drives and Distorts American Politics*. Cambridge: Cambridge University Press.

Entman, Robert M. 2003. "Cascading Activation: Contesting the White House's Frame After 9/11." *Political Communication* 20: 415–432.

Entman, Robert M. 2004. *Projections of Power: Framing News, Public Opinion, and U.S. Foreign Policy. Studies in Communication, Media, and Public Opinion*. Chicago: University of Chicago Press.

Erikson, Robert, and Laura Stoker. 2011. "Caught in the Draft: The Effects of Vietnam Draft Lottery Status on Political Attitudes." *American Political Science Review* 105 (2): 221–237.

Eysenck, Michael W. 1992. *Anxiety: The Cognitive Perspective*. Essays in Cognitive Psychology. Mahwah, NJ: Lawrence Erlbaum.

Feldman, Lauren, Edward Maibach, Connie Roser-Renouf, and Anthony Leiserowitz. 2012. "Climate on Cable: The Nature and Impact of Global Warming Coverage on Fox News, CNN, and MSNBC." *International Journal of Press/Politics* 17: 3–31.

Feldman, Stanley, and Leonie Huddy. Unpublished manuscript. "The Paradoxical Effects of Anxiety on Political Knowledge." New York: SUNY, Stony Brook.

Ferejohn, J. 1999. "Accountability and Authority: Toward a Theory of Political Accountability." *Democracy, Accountability, and Representation* 131: 137.

Fernandez, Manny, and Michael D. Shear. 2014. "Texas Governor Bolsters Border, and His Profile." *The New York Times*, July 21. www.nytimes.com /2014/07/22/us/perry-to-deploy-national-guard-troops-to-mexico-border.html.

Fessy, Thomas. 2014. "Ebola: Fear and Denial in West Africa." *Newshour*. BBC World Service. www.bbc.co.uk/programmes/po23rpz4.

Fiorina, Morris P. 1981. *Retrospective Voting in American National Elections*. New Haven, CT: Yale University Press.

Fischhoff, Baruch, Roxana M. Gonzalez, Deborah A. Small, and Jennifer S. Lerner. 2003. "Judged Terror Risk and Proximity to the World Trade Center." *Journal of Risk and Uncertainty* 26 (2/3): 137–151.

Fishkin, James S. 1995. *The Voice of the People: Public Opinion and Democracy*. New Haven, CT: Yale University Press.

Forgas, Joseph P. 1995. "Mood and Judgment: The Affect Infusion Model (AIM)." *Psychological Bulletin* 117 (1): 39–66.

Frenkel-Brunswik, E. 1949. "Intolerance of Ambiguity as an Emotional and Perceptual Personality Variable." *Journal of Personality* 18 (1): 108–143.

Frey, William, Kao-Lee Liaw, Yu Xie, and Marcia Carlson. 1996. "Interstate Migration of the US Poverty Population: Immigration 'pushes' and Welfare Magnet 'pulls.'" *Population & Environment* 17 (6): 491–533.

Frijda, Nico. 1988. "The Laws of Emotion." *American Psychologist* 43 (5): 349–358.

Frijda, Nico, Peter Kuipers, and Elisabeth ter Schure. 1989. "Relations among Emotion, Appraisal, and Emotional Action Readiness." *Journal of Personality and Social Psychology* 57 (2): 212–228.

Gadarian, Shana Kushner. 2008. "The Politics of Threat: Terrorism, Media, and Foreign Policy Opinion." Ph.D., Princeton, NJ: Princeton University. http:// search.proquest.com.ezproxy.lib.utexas.edu/pqdtft/docview/304500496/ abstract/13ED733CB444C1694C8/1?accountid=7118.

Gadarian, Shana Kushner. 2013. "Beyond the Water's Edge: Threat, Partisanship, and the Media." In *The Political Psychology of Terrorism Fears*, edited by Samuel Justin Sinclair and Daniel Antonius. New York: Oxford University Press, 67–84.

Gadarian, S. K. and Albertson, B. (2014), Anxiety, Immigration, and the Search for Information. Political Psychology, 35: 133–164. doi: 10.1111/pops.12034

Garrett, Laurie. 2009. "The Path of a Pandemic." *Newsweek*, May 18.

Garsten, Bryan. 2006. *Saving Persuasion: A Defense of Rhetoric and Judgment*. Cambridge, MA: Harvard University Press.

Geer, John. 2012. "The News Media and the Rise of Negativity in Presidential Campaigns." In *Can We Talk?*, edited by Dan Shea and Morris Fiorina. New York: Pearson.

Getmansky, Anna, and Thomas Zeitzoff. 2014. "Terrorism and Voting: The Effect of Rocket Threat on Voting in Israeli Elections." *American Political Science Review* 108 (3): 588–604.

Gilens, Martin, and Naomi Murakawa. 2002. "Elite Cues and Political Decision-Making." In *Research in Micropolitics*, edited by Michael X. Delli Carpini, Leonie Huddy, and Robert Y. Shapiro. Greenwich, CT: JAI Press, 15–50.

Gilliam, F. D., N. A. Valentino, and M. N. Beckmann (2002). "Where You Live and What You Watch: The Impact of Racial Proximity and Local Television

Ginsberg, Jeremy, Matthew Mohebbi, Rajan Patel, Lynnette Brammer, Mark Smolinski, and Larry Brilliant. 2008. "Detecting Influenza Epidemics Using Search Engine Query Data." *Nature* (457): 1012–1014.

Goble, Hannah, and Peter M. Holm. 2009. "Breaking Bonds? The Iraq War and the Loss of Republican Dominance in National Security." *Political Research Quarterly* 62 (2): 215–229.

Godlee, F., J. Smith, and H. Marcovitch. 2011. "Wakefield's Article Linking MMR Vaccine and Autism Was Fraudulent." *BMJ* 342 (January 5): c7452–c7452. doi:10.1136/bmj.c7452.

Goldsteen, Raymond L., Karen Goldsteen, and John K. Schorr. 1992. "Trust and Its Relationship to Psychological Distress: The Case of Three Mile Island." *Political Psychology* 13 (4): 693–707.

Gore, Al. 2006. *An Inconvenient Truth: The Planetary Emergency of Global Warming and What We Can Do about It.* 2nd edition. New York: Rodale Books.

Gravatt, Steven, and Michael J. Brown. 2011. "*Health Anxiety* and Internet Use." Working Paper. New York: Brooklyn College–City University of New York.

Gray, Elizabeth, and David Watson. 2007. "Assessing Positive and Negative Affect via Self-Report." In *Handbook of Emotion Elicitation and Assessment*, edited by James Coan and John Allen. New York: Oxford University Press, 171–183.

Green, D. P., and A. S. Gerber (2002). "The Downstream Benefits of Experimentation." *Political Analysis* 10 (4): 394–402.

Green, Edward, and Kim Witte. 2003. "Can Fear Arousal in Public Health Campaigns Contribute to the Decline of Health Prevalence?" *Journal of Health Communication* 11 (3): 245–259.

Green, Emily. 1999. "Britain Details the Start of Its 'Mad Cow' Outbreak – New York Times." *New York Times*, January 26. www.nytimes.com/1999/01/26/science/britain-details-the-start-of-its-mad-cow-outbreak.html?pagewanted=all&src=pm.

Greenberg, Jeff, Andy Martens, Eva Jonas, Donna Eisenstadt, Tom Pyszczynski, and Solomon Sheldon. 2003. "Psychological Defense in Anticipation of Anxiety: Eliminating the Potential for Anxiety Eliminates the Effect of Mortality Salience on Worldview Defense." *Psychological Science* 14 (5): 516–519.

Greenberg, Jeff, Tom Pyszczynski, Sheldon Solomon, Abram Rosenblatt, Mitchell Veeder, Shari Kirkland, and Deborah Lyon. 1990. "Evidence for Terror Management Theory II: The Effects of Mortality Salience on Reactions to Those Who Threaten or Bolster the Cultural Worldview." *Journal of Personality and Social Psychology* 58 (2): 308–318.

Groenendyk, Eric, Ted Brader, and Nicholas Valentino. 2011. "Appraising Political Emotions: Appraisals, Emotions, and Behavior in Response to Threatening News." University of Memphis, unpublished paper.

Gross, James. 2009. *Handbook of Emotion Regulation.* New York: Guilford Press.

Gross, James, and Robert Levenson. 1995. "Emotion Elicitation Using Films." *Cognition and Emotion* 9 (1): 87–108.

Gross, James, and Ross Thompson. 2009. "Emotion Regulation: Conceptual Foundations." In *Handbook of Emotion Regulation*, edited by James Gross. New York: Guilford Press, 3–26.

Ha, Shang E. 2010. "The Consequences of Multiracial Contexts on Public Attitudes toward Immigration." *Political Research Quarterly* 63 (1): 29–42.

Haber, Gillian, Robert M. Malow, and Gregory D. Zimet. 2007. "The HPV Vaccine Mandate Controversy." *Journal of Pediatric and Adolescent Gynecology* 20 (6) (December): 325–331. doi:10.1016/j.jpag.2007.03.101.

Habermas, Jurgen. 1989. *The Structural Transformation of the Public Sphere: An Inquiry into a Category of Bourgeois Society.* Studies in Contemporary German Social Thought. Cambridge, MA: MIT Press.

Halperin, Eran, Daphna Canetti-Nisim, and Sivan Hirsch-Hoefler. 2009. "The Central Role of Group-Based Hatred as an Emotional Antecedent of Political Intolerance: Evidence from Israel." *Political Psychology* 30 (1): 93–123.

Halperin, Eran, Keren Sharvit, and James Gross. 2011. "Emotion and Emotion Regulation in Intergroup Conflict: An Appraisal Based Framework." In *Intergroup Conflicts and Their Resolution: Social Psychological Perspective,* edited by Daniel Bar-Tal. New York: Psychology Press, 83–104.

Hamilton, Alexander, John Jay, and James Madison. 1961. *The Federalist Papers.* Vol. 558. New York: New American Library.

Hansen, James E. 1988. *The Greenhouse Effect: Impacts on Current Global Temperature and Regional Heat Waves.* (Congressional testimony.) Washington, DC: Senate Energy and Natural Resources Committee.

Hayes, Danny. 2011. "Media Frames and the Immigration Debate." George Washington University, unpublished manuscript.

Hendrickx, L., C. Vlek, and H. Oppewal. 1989. "Relative Importance of Scenario Information and Frequency Information in the Judgment of Risk." *Acta Psychologica* 72 (1): 41–63.

Hetherington, Marc. 1998. "The Political Relevance of Political Trust." *American Political Science Review* 92 (4): 791–808.

Hetherington, Marc. 2005. *Why Trust Matters: Declining Political Trust and the Demise of American Liberalism.* Princeton, NJ: Princeton University Press.

Hetherington, Marc, and Thomas Rudolph. 2008. "Priming, Performance, and the Dynamics of Political Trust." *Journal of Politics* 70 (2): 498–512.

Hicks, Raymond, and Dustin Tingley. 2011. Mediation: STATA Package for Causal Mediation Analysis. http://scholar.harvard.edu/dtingley/software/mediation-stata.

Hill, Seth, James Lo, Lynn Vavreck, and John Zaller. 2007. "The Opt-in Internet Panel: Survey Mode, Sampling Methodology and the Implications for Political Research." UCLA, unpublished manuscript.

Hobbes, Thomas. 2008. *Leviathan: Or the Matter, Forme, and Power of a Commonwealth Ecclesiasticall and Civil.* New York: Simon & Schuster.

Hopkins, Daniel. July 2014. "One Language, Two Meanings: Partisanship and Responses to Spanish." *Political Communication* 31 (3): 421–445.

Huddy, Leonie, Stanley Feldman, and Erin Cassese. 2007. "On the Distinct Political Effects of Anxiety and Anger." In *The Affect Effect: Dyanmics of Emotion in Political Thinking and Behavior,* edited by W. Russell Neuman, George E. Marcus, Ann N. Crigler, and Michael MacKuen. Chicago: University of Chicago Press, 202–230.

Huddy, Leonie, Stanley Feldman, Gallya Lahav, and Charles S. Taber. 2003. "Fear and Terrorism: Psychological Reactions to 9/11." In *Framing Terrorism: The News Media, the Government, and the Public*, edited by Pippa Norris, Montague Kern, and Marion R. Just. New York: Routledge.

Huddy, Leonie, Stanley Feldman, Charles Taber, and Gallya Lahav. 2005a. "Threat, Anxiety, and Support of Antiterrorism Policies." *American Journal of Political Science* 49 (3): 593–608.

Huddy, Leonie, Stanley Feldman, Charles S. Taber, and Gallya Lahav. 2005b. "The Politics of Threat: Cognitive and Affective Reactions to 9/11." *American Journal of Political Science* 49 (3): 610–625.

Huddy, Leonie, and Anna Gunnthorsdottir. 2000. "The Persuasive Effects of Emotive Visual Imagery: Superficial Manipulation or the Product of Passionate Reason?" *Political Psychology* 21 (4): 745–778.

Huntington, Samuel P. 2004. "The Hispanic Challenge." *Foreign Policy* (141): 30–45.

Imai, Kosuke, Luke Keele, and Dustin Tingley. 2010. "A General Approach to Causal Mediation Analysis." *Psychological Methods* 15 (4): 309–334.

Imai, Kosuke, Luke Keele, Dustin Tingley, and Teppei Yamamoto. 2011. "Unpacking the Black Box of Causality: Learning about Causal Mechanisms from Experimental and Observational Studies." *American Political Science Review* 105 (4): 765–789.

Isbell, Linda, and Victor Ottati. 2002. "The Emotional Voter: Effects of Episodic Affective Reactions on Candidate Evaluation." In *The Social Psychology of Politics. Social Psychological Application to Social Issues*, edited by Emil Posavac Ottati et al. New York: Kluwer Academic-Plenum Publishers, chap. 5:55–74.

Iyengar, Shanto. 1991. *Is Anyone Responsible?: How Television Frames Political Issues*. Chicago: University of Chicago Press.

Iyengar, Shanto, and Donald Kinder. 1987. *News That Matters: Television and American Opinion*. American Politics and Political Economy. Chicago: University of Chicago Press.

James, William. 1884. "What Is an Emotion?" *Mind* 34: 188–205.

Jarymowicz, Mary, and Daniel Bar-Tal. 2006. "The Dominance of Fear over Hope in the Life of Individuals and Collectives." *European Journal of Social Psychology* 36: 367–392.

Jones, Bryan D. 1994. *Reconceiving Decision-Making in Democratic Politics: Attention, Choice, and Public Policy*. Chicago: University of Chicago Press.

Jones, Jeffrey. 2001. "Americans Now Less Concerned about Being Terrorism Victim." *Gallup*. November 7. www.gallup.com/poll/5041/americans-now-less-concerned-about-being-terrorism-victim.aspx.

Jones, Jeffrey, and Lydia Saad. 2013. "Gallup Poll Social Series: Environment." 13-03-003. www.gallup.com/file/poll/161663/Global_Warming_130408.pdf.

Jost, John T., and Mahzarin R. Banaji. 1994. "The Role of Stereotyping in System-justification and the Production of False Consciousness." *British Journal of Social Psychology* 33: 1–27.

Jost, John T., Mahzarin R. Banaji, and Brian Nosek. 2004. "A Decade of System Justification Theory: Accumulated Evidence of Conscious and Unconscious Bolstering of the Status Quo." *Political Psychology* 25 (6): 881–919.

Jost, John T., Jack Glaser, Arie Kruglanski, and Frank Sulloway. 2003. "Political Conservatism as Motivated Social Cognition." *Psychological Bulletin* 129 (3): 339–375.

Jost, John T., Janina Pietrzak, Ido Liviatan, Anesu Mandisodza, and Jaime Napier. 2008. "System Justification as Conscious and Nonconscious Goal Pursuit." In *Handbook of Motivation Science*, edited by James Shah and Wendi L. Gardner. New York: Guilford Press, 591–606.

Jost, John T., and J. van der Toorn. 2011. "System Justification Theory." In *Handbook of Theories of Social Psychology: Volume Two*, edited by Paul A. M. Van Lange, Arie W. Kruglanski, and E. Tory Higgins. London: Sage, 313.

Kahan, Dan, Donald Braman, Geoffrey Cohen, John Gastil, and Paul Slovic. 2010. "Who Fears the HPV Vaccine, Who Doesn't and Why? An Experiment in the Study of Mechanisms of Cultural Cognition." *Law and Human Behavior* 34 (6): 501–516.

Kahneman, Daniel, and Amos Tversky. 1979. "Prospect Theory: An Analysis of Decision Under Risk." *Econometrica* 47 (2): 263–292.

Karl, Thomas R., Jerry M. Melillo, Thomas C. Peterson, and Susan J. Hassol, eds. 2009. *Global Climate Change Impacts in the United States*. 1st ed. New York: Cambridge University Press.

Keith, Bruce, David Magleby, Candice Nelson, Elizabeth Orr, Mark Westlye, and Raymond Wolfinger. 1992. *The Myth of the Independent Voter*. Berkeley: University of California Press.

Kern, Montague. 1989. *30-Second Politics: Political Advertising in the Eighties*. New York: Praeger Publishers.

Key, V. O. 1966. *The Responsible Electorate: Rationality in Presidential Voting, 1936–1960*. New York: Vintage Books.

Kiely, K. 2006. "Immigration Issue Takes Flight: Campaign Topic Even in States Far from Border." *USA Today*, July 20, 4A.

Kinder, Donald. 1994. "Reason and Emotion in American Political Life." In *Beliefs, Reasoning, and Decision Making: Psycho-Logic in Honor of Bob Abelson*, edited by Robert Schank and Ellen Langer. Hillsdale, NJ: Lawrence Erlbaum, 277–314.

Kinder, Donald, Robert Abelson, and Susan T. Fiske. 1979. "Developmental Research on Candidate Instrumentation: Results and Recommendations." Center for Political Studies, Institute for Social Research, University of Michigan.

Klapper, Joseph. 1960. *The Effects of Mass Communication*. New York: Free Press.

Knoll, Benjamin, David P. Redlawsk, and Howard Sanborn. 2011. "Framing Labels and Immigration Policy Attitudes in the Iowa Caucuses: 'Trying to Out-Tancredo Tancredo.'" *Political Behavior* 33 (3): 433–454.

Kubey, Robert, and Thea Peluso. 1990. "Emotional Response as a Cause of Interpersonal News Diffusion: The Case of the Space Shuttle Tragedy." *Journal of Broadcasting and Electronic Media* 34: 69–76.

Kuhnhenn, Jim. 2014. "Immigration Debate Upended by a Flood of Children." *ABC News*. July 21. http://abcnews.go.com/Politics/wireStory/flood-kids-upended-immigration-debate-24637501.

Kuklinski, James H., Ellen Riggle, Victor Ottati, Norbert Schwarz, and Robert S. Wyer, Jr. 1991. "The Cognitive and Affective Bases of Political Tolerance Judgments." *American Journal of Political Science* 35 (1): 1–27.

Kunda, Ziva. 1987. "Motivated Inference: Self-serving Generation and Evaluation of Causal Theories." *Journal of Personality and Social Psychology* 53 (4): 636–647.

Lake, David A., and Donald Rothchild. 1996. "Containing Fear: The Origins and Management of Ethnic Conflict." *International Security* 21 (2): 41. doi:10.2307/2539070.

Lambert, A. J., L. D. Scherer, J. P. Schott, K. R. Olson, R. K. Andrews, T. C. O'Brien, and A. R. Zisser. 2010. "Rally Effects, Threat, and Attitude Change: An Integrative Approach to Understanding the Role of Emotion." *Journal of Personality and Social Psychology* 98 (6): 886.

Landau, Mark J., Sheldon Solomon, Jeff Greenberg, Florette Cohen, Tom Pyszczynski, Jamie Arndt, Claude H. Miller, Daniel M. Ogilvie, and Alison Cook. 2004. "Deliver Us from Evil: The Effects of Mortality Salience and Reminders of 9/11 on Support for President George W. Bush." *Personality and Social Psychology Bulletin* 30 (9): 1136–1150.

Lane, Robert. 1962. *Political Ideology: Why the American Common Man Believes What He Does*. Oxford: Free Press of Glencoe.

Langer, Gary. 2009. "Swine Flu Poll: Vaccine Supply and Safety." *ABC News*. November 18. http://abcnews.go.com/PollingUnit/SwineFlu/swine-flu-vaccine-abc-news-washington-post-poll/story?id=9114768.

Lapinski, John, P. I. A. Peltola, Greg Shaw, and Alan Yang. 1997. "Trends: Immigrants and Immigration." *Public Opinion Quarterly* 61 (2): 356–383.

Lasswell, Harold. 1927. "The Theory of Political Propaganda." *The American Political Science Review* 21 (3): 627–631.

Lau, Richard. 1982. "Negativity in Political Perspective." *Political Behavior* 4 (4): 353–378.

Lau, Richard, and David P. Redlawsk. 2001. "An Experimental Study of Information Search, Memory, and Decision-Making in a Political Campaign." In *Citizens and Politics: Perspectives from Political Psychology*, edited by James H. Kuklinski. New York: Cambridge University Press, 136–159.

Lau, Richard, and David P. Redlawsk. 2006. *How Voters Decide: Information Processing During Election Campaigns*. New York: Cambridge University Press.

Lazarus, Richard S. 1991. "Cognition and Motivation in Emotion." *American Psychologist* 46 (4): 352–367.

Leavitt, J. W. 2003. "Public Resistance or Cooperation? A Tale of Smallpox in Two Cities." *Biosecurity and Bioterrorism: Biodefense Strategy, Practice, and Science* 1 (3): 185–192.

LeDoux, Joseph. 2000. "Emotion Circuits in the Brain." *Annual Review of Neuroscience* 23: 155–184.

Lee, Yueh-Ting, and Victor C. Ottati. 2002. "Attitudes toward U.S. Immigration Policy: The Roles of In-group-out-group Bias, Economic Concern, and Obedience to Law." *The Journal of Social Psychology* 142 (5): 617–634.

Lerner, Jennifer S., and Dacher Keltner. 2000. "Beyond Valence: Toward a Model of Emotion-specific Influences on Judgement and Choice." *Cognition and Emotion* 14: 473–494.

Lerner, Jennifer S., and Dacher Keltner. 2001. "Personality Processes and Individual Differences – Fear, Anger, and Risk." *Journal of Personality and Social Psychology* 81 (1): 146.

Levendusky, Matthew. 2009. *The Partisan Sort: How Liberals Became Democrats and Conservatives Became Republicans.* Chicago: University of Chicago Press.

Levi, Margaret. 1988. "A State of Trust." In *Trust & Governance*, edited by Valerie Braithwaite and Margaret Levi. New York: Russell Sage Foundation, 77–101.

Levi, Margaret, and Laura Stoker. 2000. "Political Trust and Trustworthiness." *Annual Review of Political Science* 3 (1): 475–507.

Lichtenstein, S., P. Slovic, B. Fischoff, M. Layman, and B. Combs. 1978. "Judged Frequency of Lethal Events." *Journal of Experimental Psychology: Human Learning and Memory* 4: 551–578.

Lippmann, Walter. 1946. *Public Opinion.* New York: Transaction.

Locke, John. 1950. *An Essay Concerning Human Understanding.* New York: Dover.

Lodge, Milton, and Charles S. Taber. 2005. "The Automaticity of Affect for Political Leaders, Groups, and Issues: An Experimental Test of the Hot Cognition Hypothesis." *Political Psychology* 26 (3): 455–482.

Loewenstein, George, Elke Weber, Christopher Hsee, and Ned Welch. 2001. "Risk as Feelings." *Psychological Bulletin* 127 (2): 267.

Lord, C. G., Ross, L., & Lepper, M. R. 1979. "Biased Assimilation and Attitude Polarization: The Effects of Prior Theories on Subsequently Considered Evidence." *Journal of Personality and Social Psychology* 37(11): 2098–2109.

Los Angeles Times. 1996. "Dole's California Campaign Plays the Fear Card." October 30. http://articles.latimes.com/1996-10-30/local/me-59224_1_dole-campaign.

Lupia, Arthur. 1994. "Shortcuts Versus Encyclopedias: Information and Voting Behavior in California Insurance Reform Elections." *The American Political Science Review* 88 (1): 63–76.

Lupia, Arthur, Mathew D. McCubbins, and Samuel L. Popkin. 2000. *Elements of Reason: Cognition, Choice, and the Bounds of Rationality.* Cambridge Studies in Political Psychology and Public Opinion. New York: Cambridge University Press.

Lupia, Arthur, and Jesse Menning. 2009. "When Can Politicians Scare Citizens into Supporting Bad Policies?" *American Journal of Political Science* 53 (1): 90–106.

Lyall, Sarah. 1996. "Tories Lose Local Elections, But Major Sees a Comeback – New York Times." *New York Times*, May 4. www.nytimes.com/1996/05/04/world/tories-lose-local-elections-but-major-sees-a-comeback.html.

Machiaveli, Niccolo. 1997. *The Prince.* New Haven, CT: Yale University Press.

MacKuen, Michael, Jennifer Wolak, Luke Keele, and George Marcus. 2010. "Civic Engagements: Resolute Partisanship or Reflective Deliberation." *American Journal of Political Science* 54 (2): 440–458.

Malhotra, Neil, and Alexander G. Kuo. 2008. "Attributing Blame: The Public's Response to Hurricane Katrina." *The Journal of Politics* 70 (1): 120–135.

Malka, Ariel, Jon A. Krosnick, and Gary Langer. 2009. "The Association of Knowledge with Concern about Global Warming: Trusted Information Sources Shape Public Thinking." *Risk Analysis* 29 (5): 633–647.

Malnick, Edward. January 1, 2012. "Hundreds of Frontline Health Workers Vaccinated against Smallpox." *The Telegraph*. www.telegraph.co.uk/sport/olympics/news/8986211/Hundreds-of-frontline-health-workers-vaccinated-against-smallpox.html.

Mansbridge, J. 1997. "Social and Cultural Causes of Dissatisfaction with US Government." In *Why People Don't Trust Government*, edited by J. Nye, S. Joseph, P. Zelikow, and D. King. Cambridge, MA: Harvard University Press, 133–153.

Marcus, George. 2002. *The Sentimental Citizen: Emotion in Democratic Politics*. University Park: Pennsylvania State University Press.

Marcus, George, and Michael B. MacKuen. 1993. "Anxiety, Enthusiasm, and the Vote: The Emotional Underpinnings of Learning and Involvement During Presidential Campaigns." *American Political Science Review* 87 (3): 672–685.

Marcus, George, W. Russell Neuman, and Michael MacKuen. 2000. *Affective Intelligence and Political Judgment*. Chicago: University of Chicago Press.

Marcus, George, John L. Sullivan, Elizabeth Theiss-Morse, Sandra L. Wood, and James L. Gibson. 1996. "With Malice toward Some: How People Make Civil Liberties Judgments." *The American Political Science Review* 90 (4): 916.

Maslow, Abraham H. 1963. "The Need to Know and the Fear of Knowing." *The Journal of General Psychology* 68 (1): 111–125.

Mathews, Andrew. 1990. "Why Worry? The Cognitive Function of Anxiety." *Behaviour Research and Therapy* 31: 57–62.

Mathews, Andrew, and Colin MacLeod. 1986. "Discrimination of Threat Cues Without Awareness in Anxiety States." *Journal of Abnormal Psychology* 95 (2): 131–138.

McAdams, E. S., Anand Sokhey, and Herbert Weisberg. 2008. "Group Labels, Group Affect and Immigration: What's in a Name?" Paper presented at annual meeting of Midwest Political Science Association. April 3–5, 2008. Chicago, Illinois.

McDermott, Rose. 2004. "The Feeling of Rationality: The Meaning of Neuroscientific Advances for Political Science." *Perspectives on Politics* 2 (4): 691–706.

McDermott, Rose, James H. Fowler, and Oleg Smirnov. 2008. "On the Evolutionary Origin of Prospect Theory Preferences." *The Journal of Politics* 70 (2): 335–350.

McRae, Kateri, Supriya Misra, Aditya Prassad, Sean Pereira, and James Gross. 2011. "Bottom-up and Top-down Emotion Generation: Implications for Emotion Regulation." *Social Cognitive and Affective Neuroscience* 7 (3): 1–10.

Meijnders, Anneloes L., Cees J. H. Midden, and Henk A. M. Wilke. 2001. "Communications about Environmental Risks and Risk-Reducing Behavior: The Impact of Fear on Information Processing." *Journal of Applied Social Psychology* 31 (4): 754–777.

Meinhardt, Theodore, William Pollard, Robert Blendon, Catherine DesRoches, and Martin Cetron. 2006. "Attitudes toward the Use of Quarantine in a Public Health Emergency." *Health Affairs* 25 (2): 15–25.

Merolla, Jennifer, J. Daniel Montalvo, and Elizabeth Zechmeister. 2012. "Terrorism and Democracy in Latin America and the Caribbean." Claremont Graduate University, unpublished manuscript.

Merolla, Jennifer, Jennifer Ramos, and Elizabeth Zechmeister. 2007. "Crisis, Charisma, and Consequences: Evidence from the 2004 U.S. Presidential Election." *The Journal of Politics* 69 (1): 30–42.

Merolla, Jennifer, and Elizabeth Zechmeister. 2009. *Democracy at Risk: How Terrorist Threats Affect the Public*. Chicago: University of Chicago Press.

Miller, Arthur. 1974. "Political Issues and Trust in Government: 1964–1970." *American Political Science Review* 68 (3): 951–972.

Miller, Joanne M. 2007. "Examining the Mediators of Agenda Setting: A New Experimental Paradigm Reveals the Role of Emotions." *Political Psychology* 28 (6): 689–717.

Mintz, Alex. 2004. "How Do Leaders Make Decisions?: A Poliheuristic Perspective." *The Journal of Conflict Resolution* 48 (1): 3–13.

Mintz, Alex, Nehemia Geva, Steven B. Redd, and Amy Carnes. 1997. "The Effect of Dynamic and Static Choice Sets on Political Decision Making: An Analysis Using the Decision Board Platform." *The American Political Science Review* 91 (3): 553–566.

Mogg, Karin, and Brendan P. Bradley. 2002. "Selective Orienting of Attention to Masked Threat Faces in Social Anxiety." *Behaviour Research and Therapy* 40 (12): 1403.

Mogg, Karin, Andrew Mathews, Carol Bird, and Rosanne Macgregor-Morris. 1990. "Effects of Stress and Anxiety on the Processing of Threat Stimuli." *Journal of Personality and Social Psychology* 59 (6): 1230–1237.

Mondak, Jeffery J., and Jon Hurwitz. 2012. "Examining the Terror Exception." *Public Opinion Quarterly* 76 (2): 193–213.

Mueller, John E. 1973. *War, Presidents, and Public Opinion*. New York: Wiley.

Mueller, John E. 2006. *Overblown: How Politicians and the Terrorism Industry Inflate National Security Threats, and Why We Believe Them*. New York: Free Press.

Myers, C. Daniel, and Dustin Tingley. 2011. "The Influence of Emotion on Trust." Princeton University, unpublished paper.

Nabi, Robin. 1999. "A Cognitive-Functional Model for the Effects of Discrete Negative Emotions on Information Processing, Attitude Change, and Recall." *Communication Theory* 9 (3): 292–320.

Nacos, Brigitte Lebens. 1990. *The Press, Presidents, and Crises*. New York: Columbia University Press.

Nacos, Brigitte Lebens, Yaeli Bloch-Elkon, and Robert Shapiro. 2011. *Selling Fear: Counterterrorism, The Media, and Public Opinion*. Chicago: University of Chicago Press.

National Commission on Terrorist Attacks upon the United States. 2004. *The 9/11 Commission Report: Final Report of the National Commission on Terrorist Attacks Upon the United States*. New York: Norton.

Neblo, Michael. 2007. "Philosophical Psychology with Political Intent." In *The Affect Effect*, edited by W. Russell Neuman, George Marcus, Ann Crigler, and Michael MacKuen. Chicago: University of Chicago Press, 25–47.

Neiman, Max, Martin Johnson, and Shaun Bowler. 2006. "Partisanship and Views about Immigration in Southern California: Just How Partisan Is the Issue of Immigration?" *International Migration* 44 (2): 35–56.

Nelson, Thomas, and Donald Kinder. 1996. "Issue Frames and Group-Centrism in American Public Opinion." *The Journal of Politics* 58 (4): 1055–1078.

Neuman, W. Russell, George Marcus, Ann N. Crigler, and Michael MacKuen. 2007. *The Affect Effect: Dynamics of Emotion in Political Thinking and Behavior*. Chicago: University of Chicago Press.

New York Times. 2000. "British Wrongly Lulled People on 'Mad Cow,' Report Finds." *The New York Times*, October 27, sec. World. www.nytimes.com/2000/10/27/world/27BRIT.html.

Newport, Frank. 2012. "Americans' Worries about Global Warming Up Slightly." *Gallup*. March 30. www.gallup.com/poll/153653/Americans-Worries-Global-Warming-Slightly.aspx.

Nisbet, Matthew C., and Teresa Myers. 2007. "The Polls – Trends Twenty Years of Public Opinion about Global Warming." *Public Opinion Quarterly* 71 (3) (September 21): 444–470.

NPR. 2010. "A Reagan Legacy: Amnesty for Illegal Immigrants: NPR." *NPR.org*. July 4. www.npr.org/templates/story/story.php?storyId=128303672.

Ortony, Anthony, Gerald L. Clore, and Allan Collins. 1990. *The Cognitive Structure of Emotions*. New York: Cambridge University Press.

Osgood, Charles Egerton, George Suci, and Percy Tannenbaum. 1957. *The Measurement of Meaning*. Urbana: University of Illinois Press.

Oshinsky, David M. 2006. *Polio: An American Story*. Second printing. New York: Oxford University Press.

Ottati, Victor. 1997. "When the Survey Question Directs Retrieval: Implications for Assessing the Cognitive and Affective Predictors of Global Evaluation." *European Journal of Social Psychology* 27 (1): 1–21.

Ottati, Victor, and Robert S. Wyer Jr. 1993. "Affect and Political Judgment." In *Explorations in Political Psychology*, edited by Shanto Iyengar and William McGuire. Durham, NC: Duke University Press, 296–315.

Page, Benjamin, and Robert Shapiro. 1992. *The Rational Public: Fifty Years of Trends in Americans' Policy Preferences*. Chicago: University of Chicago Press.

Pantoja, Adrian, and Gary Segura. 2003. "Fear and Loathing in California: Contextual Threat and Political Sophistication among Latino Voters." *Political Behavior* 25 (3): 265–286.

Petrocik, John R. 1996. "Issue Ownership in Presidential Elections, with a 1980 Case Study." *American Journal of Political Science* 40 (3): 825–850.

Petrocik, John R., William L. Benoit, and Glenn J. Hansen. 2003. "Issue Ownership and Presidential Campaigning, 1952–2000." *Political Science Quarterly* 118 (4): 599–626.

Petty, Richard, Sarah Baker, and Faith Gleicher. 1991. "Attitudes and Drug Abuse Prevention: Implications of the Elaboration Likelihood Model of Persuasion." In *Persuasive Communication and Drug Abuse Prevention*, edited by Lewis Donohew, Howard Sypher, and William Bukoski. Hillsdale, NJ: Lawrence Erlbaum, 71–90.

Petty, Richard E., and John T. Cacioppo. 1986. *Communication and Persuasion: Central and Peripheral Routes to Attitude Change*. Springer Series in Social Psychology. New York: Springer. http://link.springer.com/chapter/10.1007/978-1-4612-4964-1_1.

Pew Research Center for the People and the Press. 2006a. "America's Immigration Quandary." March 30. www.people-press.org/2006/03/30/americas-immigration-quandary/.

Pew Research Center for the People and the Press. 2006b. "Little Consensus on Global Warming." *Pew Research Center for the People and the Press*. July 12. www.people-press.org/2006/07/12/little-consensus-on-global-warming/.

Pew Research Center for the People and the Press. 2006c. "Baker-Hamilton Report Evokes Modest Public Interest: Growing Number Sees Iraq Becoming 'Another Vietnam': News Interest Index." December. www.people-press.org/2006/12/12/baker-hamilton-report-evokes-modest-public-interest/.

Pew Research Center for the People and the Press. 2010a. "Broad Approval for New Arizona Immigration Law." May 12. www.people-press.org/2010/05/12/broad-approval-for-new-arizona-immigration-law/.

Pew Research Center for the People and the Press. 2010b. "Little Change in Opinions about Global Warming." *Pew Research Center for the People and the Press*. October 27. www.people-press.org/2010/10/27/little-change-in-opinions-about-global-warming/.

Pew Research Center for the People and the Press. 2010c. "Despite Years of Terror Scares, Public's Concerns Remain Fairly Steady." December 2. www.people-press.org/2010/12/02/despite-years-of-terror-scares-publics-concerns-remain-fairly-steady/.

Pew Research Center for the People and the Press. 2011. "Partisan Divide Over Alternative Energy Widens." November 10. www.people-press.org/2011/11/10/partisan-divide-over-alternative-energy-widens/.

Pollard, William E. 2003. "Public Perceptions of Information Sources Concerning Bioterrorism Before and After Anthrax Attacks: An Analysis of National Survey Data." *Journal of Health Communication* 8 (1): 148–151.

Pratto, Felicia, and Oliver P. John. 1991. "Automatic Vigilance: The Attention-grabbing Power of Negative Social Information." *Journal of Personality and Social Psychology* 61 (3): 380–391.

Prior, Markus. 2007. *Post-broadcast Democracy: How Media Choice Increases Inequality in Political Involvement and Polarizes Elections*. Cambridge Studies in Public Opinion and Political Psychology. New York: Cambridge University Press.

Prior, Markus. 2009. "The Immensely Inflated News Audience: Assessing Bias in Self-Reported News Exposure." *Journal of Politics* 73 (1): 130–143.

Putnam, Robert. 1994. *Making Democracy Work: Civic Traditions in Modern Italy*. Princeton, NJ: Princeton University Press.

Quick, Brian, and Michael Stephenson. 2008. "Examining the Role of Trait Reactance and Sensation Seeking on Perceived Threat, State Reactance, and Reactance Restoration." *Human Communication Research* 34: 448–476.

Rabinowitz, George, and Stuart Elaine Macdonald. 1989. "A Directional Theory of Issue Voting." *The American Political Science Review* 83 (1): 93–121.

Redlawsk, David P., Andrew J. W. Civinetti, and Richard R. Lau. 2007. "Affective Intelligence and Voting: Information Processing and Learning in a Campaign." In *The Affect Effect: Dynamics of Emotion in Political Thinking and Behavior*, edited by W. Russell Neuman, George E. Marcus, Ann N. Crigler, and Michael MacKuen. Chicago: University of Chicago Press, 152–179.

Renshon, Jonathan, Jooa Julia Lee, and Dustin Tingley. 2014. "Physiological Arousal and Political Beliefs." *Political Psychology*. Article first published online February 12, 2014. doi: 10.1111/pops.12173.

Renshon, Jonathan, and Jennifer Lerner. 2012. "The Role of Emotion in Foreign Policy Decision Making." In *The Encyclopedia of Peace Psychology*, edited by Daniel J. Christie. West Sussex: Blackwell Publishing, 313–317.

Republican Party, The. 2012. "2012 Republican Platform." www.gop.com/wp-content/uploads/2012/08/2012GOPPlatform.pdf.

Ridout, Travis N., and Kathleen Searles. 2011. "It's My Campaign I'll Cry If I Want To: How and When Campaigns Use Emotional Appeals." *Political Psychology* 32 (3): 439–458.

Robin, Corey. 2006. *Fear: The History of a Political Idea*. New York: Oxford University Press.

Rogers, Ronald W. 1975. "A Protection Motivation Theory of Fear Appeals and Attitude Change." *The Journal of Psychology* 91 (1): 93–114.

Rokeach, M. 1960. *The Open and Closed Mind: Investigations into the Nature of Belief Systems and Personality Systems*. New York: Basic Books.

Rose, William, Rysia Murphy, and Max Abrahms. 2007. "Does Terrorism Ever Work? The 2004 Madrid Train Bombings." *International Security* 32 (1): 185–192.

Roseman, Ira. 1984. "Cognitive Determinants of Emotions: A Structural Theory." In *Review of Personality and Social Psychology*, edited by Phillip Shaver. Beverly Hills, CA: Sage Publications, chap. 5: 11–36.

Roseman, Ira, and A. Evdokas. 2004. "Appraisals Cause Experienced Emotions: Experimental Evidence." *Cognition and Emotion* 18: 1–18.

Roseman, Ira, Martin Spindel, and Paul Jose. 1990. "Appraisals of Emotion-eliciting Events: Testing a Theory of Discrete Emotions." *Journal of Personality and Social Psychology* 59 (5): 899–915.

Rough, Ginger. 2010. "Immigrants Bring Drugs, Brewer Says." *The Arizona Republic*, June 26. www.azcentral.com/news/articles/2010/06/25/20100625arizona-governor-says-most-illegal-immigrants-smuggle-drugs.html.

Rubin, Alan M., Paul M. Haridakis, Gwen A. Hullman, Shaojing Sun, Pamela M. Chikombero, and Vikanda Pornsakulvanich. 2003. "From an Academic: Television Exposure Not Predictive of Terrorism Fear." *Newspaper Research Journal* 24 (1): 128.

Rudolph, T. J., and J. Evans. 2005. "Political Trust, Ideology, and Public Support for Government Spending." *American Journal of Political Science* 49 (3): 660–671.

Saad, Lydia. 2012. "Economic Issues Still Dominate Americans' National Worries." Gallup. www.gallup.com/poll/153485/economic-issues-dominate-americans-national-worries.aspx.

Scherer, Klaus. 2003. "Introduction: Cognitive Components of Emotion." In *Handbook of Affective Sciences*, edited by R. Davidson, H Goldsmit, and K. Scherer. New York: Oxford University Press, 563–572.

Schlenger, William E., Juesta M. Caddell, Lori Ebert, B. Kathleen Jordan, Kathryn M. Rourke, David Wilson, Lisa Thalji, J. Michael Dennis, John A. Fairbank, and Richard A. Kulka. 2002. "Psychological Reactions to Terrorist Attacks: Findings From the National Study of Americans' Reactions to September 11." *JAMA: The Journal of the American Medical Association* 288 (5): 581.

Scholz, J. T., and M. Lubell. 1998. "Trust and Taxpaying: Testing the Heuristic Approach to Collective Action." *American Journal of Political Science* 42 (2): 398–417.

Schuster, Mark A., Bradley D. Stein, Lisa H. Jaycox, Rebecca L. Collins, Grant N. Marshall, Marc N. Elliott, Annie J. Zhou, David E. Kanouse, Janina L. Morrison, and Sandra H. Berry. 2001. "A National Survey of Stress Reactions After the September 11, 2001, Terrorist Attacks." *New England Journal of Medicine* 345 (20): 1507–1512.

Schwarz, Norbert, and Gerald L. Clore. 1983b. "Mood, Misattribution, and Judgments of Well-being: Informative and Directive Functions of Affective States." *Journal of Personality and Social Psychology* 45 (3): 513–523.

Sears, David. 1986. "College Sophomores in the Laboratory: Influence of a Narrow Data Base on Social Psychology's View of Human Nature." *Journal of Personality and Social Psychology* 51: 515–530.

Sears, David O. 1993. "Symbolic Politics: A Socio-Political Theory." In *Explorations in Political Psychology*, edited by Shanto Iyengar and William J. McGuire. Durham, NC: Duke University Press, 113–148.

Sears, David O., Richard Lau, Tom Tyler, and Harris Allen. 1980. "Self-interest vs. Symbolic Politics in Policy Attitudes and Presidential Voting." *The American Political Science Review* 74 (3): 670–684.

Sebelius, Kathleen. 2011. "Why We Still Need Smallpox." *The New York Times*, April 25. The Opinion Pages: www.nytimes.com/2011/04/26/opinion/26iht-edsebelius26.html?_r=0.

Shani, Danielle. 2006. "Can Knowledge Correct for Partisan Bias in Political Perceptions?" Paper presented at the Annual Meeting of the Midwest Political Science Association, April 20–23. Chicago, Illinois.

Simon, Adam F. 2002. *The Winning Message: Candidate Behavior, Campaign Discourse, and Democracy*. Communication, Society, and Politics. New York: Cambridge University Press.

Simon, Herbert. 1967. "Motivational and Emotional Controls of Cognition." *Psychological Review* 74 (1): 29.

Simon, Rita J., and Susan H. Alexander. 1993. *The Ambivalent Welcome: Print Media, Public Opinion, and Immigration*. Westport, CT: Praeger.

Skitka, Linda, Christopher Bauman, Nicholas Armovich, and G. Scott Morgan. 2006. "Confrontational and Preventative Policy Responses to Terrorism: Anger

Wants a Fight and Fear Wants 'Them' to Go Away." *Basic and Applied Social Psychology* 28 (4): 375–384.

Skitka, Linda, Christopher W. Bauman, and Elizabeth Mullen. 2004. "Political Tolerance and Coming to Psychological Closure Following the September 11, 2001, Terrorist Attacks: An Integrative Approach." *Personality and Social Psychology Bulletin* 30 (6): 743–756.

Slovic, Paul. 1993. "Perceived Risk, Trust, and Democracy." *Risk Analysis* 13 (6): 675–682.

Slovic, Paul, E. Peters, M. L. Finucane, and D. G. MacGregor. 2005. "Affect, Risk, and Decision Making." *Health Psychology* 24 (4S): S35.

Smith, Craig A., and Phoebe C. Ellsworth. 1985. "Patterns of Cognitive Appraisal in Emotion." *Journal of Personality and Social Psychology* 48 (4): 813–838.

Smith, Kevin, Douglas Oxley, Matthew Hibbing, John Alford, and John Hibbing. 2012. "The Ick Factor: Disgust Sensitivity as a Predictor of Political Attitudes." Paper presented at the 2009 Midwest Political Science Association.

Sniderman, P. M., R. A. Brody, and P. Tetlock. 1993. *Reasoning and Choice: Explorations in Political Psychology*. New York: Cambridge University Press.

Spielberger, Charles Donald, Richard L. Gorsuch, and Robert E. Lushene. 1984. *STAI Manual for the State-trait Anxiety Inventory (Self-evaluation Questionnaire)*. Palo Alto, CA: Consulting Psychologists Press.

Starcevic, Vladan, and Davide Berle. 2006. "Cognitive Specificity of Anxiety Disorders: A Review of Selected Key Constructs." *Depression and Anxiety* 23: 51–61.

Steenbergen, Marco, and Christopher Ellis. 2006. "Fear and Loathing in American Elections: Context, Traits, and Negative Candidate Affect." In *Feeling Politics: Emotion in Political Information Processing*, edited by David P. Redlawsk. New York: Palgrave Macmillan, 109–134.

Steinhauser, Paul. 2009. "CNN Poll: Concerns over H1N1 Virus on the Rise." September 2. http://politicalticker.blogs.cnn.com/2009/09/02/cnn-poll-con cerns-over-h1n1-virus-on-the-rise/.

Stern, Jessica. 2006. "The Song Is Still the Same: Responses to 'Is There Still a Terrorist Threat?'" *Foreign Affairs*. 11. www.foreignaffairs.com/discussions/ roundtables/are-we-safe-yet.

Stern, Paul, and Harvey Fineberg. 1996. "Understanding Risk: Informing Decisions in a Democratic Society." National Research Council. Washington, DC: National Academy Press.

Taylor-Clark, Kalahn, Robert Blendon, Alan Zaslavsky, and John Benson. 2005. "Confidence in Crisis? Understanding Trust in Government and Public Attitudes toward Mandatory State Powers." *Biosecurity and Bioterrorism: Biodefense Strategy, Practice, and Science* 3 (2): 138–148.

Tichenor, Daniel. 2002. *Dividing Lines: The Politics of Immigration Control in America*. Princeton, NJ: Princeton University Press.

Tocqueville, A. D. (1945). *Democracy in America*. 2 vols. New York: Vintage.

Tolbert, Carolina, and Rodney Hero. 1996. "Race/Ethnicity and Direct Democracy: An Analysis of California's Illegal Immigration Initiative." *Journal of Politics* 58 (3): 806–818.

Tooby, John, and Leda Cosmides. 2008. "The Evolutionary Psychology of the Emotions and Their Relationship to Internal Regulatory Variables." In *Handbook of Emotions*, edited by Michael Lewis, Jeanette Haviland-Jones, and Lisa Feldman Barrett, 3rd edition. New York: Guilford Press, 114–137.

Tversky, Amos, and Daniel Kahneman. 1973. "Availability: A Heuristic for Judging Frequency and Probability." *Cognitive Psychology* 5: 207–232.

Tyler, Tom R., and P. Degoey. 1995. "Collective Restraint in Social Dilemmas: Procedural Justice and Social Identification Effects on Support for Authorities." *Journal of Personality and Social Psychology* 69 (3): 482.

Tyler, Tom R., Kenneth A. Rasinski, and Kathleen M. McGraw. 1985. "The Influence of Perceived Injustice on the Endorsement of Political Leaders1." *Journal of Applied Social Psychology* 15 (8): 700–725.

Valentino, Nicholas A., Antoine Banks, Vincent Hutchings, and Anne K. Davis. 2009. "Selective Exposure in the Internet Age: The Interaction between Anxiety and Information Utility." *Political Psychology* 30 (4): 591–613.

Valentino, Nicholas A., Vincent L. Hutchings, Antoine J. Banks, and Anne K. Davis. 2008. "Is a Worried Citizen a Good Citizen? Emotions, Political Information Seeking, and Learning via the Internet." *Political Psychology* 29 (2): 247–273.

Vallone, Robert P., Lee Ross, and Mark R. Lepper. 1985. "The Hostile Media Phenomenon: Biased Perception and Perceptions of Media Bias in Coverage of the Beirut Massacre." *Journal of Personality and Social Psychology* 49 (3): 577–585.

Verba, Sideny, Schlozman, Kay Lehman, Henry E. Brady, and H. E. Brady (1995). *Voice and Equality: Civic Voluntarism in American Politics*. New York: Cambridge University Press.

Wattenberg, M. P., and C. L. Brians (1999). "Negative Campaign Advertising: Demobilizer or Mobilizer?" *American Political Science Review* 93 (4): 891–899.

Weyland, Kurt. 1996. "Risk Taking in Latin American Economic Restructuring: Lessons from Prospect Theory." *International Studies Quarterly* 40: 185–208.

White House. 2008. *President Bush Discusses Protect America Act, February 13, 2008*. Vol. 2008. February 20, 2008.

Willman, David. 2011. "Cost, Need Questioned in $433-Million Smallpox Drug Deal." *Los Angeles Times*, November 13. http://articles.latimes.com/2011/nov/13/nation/la-na-smallpox-20111113.

Witte, Kim. 1992. "Putting the Fear Back in Fear Appeals: The Extended Parallel Processing Model." *Communication Monographs* 59: 329–349.

Witte, Kim, and Mike Allen. 2000. "A Meta-Analysis of Fear Appeals: Implications for Effective Public Health Campaigns." *Health Education & Behavior* 27 (5): 591–615.

Wood, Daniel B. 2005. "What 'Minuteman' Vigil Accomplished." *Christian Science Monitor*, May 2. www.csmonitor.com/2005/0502/p01s04-ussc.html.

Wood, Jacqueline, Andrew Mathews, and Tim Dalgleish. 2001. "Anxiety and Cognitive Inhibition." *Emotion* 1 (2): 166–81.

World Health Organization. 2001. *Smallpox: WHO Fact Sheet*. Vol. 2012. April 25. www.who.int/topics/smallpox/en/.

Wright, Rex A., and Sharon Brehm. 1982. "Reactance as Impression Management: A Critical Review." *Journal of Personality and Social Psychology* 42 (4): 608–618.

Yiend, Jenny, and Andrew Mathews. 2001. "Anxiety and Attention to Threatening Pictures." *The Quarterly Journal of Experimental Psychology* 54 (3): 665–681.

Youngdahl, Karie. 2012. "Polio and Swimming Pools: Historical Connections." *History of Vaccines Blog: A Project of the College of Physicians of Philadelphia.* www.historyofvaccines.org/content/blog/polio-and-swimming-pools-historical-connections.

Zajonc, Robert. 1980. "Feeling and Thinking: Preferences Need No Interference." *American Psychologist* 35 (2): 151–175.

Zaller, John. 1992. *The Nature and Origin of Public Opinion.* New York: Cambridge University Press.

Zaller, John. 1999. "A Theory of Media Politics: How the Interests of Politicians, Journalists, and Citizens Shape the News." Unpublished manuscript. University of California–Los Angeles.

Zaller, John. 2002. "The Statistical Power of Election Studies to Detect Media Exposure Effects in Political Campaigns." *Electoral Studies* 21 (2): 297.

Zeitzoff, Thomas. 2014. "Anger, Exposure to Violence, and Intragroup Conflict: A 'Lab in the Field' Experiment in Southern Israel." *Political Psychology* 35 (3) (June 1): 309–335. doi:10.1111/pops.12065.

Index

Abelson, Robert, 3
Achen, Christopher, 154
Achille Lauro hijacking (1985), 31
Adorno, T.W., 102
Affective intelligence theory
    anxiety and, 8–9, 140–141
    information seeking and, 44
Affect versus emotion, 5–6
Amazon, 42, 89, 132
Ambiguity intolerance theory, 102
American Medical Association (AMA)
    H1N1 influenza and, 80–81
    smallpox and, 85
American National Election Studies
    (1994), 125–126
Anger
    anxiety versus, 36, 95, 97–98
    immigration and, 96
    political trust and, 95, 97–98
    terrorism and, 118
Anthrax, 44, 76
Anxiety, effect of
    overview, xix–xxii, 1–2, 4–5,
        9–10, 18
    affective intelligence theory and,
        8–9, 140–141
    anger versus, 36, 95, 97–98
    on civic life broadly, 140
    climate change, regarding, 112–113
    conservatism and, 145

counterbalancing of threats, 155
dangers of, 153
definition of anxiety, 8
on democratic theory (See
    Democratic theory, effect of
    anxiety on)
duration of, 151–152
external threats, 76
framed threats and, 147–148
H1N1 influenza, regarding, 76
immigration, regarding, 125, 127,
    131, 132, 212
on information seeking, 10–11, 44–47
internal threats, 76
manipulation of anxiety (See
    Manipulation of anxiety)
measurement of anxiety, 127,
    148–151, 185
non-immediate threats, 155
partisanship and, 15, 140–141, 142
political elites, use by, 144
on political environment, 103–105
on political trust, 11–13, 75–77
on protective policies, 13–15,
    105–106
relevance of threats, 154–155
risk aversion and, 103
risk seeking and, 103
smallpox, regarding, 76, 202–205,
    208